Recording in the Digital World

Complete Guide to Studio Gear and Software

Thomas E. Rudolph and Vincent A. Leonard, Jr.

Berklee Press

Director: Dave Kusek
Managing Editor: Debbie Cavalier
Marketing Manager: Ola Frank
Sr. Writer/Editor: Jonathan Feist
Writer/Editor: Susan Gedutis
Product Manager: Ilene Altman

ISBN 0-634-01324-6

1140 Boylston Street
Boston, MA 02215-3693 USA
(617) 747-2146

Visit Berklee Press Online at
www.berkleepress.com

DISTRIBUTED BY

HAL•LEONARD®
CORPORATION
7777 W. BLUEMOUND RD. P.O. BOX 13819
MILWAUKEE, WISCONSIN 53213

Visit Hal Leonard Online at
www.halleonard.com

Contents

Acknowledgements

Tiiu Lutter, content editor, editor; and Jack Klotz Jr. technical advisor.

Additional thanks to Debbie Cavalier, Mary Cresse, Jonathan Feist, Dave Kusek, Lorry Lutter, David Mash, Helen Nick, Tom Petroski, Booker Raynor, and Gerson Rosenbloom.

Introduction

This book was written for professional musicians, music educators, and music hobbyists who want to explore the world of digital recording.

Its purpose is to provide an overview of current digital recording options and to include information for entry-level, mid-level, and high-end applications focusing on budgets from $1,000 to $30,000. In addition, this book contains practical tips for creating, editing, and mastering a digital recording.

If you are new to digital recording, we recommend you read the chapters sequentially from the beginning. Concepts are introduced and defined throughout each chapter. If you are experienced using digital audio, select chapters of interest.

Besides information on digital recording, there are also extensive suggestions for methods of creating a high-quality recording. The chapters on microphone techniques, mixing, and mastering include not only technical specifications but advice from experienced recording engineers that can be applied in any studio.

We hope this book will help you select the appropriate equipment and software for your studio and assist you in making the best possible digital recordings.

Vince Leonard (vincentl10@aol.com)
Tom Rudolph (terudolph@aol.com)

Chapter 1.
Digital World Fundamentals

In order to record in the digital world, a basic understanding of the fundamentals of sound is needed. This chapter is a concise overview of the most common terms. For a more in-depth study of any specific concept, consult the books and articles listed in the appendix.

Sound Waves

If a tree falls in the forest and no one is there, does it make a sound? This question might be the basis of a philosophical debate, but one thing is for certain: whether or not anyone hears it, when a tree falls in the forest, *sound waves* are produced. Sound waves can also be compared to the effect that a stone has when it is dropped into a pool of water. When the stone is dropped, it creates a series of waves. Imagine these waves as vibrations. When these vibrations reach your ear, they are received by your eardrum (also called the tympanic membrane). When the eardrum vibrates, it sends the sound waves deeper into the ear, where they are prepared for transmission to the brain. The brain recognizes these vibrations as sound. The human ear can perceive minute differences in vibrations.

If you dropped a stone into a pool of water and counted the number of waves created every second, you would determine the *frequency* of the waves. Perhaps it would be 10 waves per second. The faster the waves (20, 40, 60 waves per second), the higher the frequency. Sound may travel from a few vibrations per second to 50,000 or more. Humans can perceive a distinct pitch if the frequency of vibrations exceeds 20 per second. At a rate lower than 20 vibrations per second, the sound is heard as a series of independent clicks. As an experiment, listen to a car engine at a slow-idle speed. The sounds made by the engine at a very low frequency will sound like separate clicks. As the engine revs up to a faster speed, the frequency will increase, and a pitch will be discernable. Again, the rate at which the human ear begins to hear a distinct pitch is approximately 20 vibrations per second. Elephants and some species of whales use sounds below the level of human hearing to communicate.

At the other end of the spectrum is sound above the range of human hearing. Dogs and other animals have hearing more sensitive than that of humans and can perceive higher frequencies. A dog whistle produces sound waves that travel so rapidly they are above the level at which humans can hear. Human hearing peaks at about 20,000 vibrations per second.

Frequency = Hertz (Hz)

Frequency is related to pitch. The higher the frequency, the higher the pitch. Frequency is also referred to as cycles per second or *Hertz*, a term used in honor of German physicist Heinrich Rudolf Hertz, who conducted seminal experiments with sound. Since most sounds have a frequency in the thousands, they are abbreviated. *Kilo*, abbreviated k, equals a thousand. *Kilohertz*, abbreviated kHz, represents a frequency of one thousand vibrations per second. So, 22 kHz would represent a frequency of 22,000 vibrations per second.

Frequency response is an important concept in the world of recording. It refers to the frequency range of a specific piece of equipment. Microphones, for example, are often listed by their frequency responses (see chapter 11). For example, a 20-kHz frequency response means the unit can respond up to 22,000 vibrations per second.

Amplitude

Small and large stones have different effects when dropped into water. If each is dropped from the same height, the larger stone will create larger waves. The size or the height of the wave is referred to as its *amplitude*. Amplitude has a direct effect on the volume of a sound. If a sound wave has a larger amplitude than another sound wave, the one with the larger amplitude will be louder.

Timbre

Each sound source creates a unique set of vibrations. Musicians are familiar with the overtones of their particular instruments. Each sound produces a distinct series of overtones. The overtones, or overtone series, determine sound quality, and this is how we can tell the difference between a trumpet, a flute, or a voice. The overtone series is best demonstrated when a guitarist tunes a guitar using harmonics or when the brass player plays several notes using the same fingering or position.

Decibel

The concept of a decibel is used frequently when working with audio gear and recording. The most common use of decibels in recording is measuring the volume of sound. For example, a measurement of 0 decibels, abbreviated dB, represents the threshold of human hearing, with 130 dB representing the threshold of pain. Long-term exposure to 130 dB or more will result in permanent hearing loss. In this case, the decibel is representing the volume level of the sound.

There are other types of decibel scales that are used with audio gear. For example, dBm measures a signal's power; dBV measures voltage. Microphones are listed as having a specific signal level, or dB, as related to a specific standard measurement. The most important concept to understand is the rating of a particular microphone. For example, –60 dB tells us that the signal is 1/60 the strength of the standard signal with which it is compared. Another common use of dB is listing the output of an electronic device, such as an amplifier, which might be rated as + or – dB.

Digital and Analog

A *digital* device is one that stores information as numbers. A sound wave, for example, is represented as a series of numbers. *Analog*, an abbreviation for analogous, refers to information stored in a way that is similar to the original. Digital information is generally more useful than analog. Numbers are more easily manipulated than are grooves on a record or magnetized particles on a tape.

Because waveforms are extremely complex, in order for numbers to represent sound waves, they have to be generated at an extremely fast rate of speed. Before computer chips and microprocessors were invented, digital representation of sound wasn't feasible because the existing technologies were simply too slow.

Phonograph records are analog; compact discs are digital. The phonograph record reproduces sound when vibrations are created by the movement of the needle along the grooves on a record. The grooves are analogous to the sound waves originally produced. On a compact disc (CD) the information is stored as numbers; hence, it is digital.

Why didn't Thomas Edison use digital technology when he was experimenting with the phonograph? At that time, there were no devices capable of generating numbers at the tremendous speed required to record, store, and reproduce a musical performance. Edison used the most advanced technology at his disposal: analog. He made the first sound recordings in 1877 using a telephone repeater system. The first recorded sound was Edison saying, "hello." The sound vibrations made indentations on a sheet of paper passing over a rotating cylinder. The indentations on the paper were analogous to the original vibrations. The process of recording music using discs with grooves continued for one hundred years until the development of the digital process in the 1970s.

Today, many analog devices, such as cassette tape recorders, are still in use. However, digital devices are rapidly replacing them. The older analog tape recorders store information by arranging magnetic particles on tape in a form analogous to the sound waves produced. Digital cassette recorders store sounds as a series of numbers.

There are several distinct advantages to digital versus analog signals. Since digital information is stored as a series of numbers, there is no loss or signal degeneration when a signal is copied from one digital medium to another. Digital signals can be edited more easily than analog. Of course, sound-editing techniques were employed in the analog world. The analog recording studio included a slicing block with razor blades and tape. Small portions of the tape could be surgically removed and reordered. The tape could be turned backward and edited. However, in the digital world, editing is much easier and much more powerful. We will describe the specific advantages of digital recording and editing in the chapters that follow.

Sampling Rate

The process of digital recording has several stages. First, the original signal is recorded. This is called the *analog-to-digital* conversion stage. Analog-to-digital is abbreviated A/D. At this point the input, or original signal, is converted to a series of numbers, called a sample. These numbers are usually stored on a computer disk as a series of discrete numbers. To play back the digital sample, the reverse process, digital-to-analog conversion, is used. After the digital signal is converted to analog, it can then be amplified and sent to loudspeakers to recreate the original sound.

The more samples taken, the more accurately the sound is captured. Currently, compact discs have a sampling rate of 44,100 samples per second, abbreviated 44.1 kHz (kilohertz). Digital Audio Tape, or DAT, uses a slightly higher standard of 48 kHz. The higher the sampling rate, the more realistic the playback of the original sound. The more accurately a signal is to be sampled, the more numbers are required to represent it; therefore, more storage is needed. This is why sounds used on Web pages are often sampled at a lower rate, such as 22 kHz or 11 kHz. These sound files, while smaller, also yield a lesser-quality audio.

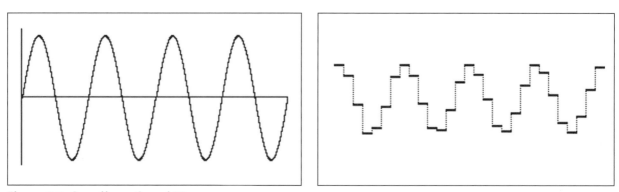

Figure 1.1. Sampling a Sound Wave

Some digital recording equipment records at higher sampling rates than the CD standard of 44.1 kHz. Most DAT recorders have a 48-kHz as well as a 44.1-kHz setting. With these devices it is possible to record at sampling rates higher than compact disc quality. However, sampling rates are not compatible with each other. If the final output is a compact disc, the signals must be resampled at 44.1 kHz before being transferred to a CD. This is made possible using a sample rate converter.

Resolution

Digital technology communicates information using numbers. Each number is referred to as a *bit*. Bit is an abbreviation for binary digit. The number of bits used to represent each measurement is referred to as the resolution. Resolution is also referred to as word length. The higher the resolution, or word length, the more accurate the waveform representation. The more accurate the representation, the better the sound quality.

The common resolution for digital recording is 8-bit, or a digital word length of eight numbers. There is also 16-bit, 20-bit, and 24-bit resolution. Higher resolutions require more storage space since they require more bits of information to represent the sound.

Quantization Noise, Aliasing, and Dithering

The compact disc format of 16-bit sampling and a 44.1-kHz sampling rate is referred to as the Red Book Standard for CD Audio. All CD players and CD-ROM drives in computers can read this format, which is why it is possible to play CDs on a variety of machines so long as they conform to it.

It would appear that the standard Red Book compact disc format (16-bit sampling and 44.1kHz sampling rate) is ideal. However, the hardware that controls these signals is not perfect and can affect the overall sound quality. For example, when an analog signal is converted to a digital signal and in the conversion process is slightly altered, a distortion called quantization noise occurs. Aliasing, another form of signal corruption, happens when the analog-to-digital converter misreads the signal and produces a lower frequency. To reduce signal distortion, some systems record at sampling rates of 44.1 kHz but with 20- or 24-bit resolution. This allows for greater dynamic range and reduced distortion or noise during production. However, before a CD is recorded, the signals must be dithered down to 16-bit. Dithering is the name given to the process of reducing the number of bits in each digital word or sample. This process involves adding some white noise to the signal. Using a process called noise shaping, this noise is usually switched to areas of the audio spectrum to which our ears are less sensitive, typically those above 10 kHz.

MIDI

Digital audio recording has become ubiquitous, although it is relatively new. The first commercial digital recorders were introduced in the early 1990s. However, in the early 1980s, prior to the advent of digital audio, another form of digital recording was launched and is still made possible through *MIDI*. MIDI, an acronym for Musical Instrument Digital Interface, is a digital computer language used to transmit information between electronic instruments and computers. MIDI is a universal language. When it is built into electronic instruments, it allows them to communicate with each other and with MIDI-equipped computers. MIDI was developed in 1983 to increase the compatibility of all electronic equipment in order to extend the capabilities available to musicians while slowing the rapid rate of hardware obsolescence. MIDI allows someone to buy keyboards, drum machines, and other devices from different manufacturers for use together. MIDI equipment from Yamaha, Korg, and Roland, for example, could be interconnected and used together in a studio or live setup.

What MIDI Transmits

The functions of MIDI can be easily compared to those of a player piano. A piano roll by itself can make no sound; it is basically a primitive program that records the performance data or notes to be played—rhythm, volume, pedals, and so on. In order to be heard, the roll, or program, must be connected to a player piano. The piano roll then tells the piano what notes to play. Similarly, MIDI tells the MIDI instrument what notes to play.

The language component of MIDI breaks down the musical performance into separate parts and represents these parts digitally. Think of MIDI as a lightning-fast analyzer. When a MIDI keyboard is played, the computer chip inside the instrument reads the performance and sends the following information:

- What keys are being pressed down. (Each key has been assigned a specific MIDI number called a MIDI *note number*.)
- The start or attack of each note. This is called *note on*.
- When the keys are let up or released, referred to as *note off*.
- How fast or hard the key is pressed, which controls the volume. This is referred to as *velocity*.
- Any use of the pitch bender to create tremolo or vibrato. This is called *pitch bend*.
- The timbre or program being used.
- Other parameters are also transmitted referred to as MIDI *controllers*.

The main concept to understand is simply that MIDI sends and receives information about the performance. There is no sound recorded, digital or audio. The sound that is heard is solely dependent upon the type of MIDI playback device used.

MIDI Channels

MIDI was originally designed to transmit on sixteen different channels. Channels are used to keep information separate. Think of each MIDI channel as being capable of transmitting a different instrument sound or timbre. Just as a television set receives different programs on different channels, MIDI transmits to the MIDI instrument the information it requires to play back separate timbres on different channels. If you want to play back timbres simultaneously, then each sound must be assigned to a separate track and a separate MIDI channel.

Computers with multimedia capabilities and almost every model of electronic keyboards manufactured today are multitimbral—that is, they can produce multiple timbres at the same time. Most instruments have a minimum of 24-voice multitimbral capability, also known as 24-note polyphonic. Some instruments have thirty-two or more voices available. Because MIDI can send information on separate channels, it can simultaneously trigger multiple sounds or timbres.

General MIDI (GM)

MIDI was created to standardize the transmission of information among electronic instruments made by different manufacturers. However, in the early days of MIDI, when a MIDI file was created with one brand of instrument, it would likely sound totally different on another. The problem was that each manufacturer used a different numbering system to access various sounds. The piano might be 41 on a Korg, 120 on a Yamaha, 45 on a Kurzweil, and so forth. Since MIDI did not transmit the actual sound, only the number of the sound, it was difficult to share MIDI files with others and have them play the instrument sound intended.

The electronic keyboard manufacturers got together to address this need and developed a standard sound set that all instruments would adhere to. They named it *General MIDI* (GM). For example, on all General MIDI instruments and computers, number 1 is *always* a piano, number 57 is *always* a trumpet, and so forth. General MIDI automatically set MIDI channel 10 to drums. Such standardization was advantageous for transmission of MIDI files over the Internet. Today's Macintosh and Windows computers have built-in General MIDI capability allowing them to play back MIDI files in GM format. The basic 128 General MIDI sounds are shown here:

Acou Piano	1	Nylon Guit	25	Strings	49	Piccolo	73	Ice Rain	97	FX-Fret	121
Brght Piano	2	Acou Guit	26	Slow Strg	50	Flute	74	Sound Trk	98	Fx-Breath	122
Elec Grand	3	Jazz Guit	27	Syn Strg 1	51	Recorder	75	Crystal	99	Sea Shore	123
Honk Tonk	4	E Guit Cln	28	Syn Strg 1	52	P Flute	76	Atmosphere	100	Bird Tweet	124
Rhodes	5	E Guit Mut	29	Choir Aahs	53	B Bottle	77	Briteness	101	Telephone	125
Elec Piano2	6	O-D Guit	30	Vocal Oohs	54	Shaku	78	Goblin	102	Helicopter	126
Harpsichord	7	Dist Guit	31	Syn Voice	55	Whistle	79	Echoes	103	Applause	127
Clav	8	Guit Harm	32	Orch Hit	56	Ocarina	80	Sci Fi	104	Gunshot	128
Celeste	9	Acou Bass	33	Trumpet	57	Sqr Wave	81	Sitar	105	DRUMS	
Glockenspl	10	Fing Bass	34	Trombone	58	Saw Wave	82	Banjo	106		
Music Box	11	Pick Bass	35	Tuba	59	Calliope	83	Shamiron	107	Standard	
Vibraphone	12	Ftless Bass	36	M Trumpet	60	Chiff Lead	84	Koto	108	Room	
Marimba	13	Slp Bass 1	37	Fr Horn	61	Charang	85	Kalimba	109	Power	
Xylophone	14	Slp Bass 2	38	Br Section	62	Vox Lead	86	Bag Pipe	110	Electronic	
Tube Bell	15	Syn Bass 1	39	Syn Br 1	63	Fifth Lead	87	Fiddle	111	Rap (808)	
Santur	16	Syn Bass 2	40	Syn Br 2	64	Bas & Lead	88	Shanai	112	Jazz	
DB organ	17	Violin	41	Sop Sax	65	New Age	89	Tinkle	113	Brush	
Per organ	18	Viola	42	Alto Sax	66	Warm Pd	90	Agogo	114		
Rock organ	19	Cello	43	Ten Sax	67	Poly Synth	91	Stl drm	115		
Ch organ	20	Ctra Bass	44	Bari Sax	68	Pd Voice	92	Wd block	116		
Reed organ	21	Tremelo	45	Oboe	69	Pd Bowed	93	Taiko drm	117		
Accordian	22	Pizzicato	46	Eng Horn	70	Pd Metal	94	Mel toms	118		
Harmonica	23	Harp	47	Bassoon	71	Pd Halo	95	Syn drums	119		
Band Neon	24	Timpani	48	Clarinet	72	Pd Sweep	96	Rev cymbl	120		

Figure 1.2. General MIDI Sound List

General MIDI established a standard location or number for sounds. The GM standard, in addition to specifying the numerical location of sounds, also required that the device provide a minimum of twenty-four polyphonic, or multitimbral voices. This guaranteed that a General MIDI instrument or computer could play back a minimum of twenty-four different sounds at the same time (referred to as 24-part multitimbral).

The downside of General MIDI is that even though number 57 is a trumpet, it may sound quite different when played on different brands of instruments and computers. For this reason, most MIDI keyboards include other banks of sounds that can be used in conjunction with GM. These other banks many times have additional sounds that complement General MIDI and employ the specific strengths of the instrument.

Yamaha and Roland have extended General MIDI specifications to include sound effects and other enhancements. Roland developed the GS format and Yamaha the XG format. These formats are downwardly compatible, which means they will play on any GM instrument. However, when played on their own equipment incorporating GS or XG enhancements, the sound quality is better than that of standard GM. As of this writing, neither of these GM-enhanced formats has been accepted by other manufacturers. However, some computer-game companies have also begun to use these enhanced GM formats.

MIDI Interface

In order for computers and electronic instruments to communicate via MIDI, they need a way to connect. The device that enables this is called a MIDI interface. There are many different types of MIDI interfaces for a wide variety of applications. Every Windows-compatible PC made today has a MIDI interface built right into the internal sound card. Also, many electronic keyboards and MIDI devices have with built-in MIDI capability. Macintosh computers require an external MIDI interface to be connected to the computer. Diagrams and descriptions of how to connect these devices are discussed in chapter 6.

In order to connect two MIDI instruments or to connect a MIDI keyboard or sound module to a computer, MIDI cables must be used. Usually a minimum of two MIDI cables are needed, one for input and one for output. Remember, MIDI only transmits MIDI data. You cannot connect your MIDI cable to a speaker. It is the actual MIDI instrument that produces the sound. See chapter 6 for more detailed information on MIDI interfaces and their application in digital recording.

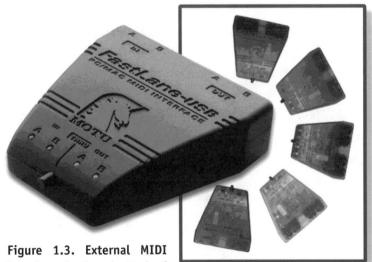

Figure 1.3. External MIDI Interface: Fastlane by Mark of the Unicorn

Standard MIDI Files

MIDI performance information is stored in a computer file format. A few years after the advent of MIDI, every instrument manufacturer and software publisher had its own proprietary MIDI file format. This meant that it was not possible to share MIDI files between different software programs, MIDI instruments, and different brands of computers. The industry addressed this problem by developing a standard MIDI file format, referred to as SMF. A MIDI file that is in SMF format can be shared between software programs. For example, a MIDI file saved in SMF format on one instrument or software program can be read into other programs produced by different publishers and manufacturers. This makes it possible to create files that can be read by any software program. Most SMF files produced today are also GM-compatible, making them instantly playable on any GM-compatible instrument or computer.

MIDI Sequencer

Analog sequencers were used long before the creation of MIDI or digital audio. In the 1960s and 1970s, sequencers were built into analog synthesizers produced by Moog, ARP, Roland, and Buchla. The original sequencers could control eight to sixteen events (or notes) at a time and were used primarily for rhythmic ostinatos. Since the dawn of microprocessor-controlled digital instruments in the 1980s, sequencers have become more and more sophisticated and can now control thousands of events at one time. It is also possible to record these events on separate tracks, creating a digital multitrack MIDI recorder, referred to as a MIDI sequencer.

As mentioned previously, with MIDI sounds are not recorded, as is the case with digital audio recording. Rather, the information about the performance is recorded—what notes were played, how long they were held, pitch bend, volume, and other performance information. A MIDI sequencer is a device that can record, store, edit, and play back MIDI performance data. MIDI is often combined with digital audio using special software. Software for sequencing will be addressed in chapters 6 and 7.

MIDI sequencers are distinctly different from digital audio recorders. A digital audio recorder records the actual sound in digital form, while MIDI records just the performance information as performed on a MIDI instrument. Since a MIDI sequencer records information or data in digital format, the data can easily be modified. For example, if you recorded a passage using a MIDI sequencer and played one wrong note, you could select the incorrect note and type in or replay the correct note. With sequencers, you can alter notes, durations, volume, and just about every aspect of the musical performance after the performance has taken place.

Unique Features of Sequencers

Just as a word processing program makes it easier for the typist to edit the text, a MIDI sequencer allows the user to more easily edit performance information. With sequencers, a melody can be transposed without affecting the tempo or speed. This is possible because the pitch and tempo are recorded as *separate* pieces of digital information. Some of the common uses of sequencers include recording music for projects such as film scores and commercials or creating practice exercises for students and professionals. Most MIDI sequencers also can record digital audio. Specific examples of MIDI sequencing software will be discussed in chapters 6 and 7.

Tracks

Both digital audio recorders and MIDI sequencers store data in digital format. They also are similar in that they both can record data on separate tracks.

Multitrack analog tape recorders came into use in the mid-1960s. Before this time, recordings were made live to tape, and no mixing was possible. Analog multitrack tape decks divided the magnetic tape into separate parts or tracks. Each of these tracks could be separately edited, erased, or changed without affecting the others. The advantage of separate tracks was independent control over each part. For example, with a 4-track tape recorder, a rock group could record the drums and bass on track 1, come back to the recording studio on another day and record the guitar parts on track 2, and then record the vocals on tracks 3 and 4. Analog tape recorders continued to develop through the 1960s and 1970s and eventually were capable of recording twenty-four separate tracks.

A MIDI sequencer can also divide information into separate tracks for independent control over performance information and therefore could function as a multitrack recording device. If a sequencer has sixteen tracks, then it is possible to store sixteen independent parts. With multiple tracks, users can create very complex sequences or compositions. Information stored on separate tracks can be edited or isolated during playback.

With today's sequencers, one can record from sixteen to an unlimited number of MIDI tracks, depending on the type and cost of the MIDI sequencer. The cost of an analog multitrack tape deck in the 1960s was in the $100,000 range. Today, thanks to the decreasing price of digital technology, digital, multitrack sequencers and sequencing software can be purchased from under $100 to more than $1,000, depending upon the features of the product. A complete review of MIDI software is presented in chapters 6 and 7.

Tracks vs. Channels

MIDI is usually transmitted on sixteen separate channels. One of the most confusing tasks when first working with MIDI sequencers is trying to distinguish between MIDI channels and MIDI sequencer tracks. Each uses the same numbering system (1, 2, 3, 4, etc.). When you record separate parts—such as a bass part, chords, and melody—each is placed on a separate track. After information is recorded, you assign the data or track to separate channels for playback. MIDI channels are synonymous with timbre. If you want separate timbres, then you must assign the tracks to separate channels. If you want all the same timbre (a string trio for example) then assign the tracks to the same channel.

Summary

Some of the most common terms used in the world of digital and MIDI recording have been introduced in this chapter. For a more in-depth investigation of these terms, consult the references listed in the appendix.

Chapter 2.

Overview of Electronic Instruments

If all you want to do in the studio is record live, acoustic sounds, then you might not need an electronic keyboard. You might only need some microphones and digital recording gear, which we will describe in the chapters that follow. Most people do include at least one or more sound sources, in the form of electronic keyboards and other instruments, when setting up a studio. For this reason, it is important to have an idea of the options available in the electronic-instrument marketplace.

MIDI Compatibility

It is easy to tell if an electronic keyboard or instrument is MIDI-capable. Just look on the instrument's back panel. If the keyboard has MIDI IN and OUT, which are known as *MIDI ports*, then the instrument is MIDI-capable. Some keyboards also have a MIDI THRU port. MIDI THRU simply passes the incoming information on to the next instrument. The THRU port is handy when you are linking several instruments. Most electronic instruments that cost more than $100 include MIDI.

Types of Electronic Keyboards

Selecting an electronic keyboard can be confusing. In order to select the appropriate instrument, some basic knowledge is needed. Almost every electronic keyboard on the market today can be placed into one of the following categories: sample player, sampler, digital piano, workstation, or analog synthesizer.

Some people use the word *synthesizer* to describe any keyboard that is electronic, while others use it in the pure sense of describing a keyboard that creates sounds by manipulating electrical currents. I limit the use of the term synthesizer to one specific type of electronic keyboard, the analog synthesizer. The more appropriate general term to use is electronic keyboard, as this is the one aspect all these instruments do have in common. The term "synth" is often used in the industry as a generic term for an electronic keyboard.

Early electronic keyboards, from the '50s, '60s, and early '70s, were analog instruments. Using oscillators and filters, they manipulated electrical current to produce an analogous representation of sound. Today, most electronic keyboards use digital means to create sound.

Sample Players: Portable Electronic Keyboards

There are portable electronic keyboards designed for the home user or for the nontechnically oriented user. The least expensive type of electronic instrument, these keyboards typically have buttons with labels such as *trumpet* or *violin*. They are considered sampler players because they reproduce samples that were recorded digitally. There are no potentially confusing, complex-looking windows with numbers. The player selects a sound merely by pressing a button. These instruments can be placed on a tabletop or stand and are easily transported. Most such models of portable electronic keyboards are equipped with features that create automatic harmonies and rhythms. Because these instruments also contain built-in speakers, no external amplification is needed. Portable electronic instruments are sold in department stores, mail order catalogs, and music stores.

Figure 2.1. Yamaha PSR-340-C Portable Electronic Keyboard

Generally, portable electronic keyboards are among the least expensive electronic instruments. Some models cost less than $200. However, to obtain quality sound production and other important features discussed below, be prepared to spend $400 or more. Be sure to listen to several models in the same price range before making a decision. Some models of portable electronic keyboards include:

- Yamaha PSR-320
- Kawai X15D
- Casio WK-1300

Most of these instruments have recording capability in the form of a built-in sequencer. This type of recording device is designed for practice and enjoyment, not professional-level recording.

Intelligent Keyboards

There are portable electronic keyboards that have many advanced features and are designed to produce high-quality accompaniments, rhythms, and rhythm patterns. Most of these instruments are designed for professional use. The enhanced applications come with a price, of course. Expect to pay about $300 for one of these instruments. Because of the significant number of built-in features, these models are usually referred to as intelligent keyboards. These keyboards are often used in stadiums to play the sound effects for athletic events. Examples of intelligent keyboards are:

- Korg I-5
- Roland EM-2000
- Yamaha PSR-7000

Figure 2.2. Roland EM-2000 Intelligent Keyboard

Programmable Keyboards

Programmable electronic keyboards have the capability to alter and create new sounds as well as to play back digital sound. As the sound quality is generally good, these instruments are frequently used in the recording studio and for performance.

Figure 2.3. Korg N-5 Programmable Keyboard

You can usually tell if a keyboard is programmable by the type of display. If you find a window displaying numbers and parameters, the keyboard is most likely programmable. If instead it has buttons that say *trumpet*, *violin*, etc., then it is most likely a portable electronic keyboard. Programmable keyboard models include:

- Alesis QS series
- Korg N series
- Roland XP series

Digital Pianos

A digital piano combines the realistic sound quality of sample players with the feel of an acoustic piano. In an effort to make the digital piano mimic the action of an acoustic piano, weights are inserted inside the keys; hence, they are called weighted keys. Weighted keys are especially important if the instrument will be played by performers who prefer the feel of an acoustic piano keyboard. Most digital pianos are smaller and less expensive than traditional acoustic pianos.

- Yamaha YDP-101
- Kurzweil SP76
- Korg C150

Figure 2.4. Kurzweil SP76

If you visit a piano outlet or manufacturer you will most likely see both acoustic and digital pianos on display. A digital piano can offer many more options than its acoustic counterpart, such as a built-in music recorder and the ability to play more than one timbre at a time.

Digital pianos are usually somewhat more expensive because of their weighted keys. They are also usually less portable. Prices for such units normally start at around $1,200. Some examples of digital pianos include:

- Kawai CA 130 and CA 230
- Korg C-150 and C-350
- Roland FP-9
- Yamaha YDP and Clavinova Series

The Workstation

The term *workstation* refers to an instrument that combines several functions in one package. Though a workstation may resemble a programmable keyboard from the outside, it is different inside: workstations have a built-in MIDI sequencer and drum sounds. Workstations usually include an effects-processing device that allows you to add digital echo and reverb to sounds and sequences. In addition, there is typically a storage device, such as a disk drive, for storing sequences. Some keyboards even offer the option of digital recording.

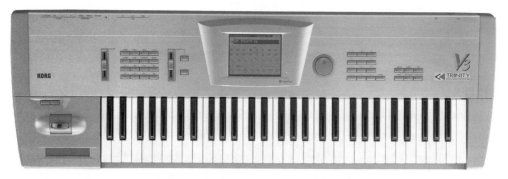

Figure 2.5. Korg Trinity Music Workstation

The purpose of a workstation is to provide an all-in-one instrument: a performance keyboard, a built-in sequencer, and effects devices for creating and playing back sequences. A workstation might serve as the main component of the low-budget studio. Examples of workstations include:

- Korg N-364
- Korg Trinity
- Ensoniq TS-12
- Kurzweil K2000

Samplers

Keyboards with sampling capability can record from external sources, using a microphone. They also can record from other sources, such as compact discs and Macintosh (aiff) and Windows (wav) file formats. Some keyboards, such as the Korg Triton and Kurzweil K2000, can function as a sample player, MIDI sequencer, and sampler. With these instruments, samples can be recorded and played back. A MIDI sequence can be recorded with mono and stereo samples. This means you can record a sample of up to eleven minutes long in stereo or mono. The trade-off for having all these features is cost. Keyboards with multiple options such as sampling and MIDI sequencing might cost $2,000 to $3,000 and up.

Figure 2.6. Korg Triton Sampling Keyboard

Samplers also come in rack-mountable versions, such as the Akai S5000. In other words, you get all of the internal sampling capability without the keyboard. This type of sampler is designed for studio use.

Figure 2.7. AKAI S5000 Rack Mount Sampler

Analog Synthesizers

In the past few years, performers have shown a renewed interest in using electronic keyboards that simulate the original analog sounds from the 1960s and 1970s. The price of these instruments is usually about $1,000 or more. Analog synthesizers are not designed to be all-purpose instruments. Examples of analog synthesizers include:

- Clavia Nord Lead by Armadillo Systems
- Korg Z-1

MIDI Sound Module

MIDI sound modules are electronic keyboards without the keys. They are also known as rack modules, as they are made to be placed in studio racks. Less expensive than their keyboard counterparts, rack modules have the advantage of letting you add extra sound sources to the studio at less expense. Most samplers and synthesizers can be purchased in module format. There are MIDI modules designed for specific purposes that can be added to the digital studio. Some modules have only piano sounds, others specialize in orchestral sounds, bass, and percussion sounds, and so forth. They are often the best means to expand the sound possibilities in the studio. Some of the available sound modules include:

- Alesis QS7
- Korg NS5R
- Roland JV-1010
- Alesis Nanopiano 64
- Alesis Nanobass 64
- Alesis Nanosynth

Figure 2.8. Proteus 2000 MIDI Sound Module

Software Synthesizers

If you buy a Macintosh or Windows computer today, it is already equipped with at least rudimentary sound-synthesis capability. A PC running Windows 95 or later comes equipped with a soundcard that can generate multitimbral sound output and MIDI. Apple Computer includes QuickTime with all PowerMac, G3, G4, and later models. This free program adds to the computer multimedia sound capability that is GM compatible. It is therefore possible to play back MIDI and General MIDI files through the computer's internal sound-synthesis capabilities.

It is also possible to purchase software synthesizers, referred to as software synths, that provide a higher-quality sound output than the built-in options. A software synthesizer is a program that has much the same function as a piece of hardware, except that it uses the memory and storage capability of the computer. With the synthesizer, the computer can generate high-quality sound and thereby eliminate the need for additional pieces of hardware. The computer's sound-producing capability can be added to the existing pieces in the studio.

Several companies are producing software synthesizers, including Roland, Bitheadz, and NemeSys. These companies offer a range of products that include software to emulate analog and digital synths and samplers. Many of these professional sound-synthesis programs can be purchased for under $500 and can be used as MIDI sound sources. Software synths can be used in conjunction with hardware units. It is possible to use multiple units for MIDI output.

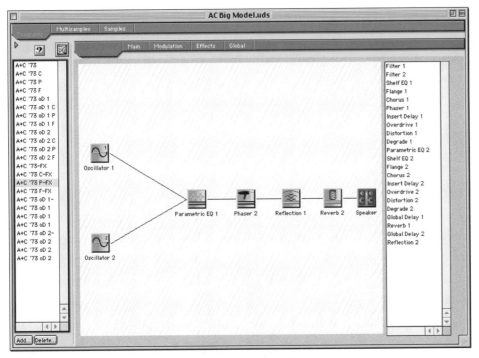

Figure 2.9. Bitheadz Unity DS-1 Software Synthesizer

Alternate MIDI Controllers

A MIDI controller is any device that connects to another MIDI instrument or sound module. In addition to keyboard controllers, there are other MIDI controllers designed to be used by percussionists, violinists, guitarists, reed players, and vocalists.

Keyboard MIDI Controllers

Keyboard controllers are keyboards that can transmit MIDI data but have a limited amount of built-in or on-board sounds. The primary function of a MIDI keyboard controller is to act as an input device and to control other MIDI modules in the studio or during a performance.

There are two categories of keyboard controllers: computer desktop models and performance controllers. The desktop MIDI keyboard controller is designed to be used with a computer and a MIDI sound module or sound card. It is light and compact and can fit in a small space. Examples of this type of keyboard include:

- Roland PC-200 MKII
- Evolution MDK 61 MIDI KEY II

Desktop MIDI keyboard controllers are less expensive than other MIDI keyboards as they have *no* sound-producing capabilities of their own. This type of MIDI keyboard controller is a good choice when there is limited space or for a desktop MIDI setup in an office or practice room. If you already own a MIDI sound module or your PC has a built-in MIDI compatible sound card, then a desktop MIDI keyboard controller could be the least expensive option. The cost of desktop MIDI keyboard controllers is in the $150 to $250 range.

The second type of MIDI keyboard controller is designed to be used primarily in live performance to control many different keyboards and MIDI devices. It also can be used in the MIDI recording studio. Examples of this type of keyboard include:

- Kurzweil PC88
- Fatar SL series
- General Music SK88
- Roland A-90

Kurzweil refers to its PC88 model as a "performance controller." The Fatar Studio 49 and Roland A-80 are examples of advanced MIDI keyboard controllers designed to be used with a complex setup of MIDI equipment. A performance MIDI keyboard controller is a good choice for live performance when many different MIDI keyboards and sound modules must be controlled at the same time or in the recording studio with multiple MIDI devices. MIDI keyboard controllers such as the Kurzweil PC88, Fatar Studio 49, and Roland A-80 are designed for the serious MIDI user. These devices are significantly more expensive than desktop MIDI keyboard controllers, ranging in cost between $1,000 and $3,000.

Figure 2.10. Kurzweil PC88 MIDI Keyboard Performance Controller

MIDI Bass Pedals

Another type of MIDI keyboard controller is designed to be played by the keyboardist who plays foot pedal bass. This instrument is used to drive a MIDI module and is primarily used to generate bass notes. The Fatar MP113 MIDI Bass Pedals is an example of a product with MIDI bass. It resembles a miniature church organ bass-pedal unit. MIDI bass pedals are designed for live performance but could be used in the studio.

Electronic Percussion

One of the fastest growing areas in the MIDI world is electronic percussion. Electronic percussion is a term used to describe any device that uses MIDI to produce percussion sounds. There are a wide variety of electronic percussion devices. Among them are the drum computer, electronic percussion MIDI controllers, and drum pads. These instruments are compact, can be used by nonpercussionists, and can produce a wide range of sounds.

Drum Computer

The drum computer is one of the oldest electronic instruments. Its predecessors were the rhythm generators that began to appear in home organs in the 1960s. The first programmable drum computers, sometimes referred to as drum machines, were introduced in the 1970s by the Oberheim and Lynn drum companies. Essentially, drum computers are devices that can store, record, and play back percussion sounds. Think of a drum computer as a specialized percussion playback unit with a built-in sequencer. Drum computers have a series of pads, which are played with the fingertips. Rhythm patterns can be created and recorded. Even the most inexpensive drum computers can store several hundred patterns.

Just about every major electronic keyboard manufacturer produces drum computers. Today's drum computers are designed for creating and recording drum patterns for use in live performance or a MIDI studio. Some examples of drum computers are:

Figure 2.11. Boss DR-770 Drum computer

- Boss DR-770 DR Rhythm
- Alesis SR-16
- Roland R8

The drum computer reproduces digitally recorded sounds or samples of percussion instruments. In other words, actual sounds from acoustic percussion instruments were digitally recorded and stored inside the drum computer's memory. Using a drum computer, you can instantly access claves, bongos, maracas, and other instrument sounds both for live performance and for recorded playback.

Since many patterns can be stored, drum parts can be created for entire songs including introduction patterns, fills, and ending patterns. Since a drum computer is similar to a sequencer, rhythm patterns can be recorded in real time (playing in time with the drum computer's metronome) or step-entered one note or one duration at a time.

The drum computer is not necessarily essential in today's MIDI studio because most MIDI keyboard workstations and most electronic MIDI keyboards can generate and record drum sounds and rhythms.

Groove Samplers

Groove samplers are designed primarily for use in rap and dance styles. A groove sampler is used in live performance or in assembling loops of audio into a composition. A sampler section records audio samples that are triggered from pads similar to a drum computer. Models have editing and processing capabilities to alter or edit the samples once they are recorded. Audio output is controlled from a mixer section where volume is controlled in real time. It is possible to send the audio signal to a mixer to combine with other MIDI devices and processing. Some units also have a built in tone generator for adding bass or keyboard parts. In addition to the Roland SP-808 and MC-505, Akai, Ensoniq, and Yamaha also offer their own designs of groove samplers.

MIDI Percussion Controllers

If you can use a piano keyboard to control a MIDI module, why not use a drumstick or xylophone mallet? Percussion controllers are devices that, when struck by a stick, hand, or pedal, can control a MIDI device.

A percussion controller is capable of triggering a MIDI sound module and hence can produce hundreds of sounds—both pitched and unpitched. MIDI percussion controllers can be used to produce sounds of instruments that are otherwise too expensive to use or not available in an ensemble. For example, a percussion controller could be used to produce the sound of a timpani, chimes, or gong.

Figure 2.12. Roland SP 808 Groovebox

There are various models of percussion controllers from which to choose. The oldest and most common type of percussion controller is a series of pads played with drumsticks.

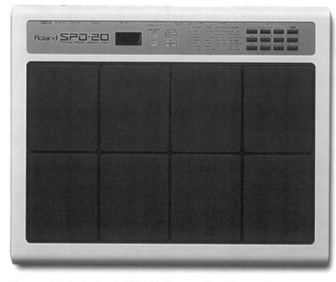

Figure 2.13. Roland SPD-20 Percussion Controller

The Roland SPD-20 is an example of a MIDI percussion controller. It must be connected to an external MIDI module to produce sound. Each pad on the instrument is assigned by the user to a separate MIDI sound.

The SPD-20, formerly the Octapad, is designed to take up a small amount of space. It would be excellent for reproducing the sounds of timpani for a musical pit orchestra, or for use on the field for a marching band show. Yamaha has a less expensive line of drum controllers (the DD series) with on-board sounds (so an external MIDI module is not required). The lower cost (from $100 to $300) makes these affordable by most budgets.

For the percussionist who wants a digital drum set that not only resembles a traditional drum set but also can be played like one, there are several options. Roland makes V-Drums and Yamaha offers the DTX Digital Percussion System, a complete set of drum triggers and a sophisticated drum sound module designed for the serious percussionist. The cost of this professional option is in the range of $1,000 to $2,000. The advantage of using a MIDI drum set is that the drums can be programmed to play or trigger any sound available from the MIDI module.

Since a percussion controller sends MIDI data, it can be connected to the input of a MIDI interface and used to input data into a sequencer or notation program. This is a natural way for percussionists to enter parts into a sequence.

MIDI String Instruments and Guitar Synthesizers

The Zeta Company produces a complete line of electronic string instruments, including several models of electronic violins, violas, and cellos, that can be easily amplified for live performance.

Figure 2.14. Roland V-Drums

Zeta also produces a MIDI violin controller that connects between four- and five-string Zeta violins, allowing these instruments to send MIDI information to MIDI sound modules and synthesizers. So, essentially two devices are needed: a Zeta MIDI violin and a MIDI violin controller. MIDI string instruments are excellent additions to an electro-acoustic ensemble, for live performance, and for entering data into sequencers and notation programs.

Suppose the cello player in a string quartet can't make the concert. With an electric violin connected to a MIDI module, an available violinist could play the cello part, using a cello sound in the correct octave. These instruments are not designed to replace their acoustic counterparts; rather, they are designed for string players to use in live performance and to control MIDI modules.

Guitar Synthesizers

Electric guitars can also send MIDI information. Several available products make this possible, for example, Roland's line of guitar synthesizers. The Roland GR series comes in various configurations, allowing guitarists to access a wide range of sounds, including acoustic instruments, effects, and even percussion sounds. Connect any guitar to a guitar synthesizer and many additional sounds are now possible.

Roland also makes a special device—the GI-10 Guitar MIDI interface—that converts a guitar's output to MIDI data. When the GI-10 is connected, a guitarist can plug into any MIDI module and access all of the available sounds. Also, with the GI-10, a guitarist can plug into the MIDI IN of a computer interface and input directly into a sequencer or notation program. This is an excellent device for guitarists who don't play the keyboard and want to record, play back, and store MIDI data.

Pitch-to-MIDI Converters

I have often been asked by musicians who are not strong keyboard players if it is possible to use an acoustic instrument or voice as a MIDI input device. With a pitch-to-MIDI converter it is possible to use acoustic instruments to input MIDI data.

21

There are MIDI converters on the market that take acoustic sound played into a microphone and convert the sound vibrations into MIDI data. Any acoustic instrument or the human voice can be used. Play or sing into a microphone and the sound is converted to MIDI data. Because the conversion process from acoustic sound to MIDI is quite complex, most pitch-to-MIDI converters are only 90 to 95 percent accurate. However, pitch-to-MIDI converters do offer a viable alternative to entering MIDI data and controlling MIDI modules with acoustic instruments and the voice.

An excellent, all-purpose pitch-to-MIDI converter is Amadeus II. Connect a standard microphone to Amadeus II and any acoustic sound can be changed into MIDI data, including the voice: simply sing into Amadeus II using a standard microphone, and the pitches are converted to MIDI information.

The advantage to using an acoustic instrument or voice to input MIDI data is that the performer does not need to learn a new instrument. The disadvantage is the significant amount of equipment needed. Also, the technology of converting acoustic sound to MIDI data is inexact. Sometimes, especially if one plays many fast notes or a combination of single notes and double stops, the converter can become overloaded. It may even sound some notes that were not played. Try out a MIDI converter before purchasing to be sure that the device can deliver the required performance level.

MIDI Wind Controllers

There are electronic instruments on the market called *wind controllers* that are designed to be used by horn players. In a manner similar to the percussion controllers and pitch-to-MIDI converters mentioned above, MIDI data is sent to a sound module via an instrument that is fingered and blown like a wind instrument.

There are several MIDI wind controllers. Casio's DH 100,

Figure 2.15. Yamaha WX-5 Wind Controller

an instrument that costs under $100, was a popular low-cost wind controller, although it is no longer produced. Akai's Electronic Wind Instrument or EWI (pronounced EE-WEE), which has fingerings similar to a recorder, also has a breath sensor so the instrument will respond to breath attacks. Yamaha also makes the WX-5, a wind controller similar to the Akai unit.

Overall, wind controllers have not been as successful as expected, especially when compared to electronic keyboards. Wind controllers have been embraced by some jazz and commercial performers. Jazz artists, including Michael Brecker and others, have featured electronic instruments on recordings and in live performance. Wind controllers do have many advantages, as they can access a variety of timbres in an unlimited range. Since wind controllers are MIDI compatible, they can produce nonpitched sounds, chords, and sound effects, in addition to any other sound a MIDI device can produce.

The are two primary limitations of wind controllers. In most cases they must be connected to an electronic keyboard or MIDI sound module in order to produce sound. Secondly, it takes practice to learn to play a wind controller and become familiar with each instrument's various performance parameters.

Summary

This section introduced the concepts and tools used in the digital studio. These options will be explored in detail in the chapters that follow.

Chapter 3.

Digital Recording: An Overview

It is amazing and sometimes mind-boggling to try to break down the number of options available in the world of digital recording. In the past few years the industry has experienced tremendous growth. This chapter is designed to provide an overview of the basic concepts and options. These options will be explained in more detail in later chapters.

There are two methods used to record in the digital world, MIDI sequencing and digital audio. Both MIDI and digital audio can be accomplished using a variety of devices and, in some cases, can be combined in the same environment. This chapter will review the various options for digital recording.

Digital Audio Tape (DAT) Recorders

The analog cassette deck is found in most every home and school stereo system. It is an analog device that can record in stereo. The digital audio tape (DAT) recorder is a digital version of the analog cassette deck. Basic 2-track stereo recording can be handled by a DAT recorder. The DAT recorder has not been well received in the consumer market but has found a niche in digital audio recording. In the studio it is used for direct-to-stereo recording and for creating the final stereo mix of a multitrack project. Portable DAT decks are available for field recording and mobile listening.

Figure 3.1. Fostex PD4 Portable DAT Recorder   Figure 3.2. TASCAM DA 45HR Rack Mount DAT Recorder

Multitrack Digital Audio

DAT is limited to stereo or 2-track recording. For multitrack recording, there are several options available. These include:

- Modular Digital Multitrack, or MDM
- Self-contained, portable hard-disk recorders
- Self-contained, rack-mount hard-disk recorders
- Computer-based hard-disk recording

Modular Digital Multitrack (MDM)

If you require the capability of recording separate tracks (multitrack), there are several possibilities. The oldest digital audio multitrack format and one of the most popular is Modular Digital Multitrack, or MDM. MDM recording is accomplished with a multitrack recorder that uses a tape format to store digital information. These tape-based digital audio recorders typically offer a minimum of eight tracks of digital recording. They are relatively easy to operate, and can be expanded to include additional tracks. Since this was the first recording option in the digital world, MDM is very popular in many home, project, and professional studios.

Multitrack digital tape recorders come in two formats, S-VHS and Super 8mm. There are S-VHS tape machines, like the Alesis ADAT family, and Super 8mm videotape machines made by TASCAM. Both units offer eight tracks of digital recording for 40 to 116 minutes, depending on the format and length of tape. The unique feature of these units is that they are modular; if you need more tracks, you simply add another unit. (They link together to function as one.) It is possible to chain up to sixteen ADATs, or DA-series multitracks, together for 128 tracks. Both systems have remote-control unit options to control multiple decks. The Alesis remote, called BRC, adds additional syncing and editing functions when multiple ADATs are connected together.

Pros and Cons of Tape-Based Systems

Tape-based modular digital multitrack systems (MDMs) have been around for quite a while and should be here for a long time to come. Digital tape machines are affordable and easy to use. The expandability of a modular system is ideal for the project studio environment, as the facility can grow gradually with technology that will not become obsolete. New generations of Alesis and TASCAM machines continually improve sonic quality and come equipped with more features.

Another advantage is that the tape used by these systems is an inexpensive storage medium. The videocassettes that each format uses are much less expensive than high quality open reel tape. Making backups of your multitracks is easy and affordable.

The other main advantage of using tape-based systems is they can be used without a Windows or Macintosh computer. MDM tracks can be edited on a computer by using separately available connections and software, such as the ADAT/Edit package from Alesis.

Tape machines are also very portable. I have an ADAT in a road case that is ready to go to record on location and to take to studios other than my own. The fact that this technology is common, affordable, and portable makes it an ideal way to record in the digital world.

What tape-based systems lack are speed and editing capabilities. Tapes take time to format. Although it is possible to format and record at the same time, it is recommended you format tapes before recording. Tape machines also take time to rewind and fast forward, especially when you are using multiple units. Sync time was a big complaint with early ADATs, but the transports have been improved with later models.

There is also the issue of tape media. Tape may be fine for storing digital information, but it is still subject to the elements. A flaw in the digital world does not mean a small drop-out or reduction in fidelity; it means disaster. Tape machines can also destroy or eat tapes, just as in the analog world. Creating backup or safety copies is recommended.

Hard Disk Recording

Hard disk recording refers to the act of storing digital audio on a computer's hard disk. The hard disk is the place where files and programs are stored. Hard disk systems offer increased editing potential compared to tape-based (MDM) systems. In the digital audio world, there are two options from which to choose: stand-alone hard disk recorders and computer-based hard disk recording systems.

Stand-alone hard disk recorders are available in track configurations from four to twenty-four tracks and can be rack-mounted in a studio or in a portable, transportable case. On the low end, this group includes portable studio models that have mixers included. The Roland V1680 portable studio can even convert the final mix to compact disc.

Computer-based hard disk systems are continuing to develop and are becoming more and more popular. Once plagued by slow computers and minimal storage capabilities, new generations of fast computers with hefty hard drives have brought about many advances and new products. Computer-based digital recording is available for almost any budget. Specific examples will be described in chapters 6, 7, and 8.

The main difference among hard disk systems is the media used to store the files. Some hard disk recorders use removable hard drives, others have connections for external hard drives. Specific descriptions of hard drives and media will take place in chapter 9.

Self-Contained, Portable Hard Disk Recorders

Another option for digital recording is a totally self-contained system. Since it includes all the necessary components in one portable unit, there is no need for an external Windows or Macintosh computer. All of the necessary hardware is included, such as microphone and line inputs, mixers, ports for connecting to external storage devices, and a hard disk for storing the digital data. There is no other equipment or computer needed. These hard disk recording units are excellent for portability and are offered in a range of models to accommodate a range of budgets. In chapter 5 we will explore some of the various modules and options in this fast-growing area.

Self-Contained, Rack-Mount Hard Disk Recorders

Self-contained, rack-mount hard disk recorders are similar to the portable hard disk recorders mentioned previously. They are all-in-one digital audio recording devices that use a hard disk to store the digital information. Since the recording takes place in a self-contained unit, a Windows or Macintosh computer can be used for MIDI sequencing, sampling, or other functions. These units will also be explored in chapter 5.

Computer-Based Digital Audio and MIDI Recording

One of the most versatile options is using a Windows or Macintosh computer with digital audio software. The advantage is that the recording takes place using the computer and can be an inexpensive way to get started in the world of digital recording. There are two types of digital audio software. There are sequencer programs that can record both MIDI and digital audio. As with most computer applications, there is a wide range of software options for all levels. Chapters 6 and 7 review some of the options in this area.

Computer-Based Digital Audio Recording

At the high end of computer-based digital recording is software that is dedicated to recording digital audio. These programs can also record MIDI, but they are not as flexible as the MIDI/digital audio programs mentioned previously. Typically, digital audio recording involves a variety of components requiring connection to a computer, as well as powerful software for recording, editing, and in some cases, mixing. These systems are designed for the professional recording studio and can cost from several to many thousands of dollars. These applications are discussed in chapter 8.

Pros and Cons of Hard Disk Systems

The strength of a hard disk system is its quick access to the media. Unlike MDMs, a hard disk system has no tape to rewind. Easy editing is also a strength. On computer-based systems there are endless possibilities. Software-based effects open up an entire studio's worth of gear on the computer desktop. Stand-alone hard disk units are easily transportable. When working between two or more studios, it is relatively simple for you to transport files on a disk or CD. CD recorders, referred to as CD burners, are common; and with the price of bulk CDs lower than that of analog cassettes, using this media for session backups is quite affordable.

A few years ago, listing the cons of a hard disk system was easy. They were prone to locking up and crashing, causing loss of data, at worst, and interruption of your session and a rise in blood pressure, at best. With computer-based systems, there are some technical considerations, and an occasional disk lockup is a possibility. It may be necessary to expand Windows or Macintosh capabilities to accommodate the requirements of a computer-based system. However, today's computer systems are much more dependable. The specifics of various systems and software are addressed in chapters 6, 7, and 8.

MIDI Sequencing

MIDI sequencing (see chapter 2) can take place either with a keyboard workstation that has a built-in MIDI sequencer or with a computer and MIDI sequencing software. Some models of electronic keyboards, referred to as workstations, have the capability to record and play back MIDI. Even less-expensive keyboards often include some MIDI sequencing capabilities. The advantages of using a MIDI-equipped electronic keyboard workstation are portability and cost.

It is also possible to record MIDI using a Windows or Macintosh computer and a software MIDI sequencer. The computer connects to a MIDI keyboard and uses the software to record and play back MIDI. The computer provides a larger screen display, and there are many software options from which to choose. However, the computer/MIDI combination is less portable than the MIDI workstations. Descriptions of specific MIDI sequencing software applications are addressed in chapter 6.

MIDI and Digital Audio

Some high-end electronic keyboard workstations with built-in MIDI-sequencing capabilities also can record digital audio tracks (see chapter 2). This makes it possible to combine MIDI sequencing and recording of digital audio recording such as acoustic instruments and vocals.

The most common combination of MIDI and digital audio occurs when using a computer and appropriate software. Some software programs are limited to recording only MIDI and are introduced in chapter 6. However, most MIDI sequencing programs can also record digital audio. Like most software applications, there is a variety of options from which to choose. Some MIDI/digital audio programs are designed for the music novice or home user, others for the project studio, and some for the professional recording studio. Each of these options is explored in chapters 6 and 7.

Cable Connections

There are many ways to connect and configure the equipment in the studio, whether you are using analog, digital, MIDI, or combinations of all three. The purpose of the following section is to present the most common terms relating to the various types of connections mentioned throughout this book.

Analog Audio Connections

There are two ways of classifying an analog audio connection: by the type of connector used and by the dB level of the signal. Line level is where most audio equipment operates. This includes mixers, tape decks, and guitar amps. Line level is before power amplification. The decibel level for most line-level equipment is –10 dBV. This number is listed in equipment specs to describe the input or output level of the jacks. Low-level sources include microphones and analog turntables. They require a preamp to boost their signals to line level.

High-end audio gear operates at a higher decibel level, +4 dBm. Feeding a higher decibel level signal into a lower level input will produce distortion. On some gear there is a switch, located on the back panel, to lower, or pad, the +4 level signal down to –10 to correct this problem. Connecting a –10 device into a +4 connection will produce a faint signal. Boosting it will only increase the noise in the signal, not the volume of the actual audio you want to record. If you want an example of this, plug a turntable into the tape inputs of your stereo or into the line inputs of your mixer. The signal will be there, but will be very faint. Increasing the volume will not correct the problem. So be sure to read the manual and understand your gear's requirements and connect the equipment accordingly.

The connectors themselves come in four types: RCA, quarter-inch (tip-ring), quarter-inch (tip-ring-sleeve), and XLR. They can be purchased individually or in a "snake." A snake is a group of eight cables enclosed in a long rubber casing; its purpose is to let users handle the cables as one wire with many connectors. The connectors are color coded for easy recognition.

Connections using a –10 dBV level are called unbalanced. Unbalanced connections use RCA or quarter-inch (tip-ring) connectors. Connections using a +4 dBm level are called balanced. Balanced connections use quarter-inch (tip-ring-sleeve) or XLR connectors. Unbalanced cables have two conductors, while balanced cables have three to make them more resistant to noise buildup. Professional level audio gear generally uses balanced connections for better sound quality.

RCA Cable

Connecting analog components is something we've all done, if not with musical or recording gear, then with home stereo equipment. Home stereo equipment uses RCA-type connectors.

Quarter-Inch Cable (Tip-Ring)

The most common connector in most project studios is the quarter-inch plug, the mono version of the standard headphone plug. These connections are on all keyboards, synths, and mixers, as well as most recorders. There are cables that have an RCA connector on one end and a quarter-inch (T-R) connector on the other to patch between equipment with different connectors. This does not present a problem to the audio signal, since both RCA and quarter-inch connectors are unbalanced. You can purchase adapter plugs, for example, to convert an RCA cable into a quarter-inch cable.

Quarter-Inch cable (Tip-Ring-Sleeve)

The actual plug of the quarter-inch (tip-ring-sleeve) connector is the same size as the quarter-inch tip-ring, but with two black bands around the connector instead of one. The actual wire used is of quality construction, reducing its susceptibility to noise and distortion.

XLR

XLR cables are most commonly used for microphone connections but are also used for balanced audio connections. It is possible to have a cable with XLR connectors at one end and quarter-inch at the other end. This is common for microphones that do not require phantom power. For more information on phantom power and microphones, see chapter 11.

Digital Audio Connections

If you think of analog audio connections as mingling at your local café, then digital connections are like visiting the United Nations. The digital connections use several different languages, referred to as protocols, and they don't understand each other, at least not without a translator. Fortunately, each language has its own proprietary connector, so it is difficult to confuse them. However, some of the connectors resemble those used for analog signals. It is very important to be sure which is which, and to connect the cables properly.

The most basic language difference is that a digital signal is expressed in numbers. The first stage an analog signal will encounter when entering the digital world is the analog-to-digital converter. This takes the audio signal and converts it to the 1s and 0s of digital language. There is a digital-to-analog converter just before the signal reaches the output jacks on digital equipment that reverses the process. When transferring digital information, don't worry about the gain. The audio information is being transmitted digitally, not as audio, so after conversion it cannot be too loud or too soft.

S/PDIF—RCA

S/PDIF, or Sony/Philips Digital Format, carries a digital stereo signal through a single cable using RCA connectors. You can use the same RCA cables as those you use with your stereo equipment. There is no special type of digital cable for S/PDIF signals. However, this does not mean you can plug a digital S/PDIF cable into an analog RCA connection, as the two signals are not compatible.

S/PDIF Optical—TOSlink

The required signal for this format is the same as the S/PDIF RCA but uses a fiberoptic cable. These jacks are common on Sony MiniDisc machines and on Kurzweil 2000 and 2500 keyboard sampling inputs. S/PDIF Optical connectors have a plastic shield over the jack and a connector that protects them from dirt when not connected.

Since the format of the data is the same, it is possible to convert between S/PDIF RCA and S/PDIF Optical connector types using an adapter box such as the Midiman CO2. The CO2 can also be used as a signal booster for long cable runs.

AES/EBU

AES/EBU was developed jointly by the Audio Engineer Society and the European Broadcast Union. This format combines a digital stereo signal using a single cable. It is more commonly found on mid-level to high-end recording gear.

For converting between AES/EBU and S/PDIF there is the Midiman CO3. It converts in either direction for complete digital transfers. The CO3 also supports the SCAMS digital copy protection system.

Figure 3.3. Midiman CO2 S/PDIF RCA and S/PDIF Optical converter

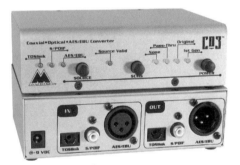

Figure 3.4. Midiman CO3 AES/EBU and S/PDIF converter

ADAT Optical (Lightpipe)

ADAT Optical (Lightpipe) is similar to the S/PDIF Optical cable in appearance, but different in content. ADAT Optical uses a fiberoptic cable to carry eight channels of digital data from one device to another. Though lightpipe was designed when ADATs recorded in 16-bit resolution, the format is able to handle up to 24-bit signals.

TDIF

TDIF, which stands for TEAC Digital Interface Format, was developed by TASCAM for the exchange of digital information between DA-88 multitrack recorders. TDIF uses a multipin connector similar to a computer hard drive.

TASCAM makes a format converter that will translate between TDIF and ADAT Optical formats for dumping tracks from one machine to another.

Figure 3.5. TDIF and ADAT Optical Converter

Syncing and Time Code: BNC

Synchronization for digital recording equipment is achieved with a feature called Word Clock. Word Clock allows for syncing between many different pieces of equipment as well as computer software. The cable for this format is the same coaxial cable used to hook up cable television to your TV and VCR.

SMPTE

SMPTE (pronounced SIM-tee) time code was developed by the Society of Motion Picture and Television Engineers. The code is in the form of hours, minutes, seconds, and frames. There are several types of sync signals used in audio and video production. SMPTE devices are capable of syncing with each other. One device serves as the master clock; all other devices chase and slave to the master's signal.

Summary

This chapter presented the many options available in the world of digital audio recording. These concepts are explored in detail in the chapters that follow. It also presented many of the most common terms used in the digital recording world.

Chapter 4.

Modular Digital Multitrack Recording (MDM)

Modular digital multitrack recording was introduced in chapter 3. This chapter will further explore the options available and the use of MDM in the digital recording studio. TASCAM and Alesis are the two major companies serving the MDM market, and we mention their products here. Over the years they have improved their products without abandoning older models.

MDM Debut

The event that launched the digital recording revolution was the introduction of the Alesis ADAT in 1992. Prior to 1992, musicians had to create and compose digitally using MIDI sequencers and the MIDI keyboard workstations that were the affordable digital technology in the 1980s. MIDI allowed a single musician to become a one-person orchestra through creation of MIDI sequenced multitimbral compositions. However, recording these MIDI masterworks at the professional level still required a trip to a commercial recording studio, which could be expensive! The Alesis ADAT lowered the boom, not to mention the noise floor, on the quality of recordings made in home and professional recording studios. Initially, digital recording took its share of hits from audio professionals, but it eventually became the

Figure 4.1. The original Alesis ADAT

choice for recording in the home studio and in many professional recording studios worldwide.

The ADAT introduced in 1992 had eight tracks of 16-bit digital recording that stored information on a conventional S-VHS tape. A standard-length S-VHS videotape offered approximately 40 minutes of audio recording. With a list price of $4,000, the 1992 ADAT was very inexpensive compared to other digital recording options. Since the ADAT is modular (hence the label Modular Digital Multitrack), it became possible to add more units over time as budget and recording needs allowed. Multiple ADAT units can be linked together to function as one unit, adding more than eight tracks to the setup. Up to sixteen ADAT machines can be chained together for a total of 128 tracks. At the time, no other products could compete with ADAT. The concept of creating a modular approach to digital recording hardware meant no more old recording devices to sell or to collect dust in the corner. In 1992, a 32-track digital recording studio setup was now available in the home or professional studio for approximately $16,000. Today, ADATs sell for less than their introductory 1992 price and have been improved from 16-bit to 20-bit resolution.

In 1993, TASCAM rolled out its version of modular digital multitrack with the DA-88 8-track digital recorder. Similar in theory to the Alesis ADAT but with a design and purpose all its own, the DA-88 became a hit, especially with those recording audio for video production. The DA-88 uses the same videotape used in Hi-8 videocassette recorders and offers 1 hour and 48 minutes of recording time per tape. While the ADAT was targeted at the music recording market, the DA-88 was aimed at the post-production market, where it quickly gained status as the machine of choice in many facilities. It even earned an Emmy award.

Figure 4.2. TASCAM D-88

The most obvious difference between the ADAT and DA-88 is the type of videotape used: S-VHS for ADAT and Super 8mm videotape for the DA-88. An inherent risk with the DA-88 was whether or not consumers would support two different formats. Fortunately for consumers, both formats have flourished. Many spinoff and add-on products for both types of videotape have been developed. Fostex, Panasonic, and Studer have offered S-VHS format units, in addition to the Alesis models. Sony offers a Hi-8 format recorder.

The original model ADAT and DA-88 are gone from the current product line. Second-generation ADATs (ADAT Type II) are 20-bit machines. TASCAM offers 24-bit recording in its top models. Each product line now has several models supporting various budget and recording needs. Both formats can be used successfully in small, medium, and large recording studios. The only decisions are what type of connectors, and extra features are required in the studio.

ADAT Inside and Outside

Working with a modular digital multitrack, or MDM, is very similar to working with analog recorders. There are the same standard transport buttons that are pressed to place tracks in record, pause, fast forward, and rewind mode. It is possible to mark specific points on the tape for easy references called locate points. Punch-in and punch-out recording is a snap. It is also quite simple to set up loop points for rehearsing and, on some decks, to bounce tracks internally. Inside, the deck more closely resembles a VCR. Videotapes are used as the recording medium, and the mechanism that loads the tape is similar to that found in a conventional VCR. MDMs use a transport similar to video recording. A drum head rotates at 3,000 revolutions per minute. The four read and write heads are positioned at equal distances around the head.

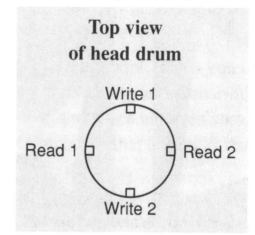

Figure 4.3. ADAT Recording Heads

The tape moves around the rotating head the same as in a VCR.

The recorder creates set of strips called helical scans. A single head records each scan as it contacts the tape. An 8-track scan looks like the following graphic.

Before it can record audio, the VHS tape must be formatted. Formatting writes an analog control track that contains time code. This is accomplished by recording the entire length of the tape in format mode. The ADAT uses the time code internally to manage the recording process. The control track is recorded by a linear head, separate from the rotary head that writes the multitrack digital data.

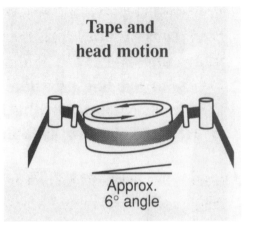

Figure 4.4. ADAT Recording Heads (Motion)

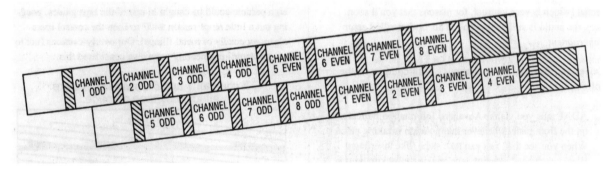

Figure 4.5. ADAT Recording Scans

The liner head reads each spike on the control track and compares it to spikes from the rotary head. If they don't happen at the same time, the deck adjusts the tape speed until they line up.

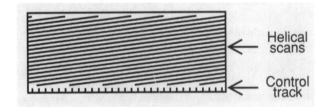

Figure 4.6. Inside the ADAT

TASCAM'S DA-88 recorders do not have a separate control track. They use Auto Track Finding (ATF), a system that embeds the timing information into the tape's subcode during the helical scan.

The ADAT Product Line

Alesis currently offers three ADAT models. All three are 20-bit machines and record at 48 kHz or 44.1 kHz. Alesis calls these ADAT Type II to differentiate them from the earlier 16-bit machines referred to as ADAT Type I. S-VHS tape is available in two lengths: 42 minutes and 60 minutes. All three models can be combined in systems with other ADATs, including the older Type I machines. ADATs come with a remote for basic transport control. It is known as an LRC—which stands for, believe it or not, "little remote control."

The ADAT Lx20 was developed after the original ADAT. It uses –10 dBV unbalanced RCA

Figure 4.7. Alesis ADAT Lx20

connectors and it can interface with most home studio equipment. It has five locate points, up from the two on the original ADAT. For rehearsing sections or punches, the recorder can loop between two of the locate points before recording.

Figure 4.8. Alesis ADAT Xt20

The ADAT xt20 has both +4 dBV servo-balanced and –10 dBV audio connections. Inside it has a few extra features like the ability to copy tracks digitally and to offset one track to correct timing errors. The xt20 is equipped with ten locate points.

The Big Remote Control

Since Alesis offers the LRC, or little remote control, why not have a BRC, or, you guessed it, "big remote control." Multiple ADATs can be slaved to a master deck or controlled by the BRC. This remote unit, developed for the original ADAT and still in use today, includes SMPTE syncing ability and adds additional locate points. It can send and receive MIDI data that can be used to create tempo maps to track bars and beats of the piece being recording. The DATA section at the beginning of each formatted ADAT tape stores BRC data.

Figure 4.9. Alesis BRC (Big Remote Control)

Alesis ADAT M20

The flagship of the Alesis ADAT line is the ADAT M20, designed for the professional studio in regard to both features and construction. The ADAT M20 records from analog and digital sources simultaneously. This ADAT does not require an external controller for syncing to other audio or video equipment as SMPTE capability is built in. It can send and receive MIDI data. It has 100 nameable locate points for marking start points on the tape.

The M20 uses XLR connectors for balanced connections to professional studio mixers. There is an optional add-on card that adds digital stereo in and out connections in four pairs. It is equipped with a jog/shuttle wheel for manually cueing to a specific location on the tape. This is a very important feature for locating an event in the picture, especially in the video post-production environment. This manual process is similar to scrubbing with analog tape, which is rocking the reels back and forth over the heads to find the exact location of an edit. The difference is that the information on the ADAT tape is digital, so it must function in a different manner when compared with analog tape. To compensate, the M20 has an analog tape head that records a composite of the data on the digital tracks onto an analog track running along the bottom of the ADAT tape. This information is played back when the tape is scrubbed with the jog/shuttle wheel. I want one for my studio!

Controller Autolocator Desktop Interface (CADI)

The M20 has different remote control requirements. Since SMPTE and MIDI sync capabilities are built into the M20, a new remote unit named

Figure 4.10. Alesis ADAT M20

CADI was developed. CADI has a feature set all its own. Designed specifically for use with the M20, it has the same vacuum fluorescent display and jog/shuttle as does the M20. It can take individual decks offline to allow formatting while recording on others. It uses a special cable to accommodate long cable runs; for example, the decks can be placed in an equipment room hundreds of yards away.

When the decks are in a remote location, a special unit, the RJ-45, can be added to the remote rack to monitor the levels going to tape. Each RJ-45 unit accommodates thirty-two tracks, provides several metering options, and has error/interpolation indicators. Metering options can be accessed from the CADI remote unit.

Figure 4.11. Alesis CADI

Figure 4.12. Alesis RJ-45

With the ADAT Lightpipe (see chapter 3), Alesis provides digital connections to other products for digital recording and digital signal processing. Some of the many devices that are equipped with ADAT optical connectors for recording directly to ADAT include Alesis electronic keyboards (QS7, QS8, and QSR) and the Alesis Q-series effects processors.

The TASCAM Family

Like the Alesis ADAT, the TASCAM DA-88 has been updated and expanded with models for different purposes. There are three basic models: the DA-88, the DA-38, and the DA-98. Tapes can be shared among the three models, as well as with the HR series if running at 16-bit resolution. It is possible to link up to sixteen separate units for a possible 128 separate digital tracks.

TASCAM DA-38

The DA-38 is TASCAM's current low-end model designed for the home or project studio. One of the advantages of the DA-38 is how quickly it can rewind and fast forward the tape. A standard 120 Hi-8mm videotape will provide 1 hour and 48 minutes of recording time, so moving quickly through that much tape is essential. As is the case with ADAT, the Hi-8 videotape must be properly formatted in order to record digital audio. It is possible to record and format on both machines at the same time, but this is only recommended for live recording, when the tape will be recorded from start to finish.

When recording a punch, it is helpful to have a few seconds of the track playback. This is referred to as a pre-roll. The DA-38 can program a pre-roll from 5 seconds to 59 minutes. The TASCAM DA multitrack series features an internal patch bay that allows for routing any input to any track. A patch bay is a place where cables can be connected or patched into various inputs and outputs. The DA-38 is a 16-bit machine, but can handle 20- or 24-bit data through its DTRS port.

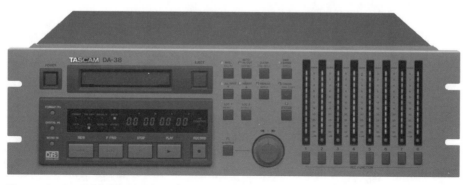

Figure 4.13. TASCAM DA-38

TASCAM DA-88

The original DA-88 is still going strong. Over the past few years it has received some software modifications but the hardware is still the rock-solid performer that has made it a staple in many production facilities. As with the entire DA series, it features a durable and speedy tape transport. It is a 16-bit machine with analog unbalanced RCA and 25-pin balanced connectors. For digital communication there is a TDIF connection (see chapter 3).

A unique feature of the DA-88 is the capability of purchasing additional add-on cards. This expandability allows additional features to be added as needed. The SY-88 SMPTE/MIDI/Chase Lock Synchronization Card is an

Figure 4.14. TASCAM DA-88

add-on card that gives the DA-88 on-board syncing capability, so no external controller is needed. For communication with stereo digital machines, consider an IF-88AE card. It adds digital AES/EBU and S/PDIF connections to the DA-88.

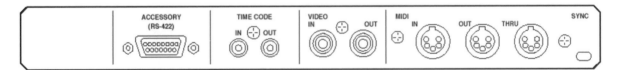

Figure 4.15. TASCAM SY-88

TASCAM DA-98

The DA-98 adds new features both inside and out to the DA series. A larger display window for navigating system parameters is the most obvious enhancement. Inside the unit, the digital patch bay allows routing of any input to any track and allows digital track copying. Monitoring options are expanded with individual input select switches. Connections include analog D-sub and digital TDIF. With the DA-98, add-on cards are not necessary for video sync. All the functions of the SY-88 add-on card mentioned previously are built into the DA-98. The IF-88AE and IF-88SD cards can be added to the DA-98 as needed.

Figure 4.16. TASCAM DA-98

The TASCAM HR Series

TASCAM's HR (High Resolution) series has the unique feature of recording in 16-bit or 24-bit resolution. These units also come equipped with Word Clock, SMPTE/EBU, MIDI Time Code, and MIDI Machine Control. The internal 8 x 2 mixer (eight tracks of input that can be assigned to any pair of tracks) has read-before-write capability and can handle panning and level controls. It is possible to mix eight tracks down to two tracks on the same recorder provided there are two open tracks available. For a complicated mix, it is possible to use MIDI messages to control the internal mixer. MIDI data from a sequencer or other controller that transmits MIDI messages can be used for this purpose.

If you move around with your recorder, you'll note there is an internal tone generator that produces a 1-kHz tone for lineup and an A-440-Hz pitch for tuning. These units can play tape that is recorded on any DA series multitrack. However, tapes recorded in 24-bit resolution can only be used in HR series machines.

DA-78HR

The DA-78HR has both RCA connectors for unbalanced connections and D-sub connectors for balanced connections. There is a S/PDIF in connection for importing digital stereo signals. Built on the DA-38 architecture, it contains the same features as its older brother, adding the features of the HR series for improved audio.

DA-98HR

As of this writing, the DA-98HR has not been released, but preliminary information is available. It is built on the DA-78 architecture but with more digital I/O (input/output connection) and sync abilities. In addition to 16-bit and 24-bit resolution at 44.1 kHz and 48 kHz, the DA-98HR can record four tracks of 24-bit/96-kHz audio and two tracks at 24-bit/192-kHz. Stereo I/O is supported with AES/EBU connections.

Figure 4.17. TASCAM DA-78HR

Figure 4.18. TASCAM DA-98HR

Remote Controllers

TASCAM MDMs do not come with separate remote control units, but there are three options that can be purchased separately. The RC-808 remote controls a single machine; the RC-828 controls up to four units; and the RC-898 controls up to six units.

Figure 4.19. RC-808 Remote   **Figure 4.20. RC-828 Remote**   **Figure 4.21. RC-898 Remote**

ADAT Computer Connection

Many recording professionals have moved to computer-based hard disk recording (see chapters 6, 7, and 8) because this technology tends to have more editing control and features than MDMs. To address this need, Alesis has developed a compromise. They now offer a PCI (Peripheral Computer Interface) computer card and ADAT/Edit, an editing software package. See chapter 7 for an in-depth discussion of this option.

Alesis AI3

The Alesis AI3 has several roles it can fill in the digital studio. It can work as the I/O with the ADAT/Edit card and software. If you have a digital mixer with an extra ADAT optical interface, the AI3 can be used to add eight analog inputs to your system. For long cable runs, the AI3 can function as a multiple input optical connector. This allows the signal to be converted, then sent digitally to an ADAT or ADAT/Edit card up to 33 feet away. Lightpipe (see chapter 2) connectors are more sensitive than normal audio cables and need to be protected in the recording environment.

The AI3 is a single rack space 20-bit A/D (analog to digital) and D/A (digital to analog) converter with eight quarter-inch ins and outs for balanced or unbalanced connections. There is a pair of ADAT optical lightpipe connectors for digital connection to an ADAT or the ADAT/Edit PCI card.

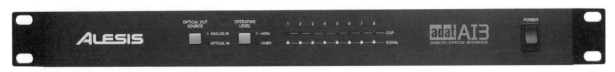

Figure 4.22. Alesis AI3 A/D, D/A Converter

Working With MDMs

I have had good experience using MDMs in a variety of recording environments. I own a first-generation ADAT that is still going strong. Following are some tips that may be helpful should you purchase an MDM for your studio.

• Formatting tape is time consuming. Use studio downtime wisely and format new tapes ahead of time so there is always a supply ready to go.

• Store tapes in a dry place out of direct sunlight.

• Use high quality tape at all times. Insist that anyone bringing tapes into your studio use approved quality tapes.

• Use quality cables for all connections. This will reduce noise in the system.

• Proper care and cleaning of MDM equipment is paramount. It is a good idea to have MDMs professionally cleaned and serviced from time to time, depending upon the level of use. Contact your local dealer or the equipment manufacturer for the name and number of a certified repair specialist.

• Tape heads also require cleaning and can be cleaned in the studio. Use only those head cleaners recommended by the manufacturer.

• Tapes used by MDMs can have imperfections. Always make a backup copy of all recording sessions.

• If you use multiple MDMs, assign each a number. Log each tape with the number of the MDM used. When reusing the tape, use the same MDM you used originally to record it. This will ensure proper playback.

Summary

MDMs started the digital revolution and continue to be a major player today. They offer a wide range of options and can fit into almost any budget. Be sure to review the various options before choosing the best system for your needs. MDMs are a viable option for the digital recording studio.

Chapter 5.

MiniDisc and Hard Disk Recording

As described in chapter 3, digital audio recording comes in a variety of formats. In this chapter, the hard disk and MiniDisc digital recording options will be explored. Hardware that does not require a Windows or Macintosh computer is covered in this chapter. Computer-based systems are covered in chapters 6, 7, and 8. The advantages of using these dedicated digital recording products include portability and ease of use.

Digital recorders can be divided into two groups: self-contained or rack-mount units. Self-contained portable units often include mixers, mic and line inputs, and ports for connecting an external storage device. The other variant is a rack unit resembling an MDM recorder (see chapter 4). It has only the electronics and interface for recording, editing, and storing data and must be connected to other devices in the studio for mixing.

Multitrack MiniDisc Recorders

Many people started recording using a multitrack cassette recorder like the TASCAM portable multitrack cassette unit. Referred to as portastudios, such recorders brought multitrack recording to the home studio. While this format is still available, it now has a digital cousin, the TASCAM 564, which uses Sony's digital MiniDisc format instead of an analog cassette.

Units such as the TASCAM 564 and the Sony MDMX4 can record 37 minutes of 4-track data on a single MiniDisc recorded at 44.1 kHz. There is sufficient memory for approximately five separate songs on each disc. The MiniDisc has several advantages, among them the ease it offers in erasing unwanted tracks. Another helpful feature is being able to divide material into segments using index markers that are similar to the locate points used with MDMs. Using this device it

Figure 5.1. TASCAM 564 MiniDisc Recorder

is possible to take apart a song, completely re-arrange it, and then recombine the segments into a totally different version. The number of segments you can create varies depending on the manufacturer; the TASCAM 564 permits twenty segments. Positioning is easy using the jog/shuttle wheel. It is even possible to specify a marker to stop playback so you can change the ending of a song.

One of the limitations of the MiniDisc portable recording units is the number of available tracks. MiniDisc recorders typically feature four tracks. It is possible to increase the number of tracks by copying tracks. This is known as bouncing. In the analog world, flexibility and fidelity were lost when a track was bounced. This is not so in the digital world. Also, after tracks were bounced, mixing was no longer an option. Digital technology to the rescue! Using the digital MiniDisc, bounces can be read from one file while recording to another. The bounced mix is written to a separate file without destroying the original. On the TASCAM 564, it is possible to record twelve first generation tracks for a song and still have access to your original tracks should you decide to change something. Want a new drum mix? Just re-bounce. Need some reverb on the keyboards? Just re-bounce. No sync track is necessary for MIDI sequencers, since the 564 offers a choice of MIDI Time Code or MIDI Clock output to sync with a sequencer.

Another luxury of a large track count is the ability to record several takes of a solo or vocal, then choose the best one for the final mix. The TASCAM 564 can record five virtual tracks that can be auditioned before recording to the track. It is even possible to set a time interval between retakes for repositioning or resetting equipment.

One of the attractions to a MiniDisc portastudio is its built-in mixer. The mixer can be used to adjust volume levels of tracks and add equalization. This enhances the portability of the unit, thus allowing rapid setup and breakdown. The mixers on most portable units are analog, not digital. The features of the mixer vary between manufacturers and models. You might wish to note the number and types of inputs available when considering the setup of your studio or your needs for live recording. An EQ (equalization) section is also a standard feature, but type and number of bands vary between machines. When it comes time for the final mix, the TASCAM 564 offers S/PDIF-compatible digital output for mixing to stereo MiniDisc, DAT, or a hard disk system—without leaving the digital domain.

Hard Disk Recorders

Hard disk recording refers to the act of storing digital audio on a computer's hard disk. A hard disk is typically found inside a Windows or Macintosh computer. It can also be housed in a dedicated recording device. The hard disk is where the digital files are stored. Hard disk systems offer increased editing potential compared to tape-based (MDM) and MiniDisc systems. In the digital audio world, there are two options from which to choose: stand-alone, or dedicated, hard disk recorders; and computer-based hard disk recording systems. As with most gear, there are various options designed to fit a variety of budgets. We break them down into entry level, mid-level, and high-end categories.

Hard Disk Portable Studios: Entry Level

Hard disk based portable studios are equipped with the same basic digital recording and editing features as the MiniDisc portastudio. The Fostex FD-4 offers a choice of media that can be used for recording. It can record on an internal hard drive or to several SCSI devices including a Zip drive, Syquest EZ Flyer, MO drive, or an external SCSI hard disk. SCSI (pronounced "scuzzy") stands for Small Computer

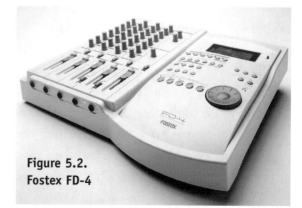

Figure 5.2. Fostex FD-4

Serial Interface. It is one way digital devices can communicate with other devices.

Although digital recording devices look like their analog ancestors, they offer significantly more power and flexibility. For example, the Fostex FD-4 hard disk portable studio actually has an extra two tracks available depending on the recording mode and media being used, so that a total of six tracks can be recorded.

The Fostex FD-8 resembles an 8-track recorder but can actually handle twenty-four tracks. The catch is that only eight tracks at a time are available for control via the mixer. The FD-8 also offers ADAT Lightpipe connectors for transferring data to and from an ADAT machine for expanding, editing, archiving, or swapping with other musicians.

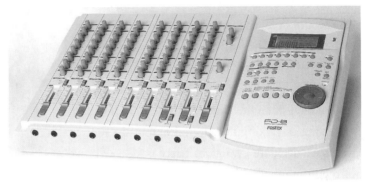

These portable hard disk units have ninety-nine "virtual reels" for separating your data into different songs or versions of songs. Digital mixing can be handled internally, without touching the original tracks, or

Figure 5.3. Fostex FD-8

dumped to a stereo DAT recorder via the S/PDIF digital outputs. Different units have different features. For example, Korg's D8 digital recorder offers internal digital effects for use in recording or mixdown.

One of the most popular lines of hard disk portable workstations is made by Roland. There are three models—one each for entry-level, mid-level, and high-end use. The VS-840EX is a 4-track recorder with a 12-channel mixer and twenty-four bands of digital EQ.

Figure 5.4. Korg D-8

Figure 5.5. Roland VS840EX

Features to keep in mind include: How many tracks can be recorded at once? How many virtual tracks are available? How many levels of undo/redo are available? Is there any compression scheme being used for the audio signal? How large is the internal drive and what, if any, options are there for expansion? Is there a limit on the size of hard drive when connected to a SCSI port? What back-up options are available for making safe copies of the original tracks and the stereo mix tracks?

Hard Disk Portable Studios: Mid-Level

The mid-level recorders are units with more tracks, among other features. Two excellent mid-level products include the Akai DPS 12 and the Roland VS-880EX.

The Akai DPS 12 can record 12 audio tracks while offering 250 virtual tracks that can be allocated to the 12 physical tracks. If you are using the DPS 12 with a MIDI sequencer, it is possible to save your mix since the machine's faders and pots generate MIDI data. There is a waveform display so you can see what you're editing and 250 levels of undo in case you change your mind about something. Original information can be stored on the virtual tracks for recall later if desired. Virtual tracks can be used in the recording process but cannot be used in the final mix. Internal effects for recording or mixing and digital output for mixing to a DAT deck are available. There is also a choice of recording media. Internally you can have either a hard disk or a Jaz drive. A Jaz drive is a disk drive that uses removable disks that store digital

Figure 5.6. Akai DPS 12

information on magnetic media (see chapter 9). There is a SCSI port for connecting external SCSI devices to provide additional recording space or to back up data from the internal drive.

The Roland VS-880EX can record eight tracks simultaneously, sixty-four virtual tracks, built-in effects board. There are two digital S/PDIF ports. With an internal software upgrade, CDs can be recorded directly from the unit.

Hard Disk Portable Units: High-End

High-end units are designed for those who need a portable device that has high-end recording features. The high-end units typically offer sixteen tracks that can be recorded simultaneously. Two examples are the Korg D16 and the Roland VS-1680.

The Korg D16 offers control of sixteen tracks of audio recorded at 16-bit resolution. It also has the option of recording at 24-bit resolution but that reduces the number of total tracks to eight and the number of tracks you can record on simultaneously to four. This unit also features a built-in tuner and metronome. It has aux (auxiliary) sends for connecting external effects devices, analog outputs for monitors, analog tape recorders, and headphone jacks.

Figure 5.7. Roland VS-880EX

Roland's high-end model is the VS-1680. It is a very powerful all-in-one unit, capable of recording, mixing, mastering, and burning a CD, with an optional CD burner attached. Although it is billed as a 24-bit machine, only the internal signals are handled at 24-bit. The A/D and D/A converters are 20-bit and any CDs burned are at the standard 16-bit resolution. The VS-1680 uses Roland Digital Audio Coding (R-DAC) to compress the amount of digital data and conserve hard drive space. In digital compression the signal is analyzed and abbreviations are used for any repeated digital words. When played back the signal is uncompressed and the full word is used. With the VS-1680 compressed data can accommodate sixteen tracks of audio. Uncompressed data is limited to eight tracks of digital audio.

Figure 5.8. Korg D16

Figure 5.9. Roland VS-1680

Like other hard disk systems, the VS-1680 uses an internal hard drive to store information. The current model supports 3.1 GB (gigabytes), but the hard drive can be replaced with one of a larger capacity if more storage space is needed. There is a SCSI port for connecting up to seven external hard drives. An Iomega Zip drive is recommended for recording and data backup. For tracking, the VS-1680 is capable of recording 8 tracks at a time and playing back 16. Each one of the 16 tracks can support 16 virtual tracks for a grand total of 256 possible tracks for recording.

On the back panel there are eight ins. Tracks 1 and 2 have XLR inputs with switchable phantom power, 3 through 8 are quarter-inch inputs. There are four stereo aux sends and two S/PDIF connections, one optical, one RCA. There are MIDI connectors for syncing a sequencer or other MIDI device and for mixer controls. MIDI Clock, MMC and MTC are supported. For guitarists there is a dedicated guitar input.

VS-1680 Mixer and Editing

On the mixer side, a routing utility allows you to set up and store twenty-nine templates of custom mixer configurations. For mixdown, the automix function provides 1,000 events of automation. Automation refers the mixer's ability to perform mixing functions controlled by the unit's microprocessor. There are three ways of automating a mix: snapshot, snapshot with smoothed transition from one snapshot to the next, and real-time changes.

Editing features include standard cut, copy, and paste features. It is possible to copy material to another track, or open space on an existing track, for experimental editing so that the original is preserved. It is also possible to copy an entire song to a later location on the same track(s) for editing alternate versions of the same song. Waveforms can be edited on the unit's large screen display and the shuttle wheel. For replacing parts, there is an auto-punch feature, and you can practice your punch before attempting it. The 999 levels of undo/redo allow you to undo your last 999 edits. This is a very helpful and cool feature. The VS-1680 also supports time compression and expansion of tracks so you can vary the tempo of a loop that has been recorded to match a sequence tempo. You can also choose to hold the pitch or alter it when performing the compression or expansion.

VS-1680 Effects and Output

On the bottom of the VS-1680 there is a slot bay with two expansion slots for a VS8F-2 effects board. This add-on device must be purchased separately. The board contains two effects processors that can be used in stereo or mono configurations. Effects can be assigned as inserts or through a bus. Using an effect as an insert means it can only be used on one track. Bus effects can have any number of tracks routed to them. Purchase two cards if your budget permits in order to have a wide variety of effects. The list of available effects includes reverb, parametric and graphic EQ, multitap delay, vocoder, chorusing, compression, distortion, lo-fi, noise suppression, auto-wah, limiter/de-esser, enhancer, pitch-shifter, and flanger.

With the effects card, there is also amp simulation. There is a rotary speaker simulation to emulate the sound of a B-3. Last, but certainly not least, is microphone simulation. Microphone emulation software imitates the qualities of various well-known mics. Digital microphones are ideal for this unit but can be expensive. Ask your local music store dealer for recommendations and test a few before you make your purchase. See chapter 11 for detailed information on microphones.

Monitoring can be done through headphones, analog speakers, or Roland's DA-90 digital monitors. When using DA-90s you can take advantage of the VS-1680's speaker emulation feature. This is similar to the microphone emulation concept. Software reproduces the response characteristics of various speaker and monitor models. This allows you to test your mix in a wide variety of situations ranging from studio monitors to car stereos.

When your mix is complete, try using Roland's VS-CDR rewritable CD drive to burn the finished product directly from the VS-1680. It even lets you back up your data files to CD. Since the drive can handle rewritable CDs, you can keep ongoing backups as you work on a project just in case the unthinkable happens—a disk crash.

Working With Self-Contained Digital Studios

For many musicians, purchasing a self-contained digital unit will be the first step in their recording careers. Digital technology has introduced many features into rooms and basements that make recordings sound much better than they did just a few short years ago. Even individuals with larger budgets will find these models attractive for working on the road.

The trick of the portable studio has always been track management and learning not to paint yourself into a corner. Digital units are a bit more forgiving but a little planning can go a long way to toward making your life easier. Get in the habit of copying or backing up frequently during and after the recording session, because hard drives are doomed to fail someday.

Modular Hard Disk Recorders

The previously discussed portable units also have studio versions. Modular hard disk recorders are designed to be used in the studio. They are similar to the modular digital multitrack devices described in chapter 4. The main difference is in the medium used to store data. MDMs store information on tape, while modular hard disk recorders use a built-in hard disk. Modular hard disk recorders function solely as a recording device, like a tape deck without the tape. They have on-board editing functions to take advantage of the hard disk format, but they need to be fed audio data from a mixer and then send it back for monitoring and processing. In other words, modular hard disk recorders are just one part of the stu-

dio. They are not as portable as the hard disk portable units described previously in this chapter.

Among the first of the modular hard disk recorders introduced were the Akai DR4 and DR8. Four DR4s can be chained together for 16-track recording.

Figure 5.10. Akai DR4

The DR8 and DR16 (8- and 16-track machines respectively) offer onscreen editing capability. Plug an SVGA-compatible computer monitor into the port on the back panel and access the SuperView

Graphic Interface. A computer keyboard can also be attached for naming files and for remote control.

Removable Hard Disk

The Fostex D-90 introduced the use of a removable hard disk in the MDHR format. This allows for easy disk swapping when a disk becomes full during a recording session and there is no time to make a full backup. It is also a convenient way to transport files between studios. The files are compatible only with Foxtex products.

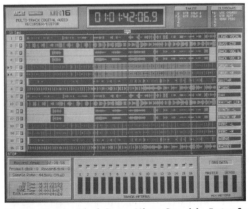

Figure 5.11. Akai SuperView Graphic Interface

The D-160 is the 16-track version of the D-90, offering the same features with double the track count and eight virtual tracks for alternate takes. Both units are equipped with ADAT lightpipe connectors for easy interfacing with MDMs for editing ADAT-recorded tracks on the hard disk, or for backing up hard disk tracks to ADAT tapes. One of the unique features of the Fostex machines is a detachable front panel that functions as a remote control. With an extender cable you can control the unit from up to 15 feet away.

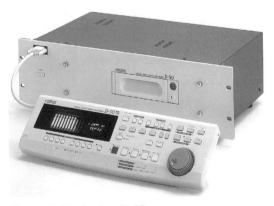

Figure 5.12. Foxtex D-90

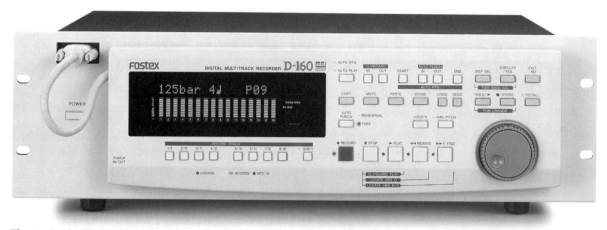

Figure 5.13. Fostex D-160

The D-160 can record approximately 18 minutes of 16-track data on a 1.6 GB disk. Insert an 8.6 GB disk, and approximately 100 minutes of 16-track data can be stored. Both the D-90 and D-160 come with unbalanced RCA connectors. Add-on cards for balanced D-sub 25-pin connectors are available for the D-160. Another card is available for additional sync options for Word Clock and syncing to video. Digital data is organized into words, and Word Clock is used to synchronize signals between different types of gear. Without a way to synchronize, digital signals would not be properly aligned causing clicks, pops, and other problems. For syncing either machine to a MIDI sequencer, MIDI Machine Control is available, as is Fostex Exclusive Message (FEX).

High-End Modular Hard Disk Recorders

The new frontier in hard disk recording includes 24-track single recorders by TASCAM and Mackie. These are currently priced in the $4,000 range. These models are 24-bit and have 96-kHz resolution, in addition to 44.1-kHz and 48-kHz. The TASCAM MX-2424 can record 50 minutes of 24-track, 24-bit data on a 9 GB drive.

The Mackie HDR 24/96 has a built-in 20-GB hard drive and 100 minutes at 48 kHz, 24-bit resolution. Both machines have a drive bay on the front. The MX-2424 can accommodate a DVD RAM drive or Kingston-compatible removable media. The HDR 24/96 also has a bay

Figure 5.14. TASCAM MX-2424

for a Kingston-compatible removable hard drive and a 3.5-inch floppy drive for installing software updates.

On the back panel, both the TASCAM and Mackie units offer a variety of connector options to accommodate a wide range of studio configurations. Options include balanced analog I/O, ADAT lightpipe, TASCAM TDIF-1, AES/EBU, or optical. Each unit easily interfaces with its manufacturer's digital mixers. SCSI connectors can be used to add an additional drive for more recording space or backup. The HDR 24/96 is planning to support a printer port so track sheets can be printed.

Figure 5.15. Mackie HDR 24/96

If you want lots of tracks, thirty-two MX-2424s can be chained together for 768 tracks at 48 kHz or 384 tracks at 96 kHz. Anyone for overdubbing some Mahler?

Editing—The Next Generation

These high-end units allow editing from the front panel or via an external computer monitor. The Mackie unit also has a connection for a computer keyboard, mouse, or trackball, and an SVGA monitor display to access the unit's functions on screen.

The TASCAM MX-2424 can interface with a Macintosh or Windows PC for editing and level control. This special application can also be used in conjunction with the RC-2424 remote. Sound files can be in outputted in Sound Designer II (Mac) or wav (Windows) formats.

Figure 5.16. Mackie HDR Software Main Screen

Both units support both destructive and non-destructive editing. Destructive editing is the permanent alteration of a sound file. This could be either a deletion of material or a digital signal processing alteration in which the actual sound of the file is changed—for example, with reverb or EQ. Nondestructive editing is one of the coolest features in digital recording. When a file is edited, a copy is created and all the edits are performed on the copy. This makes it possible to experiment with edits or DSP alterations and still be able to return to the original file if necessary. Edits are smooth and crossfades

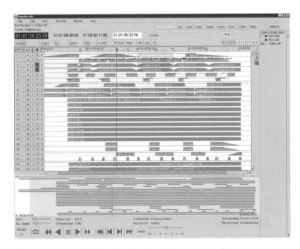

Figure 5.17. TASCAM's ViewNet MX Software

available. Timing problems can be easily fixed by nudging tracks or regions.

Working with Modular Hard Disks

One of the main advantages of using modular hard disk recorders is that they are easy to operate, as they use tape-deck type controls. They have several advantages over their modular digital multitrack counterparts (see chapter 4). Since they are hard disk based, there is no rewind time, which can be a big help in recording sessions. But the editing possibilities are where these units really shine. Being able to cut and paste parts, undo missed punches, and delete bad takes with a keystroke are just a few of the many advantages. Again, hard disk backup is essential. Making backups is a little like medical insurance—you pay for it but hope you don't have to use it.

With hard disk recorders, recording times quoted are based on the amount of data the drives will hold in average use. If you are recording only two or four tracks of data on an 8-track machine you'll be able to record for a longer period of time than if you were recording eight tracks of data. Increasing resolution also changes the machine's capabilities. For example, when the TASCAM MX-2424 is in 24-bit/96 kHz mode, it can record only a maximum of twelve tracks. The higher the resolution, the fewer the available tracks.

Summary

Portable hard disk recorders are gaining in popularity, especially with those who need a portable unit to take on the road. A variety of models is available for almost any budget. Modular hard disk recorders are designed for studio use and are less portable. There are modules available for any budget. The editing features of hard disk based recording are the main advantage. Since this medium can be quite volatile, it is important to frequently make copies and to back up data. These units, relatively easy to learn and to operate, can serve as an excellent recording media for studio and on-location recording.

Chapter 6.

Computer-Based MIDI and Digital Recording

Chapters 4 and 5 presented various stand-alone or modular digital recording options. Another possible configuration is the use of a Macintosh or Windows computer as the heart of the home or professional studio.

The main advantage of a computer in the digital studio is versatility. There is a variety of software for recording MIDI and digital audio. The disadvantage of using a computer is that it can be complex and confusing to set up and configure. It can take longer to learn a computer system than it can to learn modular and portable digital recording equipment. I recommend you use the computer as the central part of the studio only if you are fairly comfortable using software and you have a computer made within the last couple of years.

In a computer-based recording studio, the computer functions as the hard disk recorder and the software governs mixing, processing, and effects. The computer can be used in a variety of ways in the digital world. These include:

- MIDI sequencing only (no digital audio).
- MIDI sequencing and digital audio using no additional hardware.
- MIDI sequencing and digital audio with a digital audio plug-in card.
- Digital/audio recording with a digital audio plug-in card and interface.

Options 1 and 2 above will be discussed in this chapter and options 3 and 4 above will be discussed in chapters 7 and 8, respectively.

Macintosh or Windows?

One of the most common questions asked is which computer should be used for digital recording. The choices are Macintosh or Windows. There are some differences between Macintosh and Windows computers. However, either can be used as the central component for both MIDI and digital audio recording. Software is available from entry- to professional-level for both computer platforms. Many software titles are available for both Mac and Windows; such products are referred to as cross-platform software.

My advice is to purchase the computer model for which you can get the most help, support, and advice. If you are planning to record in your home, ask around to see if there are people you know that use a particular brand of computer for home recording. If you are going to operate a recording studio, check with other existing studios to see which computer model they are using. The same advice holds true if you are a music educator. The key is finding an individual or company to use as a model and a basis for comparison. It is also helpful to use equipment similar to your friends' and colleagues' so you can call on them for advice and help when needed.

Computer Hardware Considerations

The microprocessor is the heart of any computer. The faster the speed the better. Processor speed is measured in *megahertz*—a unit of frequency equal to 1 million hertz. It is abbreviated MHz. Computers running at 300 MHz or 400 MHz are common as of this writing. RAM, or random access memory, refers to the computer's temporary storage capability. RAM is where the software is loaded and where the songs you are recording are stored prior to being saved to disk. You almost can't have enough RAM if you are working with digital audio. Be sure to have enough RAM to run the software you intend to use. (I am purposely avoiding recommending specific requirements for processor speed, hard disk capacity, RAM, and other issues, as they change very quickly.)

If MIDI sequencing will be your primary function, computer processor speed and hard disk storage is not a major concern. This is because MIDI only records performance information. Therefore, the "average size of a MIDI file is relatively small, usually between 25k and 100k, depending upon the complexity of the piece. If you plan to record digital audio, the computer should have a fast processor and a large hard drive for storage. The reasoning here is that digital audio creates files that are quite large. A fast processor is needed because recording digital audio can be taxing to a computer's processor. The maker of the digital audio software you plan to purchase will list recommended system requirements for its use. Be sure your computer has the capacity to run the software. I also suggest you look for current articles in *Electronic Musician* and *Keyboard* magazines.

Storage Options

Computers can come equipped with several types of disk storage. (Disk storage is where the files are stored.) For a small studio, a computer's internal hard drive may be sufficient. In this case, be sure to purchase the most hard disk storage you can afford. Storage capacity is represented in gigabytes (GB). The more gigabytes the hard drive has, the better.

It is advisable to have a backup system for archiving files. See chapter 9 for specific recommendations on storage and backup systems. It is also a good idea to purchase an uninterruptible power supply so the computer will continue to run if there is a power outage in the studio. These devices can be purchased at computer stores. Some models cost less than $200.

When I am looking for computer hardware recommendations, I usually turn to articles by Walter Mossberg, whose writing appears in several national publications. Every six months or so he writes an article on what to look for when purchasing a computer. His articles are available online. For a complete listing of Mossberg's articles go to http://ptech.wsj.com/archive.html. Mossberg writes in a down-to-earth style and gives specific advice on hardware.

Computer System Types

There are two basic types of computers used in recording: desktop and portable (usually referred to as laptops). The desktop computer typically has two distinct parts: a case that houses the computer's processor and a separate monitor. The laptop or portable computer is an all-in-one computer that is small and light enough to fit on one's lap. The advantage is portability.

The best choice for digital audio recording at the mid and high levels is to use a desktop computer system with expansion slots. These computers have internal slots where digital audio cards can be inserted. Some desktop models, such as Apple Computer's iMac, do not have internal slots. It is possible to use entry-level audio software on these machines (discussed in this chapter). But since they currently do not support add-on digital audio cards, they are not recommended for mid- to high-level applications. Portable computers do not typically have expansion slots, so they are not as usable as desktop models. However, it is possible to add expansion slots to laptops (discussed in chapter 7).

Connecting a Macintosh via MIDI

To record and play back MIDI with a Macintosh computer, you will need a MIDI interface, as there is none built in. You can either purchase a MIDI interface separately or buy a MIDI keyboard with a built-in MIDI interface. If you are buying a separate MIDI interface, be sure that it is compatible with the model of Macintosh you are using. The iMac, G3, and G4 Macintosh computers use something called a USB, or Uniform Serial Bus, to communicate with external devices. Older Macintosh models that don't use USB require a different MIDI interface, which plugs into the Macintosh's serial port. Check with your local music store to be sure that you are purchasing the proper interface.

The interface cable connects to the back panel of the Macintosh. MIDI cables are then connected to the MIDI keyboard or MIDI instrument.

It is important to remember that MIDI itself does not make any sound. It merely transmits information about the performance. In order to hear the performance, you must connect the outputs from the MIDI keyboard to an amplifier and speaker or use headphones.

Connecting a PC to MIDI

There are basically two options with Windows computers. A MIDI interface card can be purchased and installed into one of the computer's internal slots. The second, most common, and simplest way to connect MIDI is to use the PC's built-in sound card. All sound cards that are SoundBlaster AWE32, AWE64, SB32, or are compatible with these, come with built-in MIDI capability. All you need is a MIDI cable, which you can buy for about $15. This cable connects to the game port on the computer's sound-card, which is usually located on the back panel of the central processing unit (referred to as the CPU). A game controller can also be used by plugging it to the MIDI cable.

Another option is to purchase a dedicated MIDI interface card that plugs into one of the expansion slots in the PC. This is not necessary except for older PCs that do not have a MIDI-compatible sound card. Several companies, including MusicQuest, Midiman, and Roland, make MIDI cards. The industry standard is the Roland MPU-401/AT. These cards reduce the processing requirements from the computer and result in minimal CPU load and great dependability.

There are also advantages to upgrading to a better quality sound card. Soundcards can be purchased for between $100 and $200. The basic soundcards are Creative Labs SoundBlaster cards, which currently offer several options including the AWE32, AWE64, or SB32. These cards include a MIDI interface and built-in MIDI sound synthesis. There are many other sound cards that offer better sound quality than the SoundBlaster models, including the Roland RAP-10; Turtle Beach Monterrey, MultiSound, Pinnacle, or Tropez; AVM Apex; and Ensoniq Soundscape. These cards represent the low- and mid-level soundcard options. High-end digital audio cards will be addressed in chapter 7.

Internal or External MIDI Output

MIDI information must be interpreted and converted to an audio signal. This can be done inside the MIDI keyboard. You may also use the built-in MIDI synthesis that is a part of all Macintosh and Windows computers. For Macintosh this is called QuickTime Musical Instruments, developed by Apple Computer. For Windows, the internal soundcard has built-in MIDI sound capabilities.

Usually, a MIDI keyboard will have better sound quality than the computer's built-in sound. However, if you are using an older MIDI keyboard model, the computer's built-in sound quality may be superior. If you want the sound output to come from the MIDI keyboard connect the audio outputs on the back of the keyboard to the amplifier and speakers or headphones.

If you want use the computer's built-in sounds, you can play back through the computer's built-in speakers or you can connect the sound card audio output to external speakers and/or headphones.

Software

With a computer, software is required to record MIDI and digital audio. First select the software program and then the hardware to run it. There are many different types of software for music: notation software for printing, instructional software for learning musical concepts, and MIDI sequencing and digital audio software. There are programs for all levels of applications from amateur to professional. It is relatively easy to determine the target audience for a particular piece of software. It is usually reflected in the cost. Basic, entry-level programs can cost under $150. Software for the professional recording studio can run between $250 and $1,000.

MIDI Sequencing

If budget is a primary consideration, then MIDI sequencing can be the least expensive way to enter the world of digital recording. Most MIDI sequencing software also allows for recording digital audio tracks. MIDI sequencing can be accomplished using a keyboard workstation such as the Korg Triton or Kurzweil K2000 as described in chapter 2. However, a computer can also be used for MIDI sequencing.

If you intend to record MIDI, a MIDI keyboard is recommended for note entry and playback. At this stage there are essentially three components: a computer, MIDI keyboard, and MIDI-sequencing software.

MIDI Sequencing Software

There are two types of MIDI sequencing software: programs that record only MIDI data and programs that record both MIDI and digital audio. The very basic MIDI sequencing software packages offer only MIDI sequencing without digital audio options. These packages are designed for the novice computer user, music hobbyist, or student. Some of the software titles in this area include Mastertracks Pro and FreeStyle. Each is available for Macintosh and Windows.

FreeStyle by Mark of the Unicorn (MOTU) for Macintosh and Windows is a MIDI sequencing program designed for the novice user. (The list price is $199 as of this writing.) This program includes excellent music notation printing options. FreeStyle is designed for the person with little or no sequencing background. The screen display resembles a tape recorder and can be mastered quickly. If you are interested in recording MIDI and already have a MIDI instrument and interface, check out FreeStyle. A free demo version can be downloaded at from the company's Web site that is listed in the appendix.

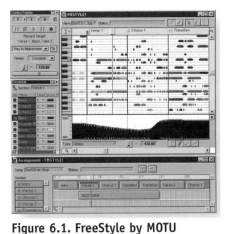

Figure 6.1. FreeStyle by MOTU

Once FreeStyle is installed and a MIDI keyboard is connected, recording can begin. Separate tracks of music, called "takes" in FreeStyle, can be recorded. The tracks/takes feature allows the user to layer multiple parts.

FreeStyle is designed to be simple and easy to use. Just click on an instrument, select the desired sound, press Record, and then input the performance on the MIDI instrument. Several takes can be recorded for each sound or part and then played back.

One of the advantages of using a MIDI sequencer is that performance information can be translated into printed music notation. FreeStyle does an especially good job of transcribing music notation, and it is easy to play in the parts from the MIDI keyboard and then print them out.

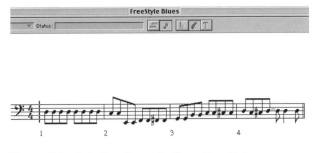

Figure 6.2. FreeStyle Takes

Keep in mind that FreeStyle is not designed to be a notation program whose primary purpose is to print out scores and parts, although it does an excellent job printing lead sheets, melodies, and parts. There are several programs designed to be used for music notation, among them Finale, Sibelius, and Encore.

Figure 6.3. Notation Example from FreeStyle

Learning to Sequence

There are several publications and other materials available to help you learn the art of sequencing. An excellent book on the topic is Paul Gilbreath's *Guide to MIDI Orchestration* (Music Works). The book is full of tips and suggestions for making musical-sounding sequences. Other products to assist the novice include Don Muro's book *The Art of Sequencing* (WB Publications). Muro's book is designed for the novice to intermediate user and provides a step-by-step method for entering a sequence using any software sequencer or integrated sequencer.

Instant Arrangement Software

Some software packages can be thought of as specialized MIDI sequencing programs designed to create arrangements. Two packages that can be useful in creating MIDI sequences include Band-in-a-Box (available for Macintosh and Windows) by PG Music and Jammer (available for Windows only) by SoundTrek. Both programs offer a range of built-in capabilities that can assist in creating professional-sounding songs and arrangements. Band-in-a-Box has more built-in options but Jammer includes 256 tracks for MIDI sequencing. Band-in-a-Box version 9 can record a single track of digital audio.

Band-in-a-Box

Band-in-a-Box is a powerful program which sells for under $100. It comes with a variety of built-in pop, jazz, and rock styles. Within some styles the program automatically creates string and guitar parts. Band-in-a-Box also has the ability to a notate and print a lead sheet.

To create a song using Band-in-a-Box, chords are typed in using the computer's typewriter keyboard. For example: C7, Cmin, and Caug, are entered into the appropriate measure.

Once the chord symbols are entered, the next step is to select a style, such as jazz, rock, bossa nova, or waltz. There are twenty-four basic styles in Band-in-a-Box and several hundred more styles from which to choose.

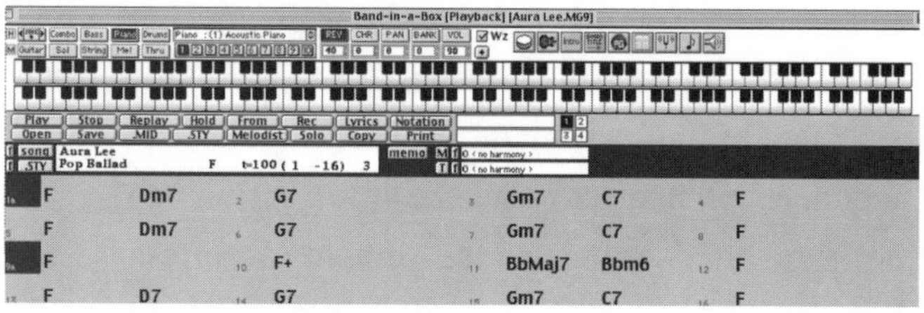

Figure 6.4. Band-in-a-Box with Chords

After entering the chords and selecting a style, click on the play button and Band-in-a-Box instantly creates an accompaniment including piano, bass, and drums. Once the chords are entered, a melody can be recorded using Band-in-a-Box's one track built-in sequencer.

Band-in-a-Box also has an automatic harmony function. After playing in a melody, select one of the two hundred harmony styles. The melody you entered will be instantly harmonized according to the selected style.

Band-in-a-Box can even create a solo in the style of many of the great jazz stars. Simply select the name of the style or artist, such as Miles Davis or John Coltrane, and Band-in-a-Box will create a solo in his or her style. Every time you press play, the solo will be slightly different.

Beginning in version 8 of Band-in-a-Box, it is possible to ask the program to create entire songs. A song can be composed by Band-in-a-Box in the style of your choice with intro, chords, melody, arrangement, and improvisations. These are all created by the program, different every time. You can actually create an original song in less than one second! Once the song is generated, the chords and melody became part of the regular Band-in-a-Box tracks and can be edited, modified, and printed. It is also possible to enter a chord progression, choose a melodic style, and ask Band-in-a-Box to create an original melody.

Band-in-a-Box also includes a printing function so that each of the various parts can be printed in music notation. You can print a copy of the bass part, melody, piano, or any other part generated by Band-in-a-Box. In fact, the notation printing option makes this an excellent program for creating lead sheets.

Transferring to Other Programs

It is possible to create a song in Band-in-a-Box and then export it to another MIDI program, such as a MIDI sequencer, to add additional tracks. It is possible to share MIDI files with other programs by saving the file as a Standard MIDI File (see chapter 2). Choose Save As from the File menu and choose Standard MIDI file. Then open a MIDI sequencer program such as FreeStyle and open the Band-in-a-Box file. The parts can now be edited and other tracks added as needed.

MIDI Input via Acoustic Instruments

In chapter 2, the concept of using alternate MIDI controllers was introduced. It is also possible to use a pitch-to-MIDI converter designed to transfer other signals into MIDI. The program AutoScore for Mac and Windows is an example of software designed to be used to convert acoustic sounds into MIDI data. The advantage of using a pitch-to-MIDI is that after the performance is converted to MIDI it can be transposed or printed out.

Editor/Librarian Software

Electronic keyboards are capable of producing hundreds of different sounds. Each sound is created by specific settings. When you look at the front panel of an electronic instrument, it may have dozens of controllers and ways to manipulate a particular sound. One advantage of using digital electronic instruments is that the sounds can be altered to better suit specific needs. For example, a string sound, sometimes referred to as a patch, could be edited to remove vibrato or tremolo. This editing could be done using the instrument's front panel display. However, it is much easier to make edits to sounds by using a computer and software designed for this purpose called editor/librarian software. Here is how it works: you connect your MIDI instrument to a Macintosh or Windows computer via a MIDI interface. Having installed the editor/librarian software, you can then edit and store the custom sounds you want to use with your instruments. The librarian portion allows you to store, organize, and recall the sounds you've created and want to use with your MIDI instruments and playback devices. The editor portion of the program gives you control over the creation of new sounds. Editing can be done on the computer screen.

Macintosh and Windows Editor/Librarian Software

Editor/librarian programs are available for Macintosh and Windows computers include Midi Quest by Sound Quest and Unisyn by Mark of the Unicorn. Midi Quest supports 360 different MIDI instruments and includes more than 55,000 patches and extensive video tutorials. The program allows the user to create, edit, and store thousands of sounds that can be used with different MIDI instruments and sound modules.

Unisyn by Mark of the Unicorn, is available for Macintosh and Windows computers and offers features

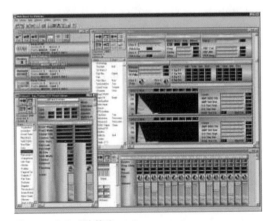

Figure 6.5. Midi Quest

similar to Midi Quest. You can modify a sound in Unisyn using graphic envelope controls and faders. It is also possible to generate entire banks of new sounds with a click of the mouse using blend, randomize, and copy/paste parameter features. Unisyn can store thousands of sounds and recall them instantly using database-style search criteria, such as "plucked electric bass" with "bright stereo flange."

Digital Signal Processing (DSP)

It is frequently desirable to record MIDI with digital audio. In other words, while you record MIDI tracks, you can plug in a microphone and record live vocals and/or instrumental parts. Thanks to digital signals processing, most MIDI sequencing software lets you do this.

As introduced in chapter 2, the term Digital Signal Processing, or DSP, is the act of sampling and editing a digital signal. In previous chapters, we discussed stand-alone hardware units that let

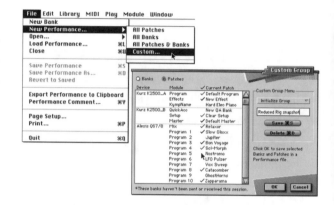

Figure 6.6. Unisyn Editor/Librarian

you record digitally. Digital recording can also be accomplished using a Windows or Macintosh computer. As with MIDI sequencing, DSP has its own hardware and software considerations. Hardware consists of the Macintosh or Windows built-in computer hardware, plus additional equipment such as DSP plug-in cards and interfaces for greater flexibility and power. These cards will be introduced in chapters 7 and 8. Software is used to record and process digital signals. The class of software ranges from packages for the hobbyist to recording professional. Each of these areas will be dealt with in following chapters.

Digital Audio Recording

A basic understanding of how computers deal with digital audio is necessary in order to make an informed decision about which digital audio recording system is best for you. Power Macintosh, G3, and G4 Macintosh models have built-in digital audio capabilities. In order to record digital audio on a Windows PC, you need a soundcard or audio card. An analog-to-digital converter is attached to the line-in or microphone in (mic in) jack, usually located on the back panel of the computer. The analog signal can be from any source, such as a microphone or electronic instrument. After the analog signal is converted to digital it is then stored on the computer's hard drive. It can be manipulated by the software to edit, add effects, and mix. To get the information out of the computer, line-out jacks are used. These function as digital-to-analog converters, referred to as DAC. The line out or speaker out is sent to the amplifier or headphones.

There are two different outputs, one for MIDI and one for digital audio. The MIDI output comes from the audio outputs on the back of a MIDI instrument. The digital audio output comes from the computer's line-out jacks. Both outputs must be connected to the mixer or amplifier.

It is also possible to use a more complex interface that will handle and route both MIDI and digital audio. This will be addressed in chapters 7 and 8.

MIDI/Digital Audio Software

So far, we have only considered software that is designed for MIDI sequencing. The next level of software allows for both MIDI sequencing and digital audio to be recorded together with the same program. As with most types of software, entry-level and high-end options are available. Entry-level MIDI/digital audio software utilizes the built-in capabilities of the Macintosh and Windows PC. High-end options require an additional DSP hardware device, called an audio card, which plugs inside the computer. This chapter will provide an overview of some entry-level software options. In chapters 7 and 8 we will deal with high-end MIDI and digital audio software.

Entry-Level Windows MIDI/Digital Audio Sequencers

In entry-level software programs, there is a limit to the number of digital audio tracks that can be used. Some programs limit the number of tracks to eight or sixteen. Also, the built-in effects are limited. The entry-level programs are designed for the home user, music hobbyist, student, or for those on a very tight budget.

For Windows computers, there are many MIDI/digital audio programs from which to choose. Entry-level software typically costs under $100. The trade-off is that the software is not designed for high-end recording, mixing, and editing. The programs in this range do include some complex features, which until just a few years ago were found only on top-of-the-line programs.

Home Studio by Cakewalk, Power Tracks Pro Audio by PG Music, Cubasis AV by Steinberg, and MicroLogic by Emagic, all with list prices under $150, are designed to be used on a Windows PC (with a minimum of a 486 processor). These products can record MIDI and multiple tracks of digital audio; they also have a music printing option. (Of course, you'll need a printer to print out parts and scores.)

Of these, Power Tracks Pro Audio (Windows only) by PGMusic is the cheapest way to get into the world of MIDI/digital audio. This software lists for an amazing $29. Don't let the price fool you! There are many high-end features that make this a very attractive entry-level program.

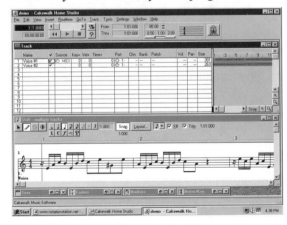

Figure 6.7. Cakewalk Home Studio

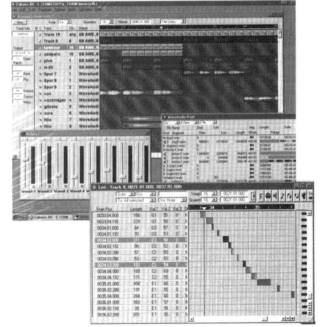

Figure 6.8. Steinberg's Cubasis

Home Studio by Cakewalk, Cubasis AV by Steinberg, and MicroLogic by Emagic are all entry-level programs, but each is part of a family of software with both low-end and high-end versions. Cakewalk, the makers of Home Studio, also produces a Pro Audio version. Steinberg, which publishes Cubasis VST PC, offers two products for the high-end user: Cubase VST and Cubase VST/24. If you find you want to upgrade to the more powerful product, the transition will be relatively easy because you will already be familiar with the basic operation and feel of the software.

With all of the above-mentioned programs, there is no additional hardware required; the built-in soundcard in the PC can be used to record and play back digital audio.

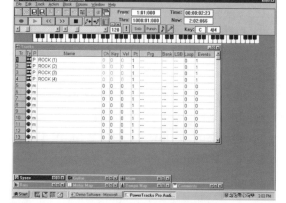

Figure 6.9. PGMusic's Powertracks Pro

Entry-Level Macintosh MIDI/Digital Audio Software

The Macintosh does not have as many entry-level MIDI/digital audio software options as Windows. Under the $150 list price are Emagic's Micrologic and Opcode's Vision DSP. Both programs offer integrated MIDI and digital audio. They can record digital audio using Sound Manager, Macintosh's built-in digital audio software. Of the two entry-level software options, MicroLogic is the better choice, as Opcode, maker of Vision DSP, is currently not upgrading.

Which Program to Buy?

All of the programs mentioned in this chapter are competitively priced, so cost is not a major factor. One way to review them is to go to the program's Web site and download a demo version. A comprehensive list of company Web sites is listed in appendix A. Spend some time using each program to see if it suits your needs. Also, contact people you know who are using digital audio software and ask for their opinions.

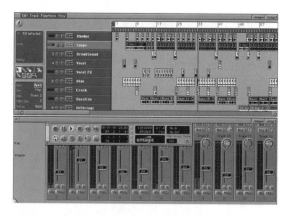

Figure 6.10. Emagic's MicroLogic

If you use the same software as your friends or coworkers, you can turn to them for help and assistance. If you think you may be upgrading to a high-end program in the future you may want to go with one of the programs supported by a line of software such as Cubase, Home Studio, and MicroLogic.

Summary

This chapter focused on some of the entry-level options. These programs are designed for the home user, music hobbyist, and student. The mid-level to high-end digital audio software is covered in chapters 7 and 8.

Chapter 7.

Mid-Level Computer-Based MIDI/Hard Disk Recording

In chapter 6, low-end MIDI sequencing/digital audio software was introduced. This chapter focuses on mid-level budget ($150 to $400) applications for the computer or software-based digital studio. Applications at this level typically include making demos, voice-overs, and other project studio applications.

As mentioned in chapter 6, Macintosh and Windows PCs can digitize audio and, with the proper software, can record and play back MIDI. A computer's built-in digital audio capabilities do have some limitations, the most serious being that the output is limited to an analog output through an RCA connector. This is sufficient for creating practice tapes, educational materials and for other uses. The output is usually limited to stereo only and there is limited capability to edit the tracks. Further, the standard PC soundcard and Macintosh Sound Manager are not designed for professional use, as there is some distortion in the sound output. They are by nature low-end digital audio products. If you are looking to do semiprofessional or professional recording, you will need to purchase hardware that was designed for digital audio and recording use. Naturally, there are several options to consider.

The Mid-Level Options

At the mid- and high-levels, output is a digital signal that can be ported or sent to other devices or burned to a CD. Of course, in order to generate a higher quality product, the cost of the hardware and software goes up.

There are several options for getting into the mid or semipro level of digital audio recording. First, a digital audio card must be added to the computer. This device makes it possible to record, edit, and transfer digital information from the computer to other devices. A digital audio card can be purchased as a stand-alone product, and the corresponding software can be chosen from several options, all designed specifically for mid-level applications. Some companies offer digital audio cards and software in one package. Others sell just a digital audio card. (You must purchase digital audio software separately.) A third option is to purchase a digital audio card and interface. An interface is a box that sits outside of the computer and allows for the connection of other devices and routing the digital signal out of the computer. At the mid-level, expect to pay from between $500 to $1,000 for a digital audio card and software. Some of the mid-level options can be expanded to take them into the high end.

Mid-Level Software Options

The following programs can be used with a variety of different audio cards. As mentioned previously, be sure that the software program you are planning to use is compatible with the digital audio card or audio card and interface package. Mid-level MIDI/digital audio software runs in the range of $200 to $400. These programs can be used with a computer's built-in hardware, such as a Windows Soundcard and Macintosh Sound Manager. However, they are also compatible with many of the audio cards or audio card/interface models described in this chapter. Some of the popular mid-level programs to consider include:

• Cakewalk (Win 95, 98). The mid-level options from Cakewalk are Cakewalk Pro ($269) and Cakewalk ProAudio ($429). Cakewalk Pro supports 256 tracks of MIDI and 8 digital audio tracks. Cakewalk ProAudio supports 256 tracks of MIDI and 128 digital audio tracks, and can print up to twenty-four staves of music notation.

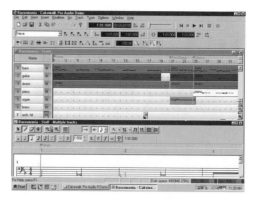

Figure 7.1. Cakewalk ProAudio 9

• Metro (Mac) by Cakewalk ($249) is a mid-level MIDI/digital audio product for the Macintosh that supports MIDI and sixty-four tracks of digital audio.

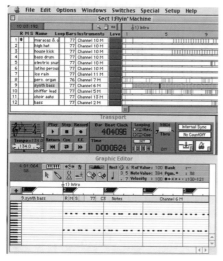

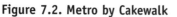

Figure 7.2. Metro by Cakewalk

Figure 7.3. Logic by Emagic

• Logic (Win 95, 98, Mac) by Emagic also boasts a line of MIDI/audio software for all levels. For the mid-level, they offer Logic Silver and Logic Gold. The basic difference is that Logic Silver ($299) is limited to sixteen digital audio tracks while Logic Gold ($499) supports forty-eight digital audio tracks.

• Cubase VST (Win 95, 98, Mac). Steinberg offers a range of versions of Cubase. Cubase VST supports an unlimited number of MIDI tracks and sixty-four tracks of digital audio and lists for $399. Quality audio effects are included and can be extended later with an ever-increasing selection of plug-ins, so you probably only need the extra ins and outs to integrate your

Figure 7.4. Cubase VST by Steinberg

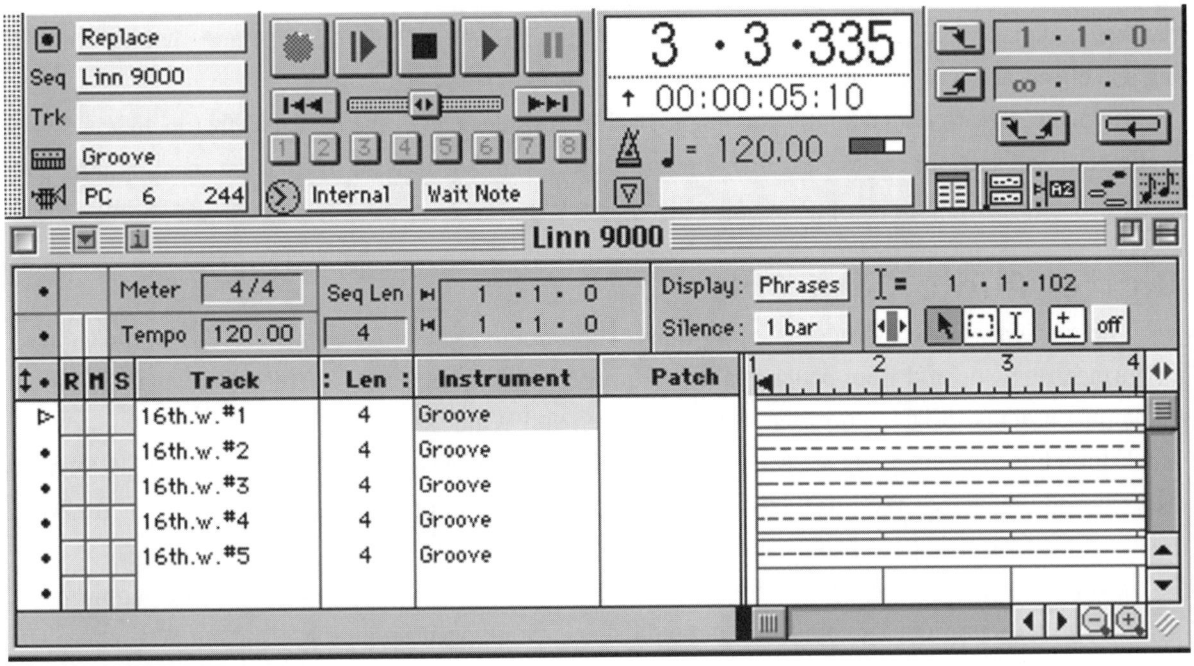

Figure 7.5. Studio Vision Pro by Opcode

current hardware effects or mixing desk. Steinberg refers to this as virtual studio technology (VST).

• Studio Vision Pro (Mac, $399) is another option offered by Opcode at the mid-level and high-end. When making your purchasing choice, be aware that as of this writing, Opcode is no longer supporting or upgrading its line of Vision products.

• Performer (Mac) by Mark of the Unicorn (MOTU) offers two products for the Macintosh: Performer and Digital Performer. Performer is priced at the upper end of the mid-level software at $495, and boasts many advanced features, including unlimited MIDI and digital audio tracks.

Which Program to Choose?

All of the companies offer demo versions that can be downloaded from their Web pages. A list of the Web addresses is located in the appendix. The companies will also send demo versions in the mail on CD-ROM at a nominal cost.

If you already use a MIDI sequencing program similar to the ones described in chapter 6 and this chapter, then I recommend that you

Figure 7.6. Performer by Mark of the Unicorn

purchase a digital audio card that is supported by that software. You will be able to do more in terms of editing and effects and will not have to learn to use a new piece of software.

If you are new to digital audio, you might want to consider one of the packages that include a digital audio card and software. These are all-in-one packages. And, if you want to have the most options with regard to signal flow, consider purchasing software packaged with a digital audio card and an interface.

Digital Audio Card Only

The card-only category is designed for those who want to use a program such as Cakewalk, Cubase, Performer, or Logic and want better quality and more options than those offered by the built-in digital signal processing available in off-the-shelf Macintosh and Windows PCs.

Within this category, there are two basic types of cards. Some support only digital audio. MIDI must be controlled by a separate MIDI card or soundcard for the PC or via a MIDI interface for the Mac. Some audio cards also have MIDI synthesis capability built in.

If you are already using a MIDI/digital audio program, find out which audio cards are supported by it. This can be found out by contacting the publisher or looking it up on the company Web page. The card should be ASIO-compatible. ASIO (Audio Stream Input/Output) is a cross-platform, multichannel audio transfer protocol that was developed by Steinberg. It is being adopted by many manufacturers of digital audio/MIDI sequencing applications. ASIO allows software to have access to the multichannel capabilities of a wide range of powerful soundcards.

Digital Audio Card Options

For mid-level recording, but not necessarily high-end studio work, there are many cards from which to choose. These cards can produce excellent results for demos and other recording projects. Descriptions of the audio cards on the market today follow. This is by no means an exhaustive list. Rather, it is intended to be an overview of some of the popular cards. There are dozens to choose from and more are coming on the market all the time. Some of the card options include Midiman Delta DiO 2496, Yamaha SW1000 XG, Yamaha DSP Factory, Korg 1212 I/0 and Oasys, Sonorus STUDI/O, Alesis PRC, Lucid PCI 24, Digital Audio Labs CardDeluxe, and others.

To work properly with your system, the cards come with software drivers that must be installed. Cards usually have a variety of driver options, including Macintosh, Windows 95 and 98, and Windows NT.

Computer Expansion Options

There are two ways to attach cards into a computer. The most common way is to plug the card into the computer's PCI slot. (PCI stands for Peripheral Component Interface.) It is also possible to purchase add-on devices that can house cards for portable or laptop computers.

Most desktop computer models have one or more PCI slots. It is not difficult to install a card. Just remove the computer case and plug the card into an existing slot. Directions are usually included with the card. If you are not comfortable performing this operation, the card can be installed by most computer service centers for approximately $100.

The other way to connect cards is via USB, which stands for Uniform Serial Bus. USB is a later advancement than PCI and is part of computers produced in 1999 and later. Check that the card you plan to purchase is compatible with your system by checking the specifications of the card.

Portable Computer Options

Digital audio isn't just for desktop computers. Portable or laptop computers have increased enough in power to handle digital audio applications. The problem is that high-end digital audio requires an audio card, and most portable computers do not have full-size, add-on card slots. The solution is an expansion chassis that adds the necessary slots and connects to the laptop. The cards are inserted into slots in the expansion chassis just as if it were a desktop computer. The chassis provides slots, power, and a cooling fan, and is rack mountable. Chassis are available in 2-, 4-, 7-, and 13-slot configurations. The 2-slot model comes with a shoulder strap and is ideal for on-location recording. Their use is not limited to laptops; they can be used with any computer that requires additional slots. A PCI card is used to connect the chassis to a desktop unit.

Figure 7.7. Magma 4 Slot Chassis

To connect the chassis to the laptop, a smaller card or host interface and cables are used. Connecting cables are available in 2- or 4-foot lengths.

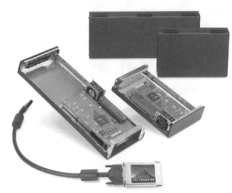

Figure 7.8. Magma PCI Cardbus Card

Figure 7.9. Magma PowerBook G3 Host Interface

Before running out and buying one, check Magma's Web site for an up-to-the minute list of supported computers, audio cards, and software. Not every computer and card is currently supported, but Magma is keeping up with computer hardware advances so an increasing number of systems will be supported. Using a laptop with Pro Tools by Digidesign was key in recording dialog on location for *Star Wars—Episode I: The Phantom Menace*. The power and flexibility allows a professional level digital recording setup that will fit on a coffee table.

Digital Audio Cards

These brief descriptions of several audio cards represent only a few of the card-only options available for Macintosh and Windows systems. I recommend you peruse one of the national catalogs that sell digital audio products, such as Sweetwater Sound, Sam Ash, B & H, Advanced Technologies, Lentine's Music, and others, to compare features and price. See the appendix for a listing of companies.

Figure 7.10. PowerBook on a Magma 2-Slot Chassis

Delta DiO 2496 (Win 95, 98, NT, Mac)

The Delta DiO 2496 by Midiman (list $299) is a digital audio card that plugs into the PCI expansion slot inside a Macintosh or Windows computer. This card has both analog and digital outputs so it can be connected to DAT, MiniDisc, DVD, CD, digital audio converter, mixer, or sound system. It offers both Optical and Coaxial S/PDIF digital audio inputs and outputs. A separate stereo analog output is provided for monitoring or analog transfers. It is designed to be used with most digital audio software applications and does not contain any synthesis capabilities.

Yamaha SW1000XG (Win 95, 98)

The Yamaha SW1000XG (list $699) includes both digital audio converters and MIDI synthesis capabilities. The card has six stereo/twelve mono tracks for playback, and processors to control dozens of effects. A special version of Yamaha's XGworks MIDI/audio sequencer and tone-generator editor is bundled with the card. SW1000XG is fully functional with many leading pro-

Figure 7.11. Delta DiO 2498

grams such as Steinberg's Cubase VST, Emagic's Logic Audio, Twelve Tone Systems' Cakewalk Pro Audio, Sonic Foundry's SoundForge, and IQS's SAW.

Korg Oasys

The Oasys (list $2,200) integrates high-quality synthesis, effects processing, and computer audio input and output into a single, professional PCI audio card designed to complement a MIDI sequencer or software-based digital audio program. The PCI card adds extra processing power to the computer and provides synthesis and effects to your studio. Oasys' built-in synthesizers include hundreds of sounds, including modeled analog synths, FM, tonewheel organ and rotary speaker, pianos, physically modeled trumpet, trombone, sax, flute, guitar, bass, vocals, pipe organ, analog percussion, analog-style sequencers, and more. Synthesis algorithms are plug-ins loaded from disk, allowing easy upgrades and expansion.

The Oasys includes more than 100 effects algorithms. All of the effects are from the Korg Trinity workstation: standard reverbs, choruses, flangers, phasers, overdrives, amp simulations, and unique effects such as random filter, stepped phaser, doppler shift, and talking modulator. Just in case that isn't enough, additional effects include tempo delays, analog style sequencers, envelope and LFO-swept filters, new high-quality analog EQ (equalization) and reverb algorithms, a 160-second maximum delay time, and more.

The Oasys features a total of twelve inputs and outputs: stereo analog, stereo S/PDIF, and 8-channel ADAT optical. All inputs and outputs are 24-bit, and can be used simultaneously with compatible multitrack audio software. The Oasys comes with Word Clock and ADAT Time Code I/O to ensure easy integration with other digital audio equipment.

The Oasys supports all major audio and MIDI standards and is compatible with virtually every audio and MIDI program. It features integration with MIDI as well as digital audio software. ASIO drivers for MacOS and Windows provide direct compatibility with Cakewalk Metro, Cubase VST, Digital Performer, Logic Audio, Vision DSP, Studio Vision Pro, and more. Standard Windows drivers provide compatibility with all popular Windows audio programs, including Cakewalk, Samplitude, SAW, Acid, Sound Forge, and more. OMS, FreeMIDI, and standard Windows MIDI drivers seamlessly connect the Oasys to all MIDI sequencers.

Audio Cards With External Interface and Software

Audio cards provide the means for sound to enter and leave the digital world, but they have a couple of disadvantages. Their size places restrictions on the number and type of connections available. Furthermore, because these cards are plugged directly inside the computer, they can pick up noise from the hard drive and other working parts of the computer. In order to address these issues, the next level of audio cards includes an external interface and a card that plugs inside the computer. Placing an interface outside of the computer reduces the amount of noise from the computer and allows additional input and outputs.

Figure 7.12. Korg Oasys

The card/interface combination provides much more flexibility and power. For example, the external interfaces typically include multiple ports for various types of analog and digital connections. The combination card and interfaces usually will cost more, but the advantages are significant, especially if your studio requires the connection of several digital and analog devices.

Midiman Delta 1010

The Delta 1010 (list $995) has 24-bit 96-kHz bandwidth and expansive flexibility. It includes eight analog I/Os, S/PDIF I/O, Word Clock I/O, and MIDI I/O to guarantee connectivity in almost any installation. To ensure that audio is not compromised by the computer's internal noise, the Delta 1010's converters reside in an external, rack mountable

Figure 7.13. Midiman Delta 1010

chassis. The power transformer is also located outside. The Delta 1010 comes with drivers for Macintosh and Windows and is compatible with most of the popular MIDI/digital audio software such as Cakewalk Metro, Cubase VST, Digital Performer, Logic Audio, Vision DSP, Studio Vision Pro, and more.

Lexicon Audio Systems

The name Lexicon is no stranger around studios large and small because its effects processors are the industry standard in studios worldwide. Lexicon currently offers two audio card and interface options. Both models feature add-on cards that incorporate Lexicon's digital effects technology into their digital audio products. Most MIDI/digital audio software can access the cards.

Core2 Desktop Audio System (Macintosh and Windows)

The Core2 system includes an audio card and external interface. There are four unbalanced ins and eight unbalanced outs for patching in synths, a mixer, or outboard effects devices. Speaking of effects, the optional MP-100 board adds effects and controls from the MPX 100 Dual Channel Effects Processor. The converters are 24-bit with selectable dbx Type IV™ soft-knee limiting on all inputs. This allows you to simulate tape compression and gives 4 dB of improved headroom.

The digital connections include a pair of RCA connectors for S/PDIF in and out and a pair of lightpipe connectors that can be used for 8-channel

Figure 7.14. Core2 Desktop Audio System by Lexicon

ADAT I/O or TOSlink S/PDIF stereo connections. Both 44.1-kHz and 48-kHz sample rates are supported. The Core2 system ships with Cool Edit Pro SE™ software for editing and control panel software for the interface settings.

Core-32 Desktop Audio System

The Core-32 system offers thirty-two simultaneous voices and an option of I/Os and more of Lexicon's trademark digital effects. The main interface is the single rack space DI-12T. Analog ins (RCA and XLR pairs) and outs (XLR only) are located on the front panel as are RCA S/PDIF connections and an XLR Time Code input. Located on the back panel are connections for ADAT sync in and out, ADAT or TOSlink S/PDIF in and out, Word Clock, and an RS 422 port.

If more analog ins and outs are required, the LDI-10T interface has eight quarter-inch balanced TRS connectors along with a pair of RCA S/PDIF connectors and a quarter-inch input for Time Code. The optional LX3 connection box allows up to three LDI10Ts to be connected to a single Core-32 card. Both interfaces use 24-bit converters and support 44.1-kHz and 48-kHz sampling rates.

Completing the system is the PC-90 Reverb Card. It contains the processor from the PCM 91 and features five algorithms, each with its own stereo in-and-out routing, that can be loaded into either of two hardware reverbs. There are 100 presets to get you started that can be controlled from your software interface.

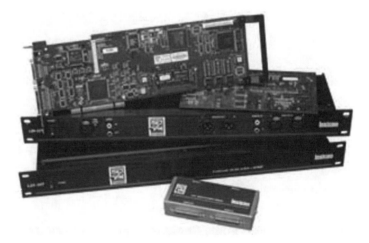

Card, Interface, and Software Combinations

Some packages provide a digital audio card, external interface, and software. These are all-in-one packages that provide all of the necessary parts. If they meet your needs, you won't have to shop any further.

Figure 7.15. Core-32 Desktop Audio System by Lexicon

Digi 001

The Digi 001 by Digidesign (list $995) is an integrated system that includes a PCI card and Pro Tools LE digital recording software. Digi001 is an all-in-one package that is ideal for the mid-level computer-based studio. This system performs the jobs of three pieces of gear. It's a 24-bit digital audio interface, a MIDI interface, and a pair of microphone preamplifiers, all in one. The unit is designed to sit on a tabletop or fit in a rack, depending on the rack's proximity to the computer. The interface offers both 44.1-kHz and 48-kHz resolutions. The total system is available for both Macintosh and Windows 98 computers.

The inputs on the Digi 001 are divided between the front and back panels. On the front panel

Figure 7.16. Digi 001 by Digidesign

there are two mic/line inputs. These inputs function as mic preamplifiers with individual gain control and phantom power. They can also be used with regular quarter-inch or XLR inputs. The other six analog inputs are on the back panel. They are quarter-inch and support both balanced and unbalanced connections.

Digital I/O is available via S/PDIF with RCA connectors and an optical I/O that can handle both ADAT lightpipe and 2-channel optical (TOSlink) S/PDIF. Also included are main and monitor outputs. Channels 1 and 2 use quarter-inch balanced (TRS) connectors, while channels 3 to 8 are unbalanced quarter-inch jacks. The unit has monitor outputs, headphone input and volume control, and MIDI in and out connectors.

Pro Tools LE is a "lite" version of Digidesign's Pro Tools digital audio recording software. The LE version of the software provides all the editing

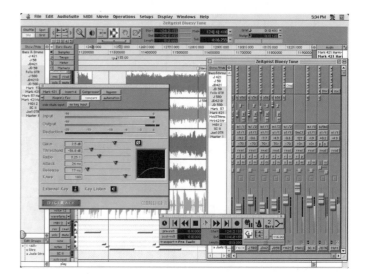

Figure 7.17. Pro Tools 5 LE

power of Pro Tools but has reduced audio capacity, twenty-four tracks maximum, and relies much more on the processing power of the computer. Pro Tools is a high-level application that will be discussed in chapter 8.

Mark of the Unicorn's (MOTU) 2408

Mark of the Unicorn's (MOTU) 2408 (list $999) system combines a single-rack space interface with a PCI card. The system also includes MOTU's AudioDesk digital audio software. The PCI 324 card and 2408 interface can be used with Macintosh and Windows computers. However, the AudioDesk digital editing software is only for Macintosh. The 2408 system supports Sound Designer II (SDII), Digidesign's standard audio file format, aiff (the standard Macintosh audio file format), and wav (the standard Windows audio file format).

With the 2408 system, audio processing is accomplished on the computer, so the amount of audio that can be processed depends on three things: the computer's processor speed, the amount of RAM, and the hard drive's speed. If you are using external drives for recording, a SCSI accelerator will be required for large track counts. A SCSI accelerator is a PCI card that adds a SCSI connection to the back of the computer. The hard drives that will be used to record audio are connected to the SCSI port. Other SCSI devices such as CD burners and scanners should be connected to the computer's SCSI port. Remember that SCSI can only handle a maximum of seven different devices.

Figure 7.18. Mark of the Unicorn's (MOTU) 2408

The PCI card that comes with the 2408 has the capability of connecting to three separate interface units. This allows for the expansion of additional units for more inputs and outputs. There is also an ADAT sync for transferring tracks to and from ADAT format. An RS-422 port rounds out the connectors which connects to MOTU's Digital Timepiece A/V synchronizer and allows sample-accurate syncing with TASCAM's DA series of multitrack recorders. The card handles all of the I/O processing and is, in effect, a 72 x 72 patch bay.

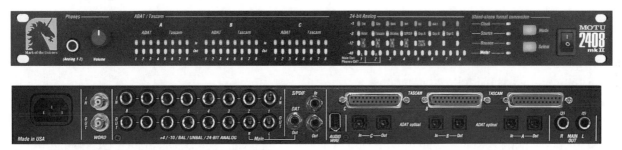

Figure 7.19. MOTO 2408's Front and Rear Panels

The 2408 external interface accommodates eight channels of unbalanced analog audio using gold plated RCA connectors, three TASCAM TDIF 8-channel digital I/O connectors, and three ADAT lightpipe 8-channel connectors. There are three 8-channel busses inside the 2408 allowing for a total of twenty-four simultaneous inputs and outputs. The A/D and D/A converters are 20-bit, but the data is handled at 24-bit internally. Therefore, Macintosh users can choose between working with 16-bit or 24-bit files in AudioDesk.

In addition to the connections for analog and MDMs, the 2408 has a S/PDIF input and two S/PDIF output connections. This means you can patch two S/PDIF devices or route one S/PDIF out to a DAT deck and one S/PDIF out to a digital mixer or patch bay. There is a pair of quarter-inch jacks for a main output stereo pair and a pair of BNC connectors for handling Word Clock sync.

On the front panel there is a headphone jack and volume control. The signal duplicates the main stereo outs. There are three sets of LEDs that indicate audio signals for the MDM digital ins and outs.

For the analog signals there are eight 4-segment LEDs that indicate the input level and a single LED to indicate output activity.

The interface also contains LEDs and buttons under the heading of stand-alone format conversion. In this mode the 1208 interface is no longer under the control of the 324 card. The primary use for this feature is bouncing tracks between ADATs and DA series MDMs. Up to twenty-four tracks can be bounced at a time. Some of the analog LEDs perform double duty and indicate settings for the interface in this mode. There are options for selecting the master deck for clock source, operating at 44.1 kHz or 48 kHz, bouncing from S/PDIF or analog connections and analog metering. Remember, you will need to use Word Clock, or other

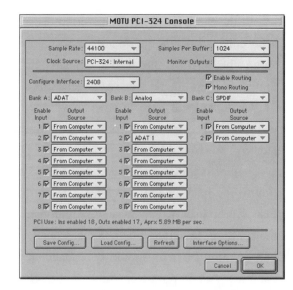

Figure 7.20. MOTU 324's Console Software for the 2408

external sync device, for the DA series decks. This feature will allow you to maintain a mixed setup of MDMs if your project requires you to work with both formats.

Routing audio signals in the 2408 is accomplished through the 324 Console software. This software is included for both Macintosh and Windows computers. The software can run separately or can be accessed from inside-supported digital audio software applications such as AudioDesk and Digital Performer.

The software is used to determine the digital-audio-specific settings and how the monitoring will be routed and for routing the audio through each of the three banks or busses. The options available are Analog, ADAT, DA88, or Disable, if nothing is being routed through the bus. Enable Routing and Mono Routing provides the following options:

Configurations can be saved so individual sessions can be easily recalled and templates can be created for specific recording situations. MOTU includes both a printed setup guide in the manual and a software setup guide that is installed with the software to help get you up and running as quickly as possible.

MOTU 2408-Supported Software

Windows users have several different options for MIDI/digital audio software to use with the 2408 system including Cubase VST 24, Logic Audio Platinum, Cakewalk Pro Audio versions 6 and 7, Samplitude, Sound Forge, SAW Plus, and Cool Edit Pro. Macintosh MIDI/digital-audio-supported software includes Logic, Cubase VST, Vision DSP, Studio Vision, and Digital Performer.

MOTU 2408 Family

Studios come in a myriad of configurations and MOTU has built on the 2408's success to provide options for those needing more analog or digital inputs. Additional units are available that can be used with the 324 card, or separately as add-ons to an existing system. The PCI 324 card has three connectors so each card can handle three additional interfaces.

MOTU 308

The MOTU 308 (list $695) is the least expensive add-on component and expands the system's digital connections. This unit adds eight channels of AES/EBU digital I/O, eight channels of S/PDIF digital I/O using RCA connectors, and eight channels of S/PDIF digital I/O using optical TOSlink connectors. Word Clock connectors are also provided. Front-panel buttons are provided, allowing the 308 to be used for 2-channel format conversion between machines with both S/PDIF connection formats and AES/EBU connectors. A signal-present LED is provided for each digital input and output along with indicator LEDs for format conversion settings.

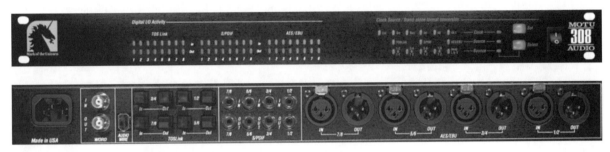

Figure 7.21. MOTU 308's Front and Back Panels

MOTU 1224

The MOTU 1224 (list $995) is a 24-bit I/O with eight channels of balanced quarter-inch TRS connectors. The unit also has two AES/EBU connectors for digital transfers. The main analog outs are XLR connectors. BNC Word Clock connectors are also included. It has a headphone jack and volume control and 6-segment LED's for metering all signals. It supports both 44.1-kHz and 48-Khz recording.

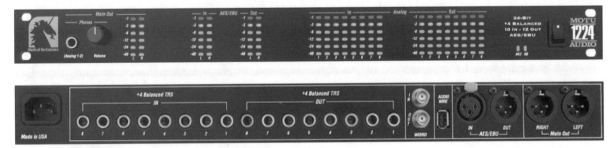

Figure 7.22. MOTU 1224's Front and Back Panels

MOTU 24i

One of the main limitations with digital recording equipment is that it typically has a relatively small number of inputs, especially when the typical studio includes several synthesizers and drum machines with six or eight outputs. The MOTU 24i (list $1,480) is ideal for setups requiring a large number of inputs. It supports twenty-four simultaneous tracks of recording at 24-bit resolution. Stereo output for monitoring and mixdown is provided in three different formats, balanced TRS quarter-inch phone jacks, TOSlink optical S/PDIF and RCA connector S/PDIF. There are 6-segment LEDs for all twenty-four inputs and the stereo output, a headphone jack, and volume knob.

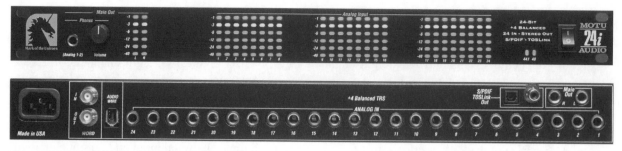

Figure 7.23. MOTU's 24i Front and Back Panels

The modular hardware approach and flexibility in software selection make this an easy system to integrate into any studio.

Effects

What about those cool effects when mixing the final product? Effects such as chorus, echo, and reverb are made available in one of two ways. They can reside on the audio card or they can be part of the software using the processing power of the computer. When effects are built into the software, they are called plug-ins. Having effects on the audio card, rather than built in to the software, can be more efficient, as the chips on the card do the processing. However, with the ever-increasing power of computers, the plug-in approach is becoming more popular. Steinberg, the producers of Cubase MIDI/Audio software, developed a widely adopted plug-in architecture called VST, or Virtual Studio Technology. This provides effects processing for those using MIDI/Audio software without additional hardware cards and rack modules.

Making the ADAT/Computer Connection

In chapter 4, we discussed MDMs, or modular digital multitrack recorders. These tape-based recorders are designed to be self-contained. However, it is possible, using a card and software, to connect a Macintosh or Windows computer for enhanced editing and processing. This is a hybrid system combining the MDM ADAT as the recording media and the computer software for editing.

Alesis offers a product called ADAT/Edit (list $399), a combination of a PCI card, interface, and software, designed to be used with ADAT recorders. The card plugs into the PCI slot inside the computer. Once the software is installed, ADAT can send and receive digital information via lightpipe technology, a multichannel digital optical connection. Using ADAT/Edit, tracks recorded on an ADAT can be sent to a computer for editing. After tracks are edited they can be sent back to the ADAT.

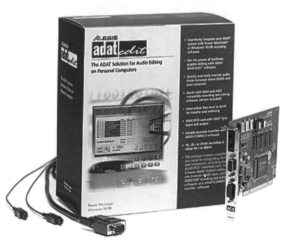

Figure 7.24. ADAT/Edit Software and Interface Card

ADAT/Edit comes with a sync cable and two optical cables to connect the ADAT to the computer card. When attaching the sync cable you must first decide whether the computer or the ADAT will be the master for the transfer, since only one sync cable can be connected. Selecting the computer as the master will allow you to use transport controls to control the ADAT. Selecting the ADAT as the source will allow you to control the software from the front panel of the ADAT, or via an LRC or BRC remote. If you are record-

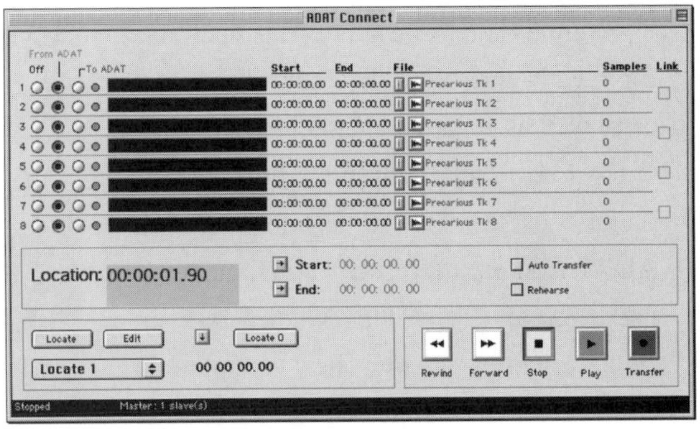

Figure 7.25. ADAT Connect Software

ing digital audio to the computer you will have to save each ADAT track as a separate file. The software will prompt for a file name, resolution (16-bit, 20-bit, or 24-bit) and the computer file type. If you plan to import the files into an audio editing program, make sure you select the type supported by the software.

It is always a good idea to make backup copies of every session. ADAT Connect software offers the option of dumping or transferring tracks to the computer so they can be backed up and archived by copying them to disk or burning a CD-ROM or DVD.

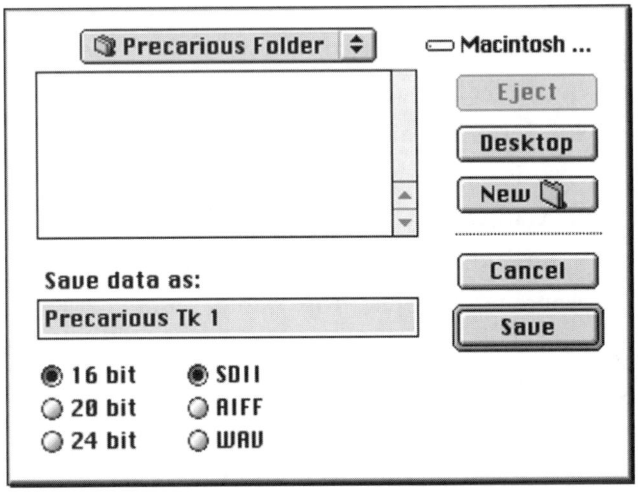

ADAT/Edit Software

The ADAT/Edit package also includes a MIDI/digital audio sequencer program made by Emagic. Based on its Logic software line, it handles both audio tracks imported from ADAT, any other audio source, and MIDI. Using this software, you now have a hybrid system including MDM, MIDI, and hard disk computer-based recording.

Figure 7.26. Save Dialog Box from ADAT Connect

The mixer window that follows provides an interface for mixing both audio and MIDI tracks with automation and plug-in effects. For MIDI tracks it controls pan, volume, and three other assignable controller options. Audio tracks can be distinguished by the presence of LED type indicators for volume and EQ settings. Audio tracks can be muted, soloed, and panned. For signal processing there is EQ on each channel strip.

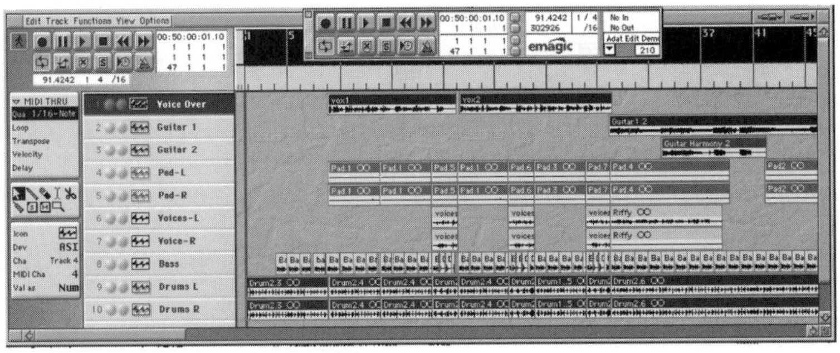

Figure 7.27. ADAT/Edit Software

Signals can be bused to plug-in effects for reverb and delay. The aux returns are displayed as separate channel strips.

Audio tracks can be edited in the Sample Editor. The audio edits made in ADAT/Edit are destructive edits, meaning the original file will be altered forever. Make backups of any files you plan to edit first so you can go back if you change your mind or make a mistake. Visually, tracks can be identified both by icon and color in the Arrange window. General MIDI is fully supported as well.

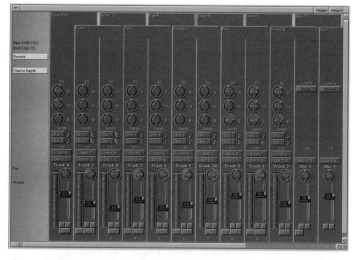

Figure 7.28. The Mixer Window of ADAT/Edit

Notation editing is also possible using the Score Editor. Using the zoom function it is possible to enlarge the view for easier reading. It can display transpositions for non-C instruments, adjust the number of staves used by keyboard instruments and handle clef changes for extreme ranges. Parts can be edited, than printed from here for use in sessions. Notation can also be exported as a PostScript file allowing it to be transferred to a page-layout program.

Digital Editing Software

All of the previously mentioned programs have built-in digital audio editing. However, there are times when you will want a dedicated 2-track hard disk tool for final editing. This software is ideal for making the final touches to the file before dumping it to DAT or burning the CD. Peak by Bias for the Macintosh and SoundForge by Sonic Foundry for Windows are examples of

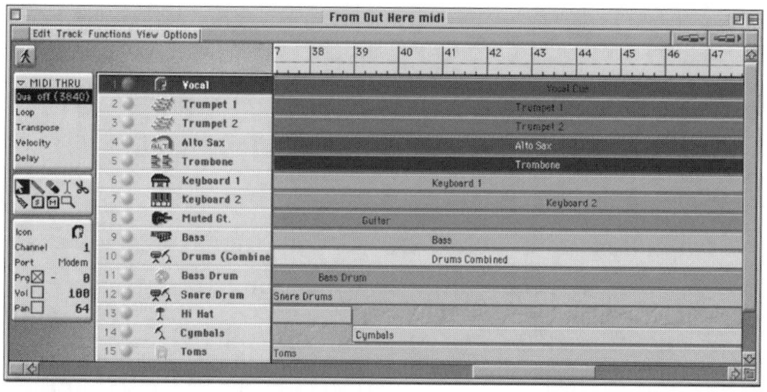

Figure 7.29. ADAT/Edit Sample Editor

digital editing software. Both companies make a "lite" version for under $100 that can be used in the entry- to mid-level studio. Peak LE and SoundForge XP cost under $100 and have many basic editing functions.

Summary

This chapter introduced some of the options for purchasing add-on digital audio cards and interfaces and mid-level studio. Several high-end options are presented in the next chapter.

Chapter 8.

High-End Computer Based MIDI/Hard Disk Recording

Chapters 6 and 7 dealt with computer software-based MIDI/digital audio recording at the entry- and mid-levels. This chapter focuses on computer software-based MIDI/digital audio recording for high-end recording. Since high-end software and hardware are designed for professional use, the capabilities will also be increased and the price will be higher.

We have drawn gray lines between each of the three levels. In fact, it is possible to use some of the entry- and mid-level audio cards described in chapter 7 with high-end software described in this chapter. With the information in chapters 6, 7, and 8, you should be able to make informed choices for your particular needs.

As with the other levels, it is possible to put together a digital audio workstation by purchasing MIDI/digital audio software and then adding an audio card, or an audio card and interface. You can also purchase a complete system that includes both hardware and software in the same package.

Selecting the Software

The most important factor in building a computer software-based digital recording setup is to select the software that best suits your needs. The same companies that make entry- and mid-level software also make high-end versions. There are two categories of software: MIDI/digital audio, and digital-audio only. Typically, high-end software supports more tracks, often an unlimited number. The software also includes high-end features like built-in effects plug-ins. The cost of high-end software alone is usually between $500 and $1,000, and includes software from Cakewalk, Steinberg, MOTU, and Emagic.

There are also complete packages at the high-end that include software, audio card, and interface. These are more expensive, between $2,000 and $10,000, and are designed to be used as stand-alone products. Pro Tools 5 and Paris are examples in this category and are explained later in this chapter.

Effects Plug-Ins

A part of every recording studio, be it an analog or digital studio, typically includes effects devices such as reverbs, equalizers, harmonizers, compressors, limiters, gates, and others. In the analog studio, these are separate units, referred to as outboard effects. Integration of outboard effects in an analog studio usually requires double the number of connections because they are normally routed through a patch bay to allow for maximum flexibility in signal routing. All of these connections multiply the noise added to the signal chain. To eliminate this noise problem and to allow for more options in the digital environment, plug-ins were developed. In digital recording software, plug-ins take on the functions of outboard effects devices.

Most high-end digital audio software comes with a few of the company's supported plug-ins, but these barely scratch the surface of what is available. A basic plug-in set usually includes EQs, filters, and reverb. Additional plug-ins not contained in the main program can be purchased and added on.

Plug-ins themselves cannot function independently; they are specifically designed to be used from within digital audio recording software. Plug-ins are covered in more detail in chapters 14, 16, 17, 18, and 19.

Real-Time and Non-Real-Time Plug-Ins

The are two types of plug-ins: real-time and non-real-time. Real-time plug-ins allow you to hear the alteration while the sound is being recorded or played back. Non-real-time plug-ins provide a short audition of the effect, but the results of the actual processing can be heard only after the file is treated and played back.

Currently there is no industry standard format for effects plug-ins. In most cases the software developers create their own format. For example Digidesign created TDM, RTAS, and Audio Suite for use with Pro Tools and Pro Tools LE. Mark of the Unicorn created MAS for Digital Performer, and Steinberg created VST for Cubase. Most plug-ins are available in several formats for both Macintosh and Windows platforms. Formats that support real-time processing include Time Division Multiplexing (TDM), Real Time Audio Suite (RTAS), Mark of the Unicorn Audio System (MAS), and Virtual Studio Technology (VST). Non-real-time plug-in formats include Audio Suite, Sound Forge, Xtras, and Adobe Primere.

High-End MIDI/Digital Audio Software

As with entry- and mid-level applications, there are many programs from which to choose. All of these programs can be used with a wide variety of digital audio cards. Some of the popular software high-end options include:

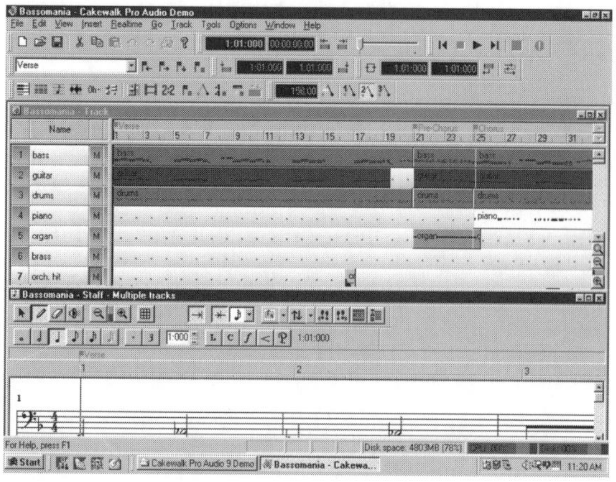

• Cakewalk Pro Audio Deluxe (Win 95, 98, list price $429). This is Cakewalk's high-end MIDI/digital audio software option. It can support 256 MIDI tracks and 128 digital audio tracks.

Figure 8.1. Cakewalk Pro Audio Deluxe

Cakewalk Pro Audio Deluxe also has a music-notation printing capability up to twenty-four staves.

• Logic Platinum (Win 95, 98, Mac, list price $799). Emagic offers Logic in several versions. Logic Platinum is the top of the line. This high-end pro version features unlimited MIDI tracks and up to ninety-six audio tracks.

• Cubase VST 24 (Win 95, 98, Mac, list price $799). Cubase VST 24 is Steinberg's high-end version of Cubase. Cubase VST supports an unlimited number of MIDI tracks and sixty-four tracks of digital audio. Quality audio effects are included and can be extended with the ever increasing selection of available plug-ins.

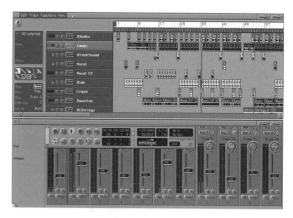

Figure 8.2. Logic Platinum

• Digital Performer (Mac, list price $795). Mark of the Unicorn (MOTU) offers two products for the Macintosh: Performer and Digital Performer. Performer, priced at the upper end of the mid-level software at $495, was discussed in chapter 7. Digital Performer boasts many advanced features, including unlimited MIDI and digital audio tracks.

High-End Digital Audio Packages

The other option at the high end is to select a digital audio all-in-one package that includes software, audio card, and interface.

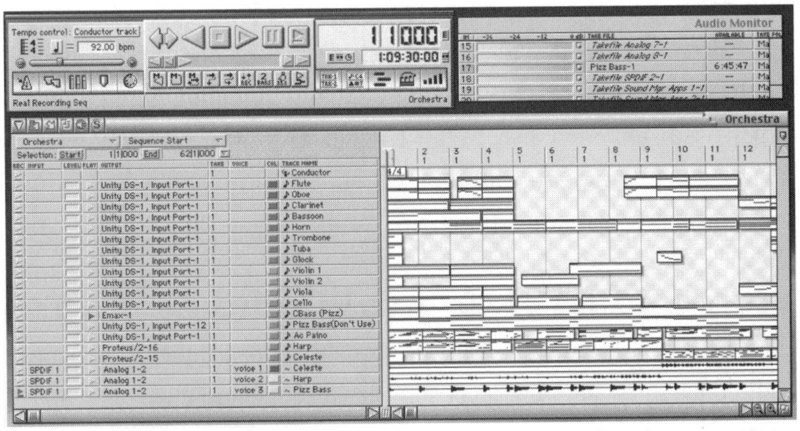

• Pro Tools (Macintosh and Windows NT, complete hardware and software package, lists between $4,000 and $10,000. Pro Tools is the high-end offering from Digidesign. Their "lite" version, Pro Tools LE, was discussed in chapter 7. Pro Tools was the first digital audio software-based program and has many high-end features. The software will be dealt with in more detail later in this chapter.

• Paris by Ensoniq (Mac and Windows NT, list price $3,895). Paris, or Professional Audio Recording Integrated System, is a complete system that includes an audio card, external interface, software, and digital mixer. It is a complete stand-alone package.

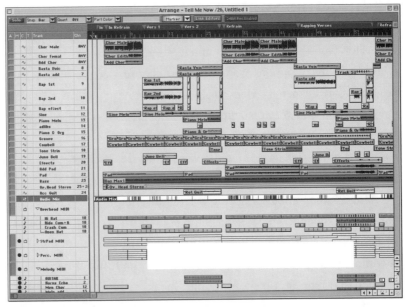

Figure 8.3. Cubase VST 24

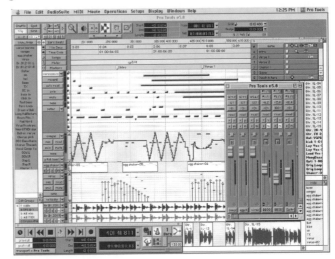

Figure 8.4. Digital Performer

Figure 8.5. Pro Tools

Making the Software Choice

The best way to choose software is to use it first-hand. However, this can be quite time-consuming, as there are many options from which to choose. Reading reviews in magazines such as *Keyboard* and *Electronic Musician* is an excellent first step. It is also a good idea to consult with local music stores and professionals and inquire what software and hardware they use or recommend.

After reading about or seeing a program that you like, consider downloading a demo copy from the company's Web site. (There is a complete list of company Web sites in the appendix.) Also, go to local music stores that have digital audio software installed and request a demonstration. Speak with people you know who use software in their studios. Ask what works for them and more importantly, what didn't? It is important to spend time reviewing software to be sure that you find the features that you need. Remember, you will only be using one main program so be sure that the one you choose is the one that best suits your needs.

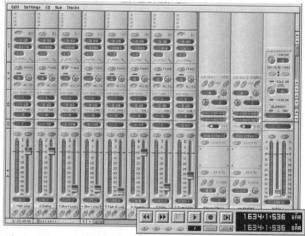

Figure 8.6. Paris Software

It would not be practical to do an exhaustive comparison of the various programs available, many of which are listed previously in this chapter. However, two programs are examined in some detail. This is intended to provide you with some baseline information on the basic features offered in typical high-end programs and a paradigm for comparison.

High-End MIDI/Digital Audio Software Features

The high-end software listed previously in this chapter have many more features for processing digital audio than entry- and mid-level software discussed in chapters 6 and 7. One high-end MIDI/digital audio program is Digital Performer (for Mac only). Like other high-end Mac and Windows programs, Digital Performer records audio using the computer's built-in audio capabilities or using plug-in digital audio cards. High-end software allows you to select the audio system or audio card that you have installed in your computer. Some of the common high-end audio cards are reviewed later in this chapter.

Audio/MIDI Tracks

MIDI/digital audio software displays audio tracks and MIDI tracks simultaneously. The audio-tracks window allows editing of the time placement of the sound files so that they are in sync with the MIDI tracks.

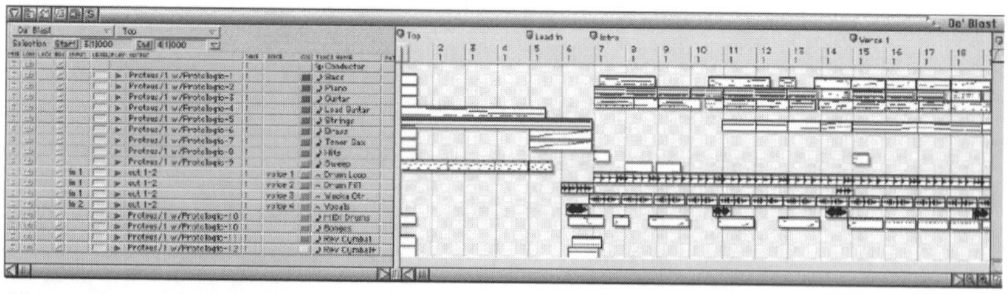

Figure 8.7. Digital Performer Audio/MIDI Tracks Window

With high-end titles, many more tracks of audio and MIDI can be recorded, usually from 128 tracks of each to an unlimited number. The number of tracks that can be recorded is limited only by the computer's processor and disk-storage capacity.

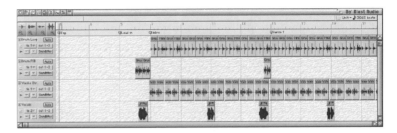

Figure 8.8. Digital Performer Audio Tracks Window

Variety of Audio Tracks

High-end software can manipulate mono or stereo tracks for audio. In addition, mono or stereo aux-sends can be routed to different effects, to outputs, or to a master fader. Software can display MIDI and audio tracks side by side and tracks can be moved for more convenient layout.

Figure 8.9. Digital Performer Mix Window

Mixing Consoles and Plug-Ins

All high-end MIDI/digital audio software includes a complete, built-in mixing console that replicates some of the functions of a stand-alone mixer including volume, panning, mute, solo, and the ability to route a signal to an effects plug-in. Effects plug-ins provide a graphic display where all parameters of each effect can be viewed. Most programs also have a different set of plug-ins for processing MIDI tracks.

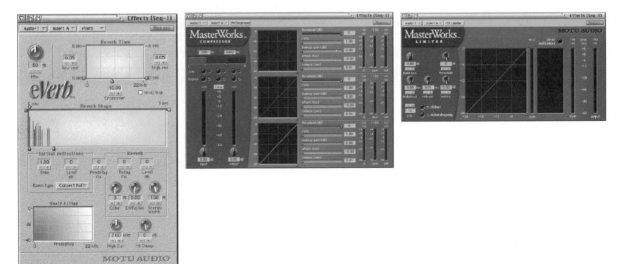

Figure 8.10. Digital Performer Effects Windows

Unique Features

Every high-end MIDI/ digital audio program also has some features that are unique to each piece of software. For example, Digital Performer has audio processing options including the Spectral Effects Processor that is designed for transposing vocals and creating other special effects. The presets available can be used to create an octave double for a vocal or a harmony part. If not, Digital Performer allows you to create and save your own effects by dragging the ball in the graphic display or entering numbers in the value boxes.

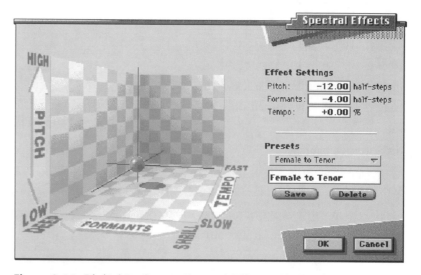

Figure 8.11. Digital Performer Spectral Effects Window

Another feature Digital Performer offers is POLAR, which stands for Performance Oriented Loop Audio Recording. POLAR takes advantage of the multiple-takes feature that allows many passes of a single phrase to be recorded. It can be used to create layers or to provide multiple takes, which can be composited, or reduced, to a single take. After recording the first pass, the take is played back and the user can then play a new take while the previous take is automatically muted. This process can be repeated until you fill up the available space in your computer's RAM.

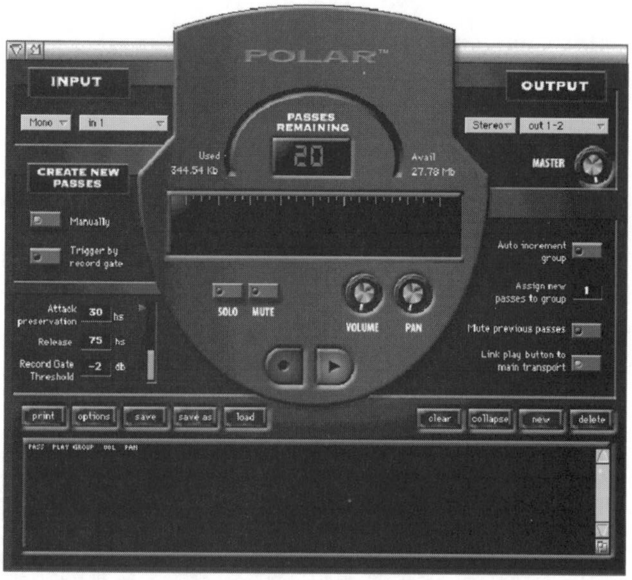

Figure 8.12. Digital Performer POLAR Window

Digital Performer can adjust the tempo of a sequence to match the length of a loop or adjust the length of the loop to fit the tempo of a sequence.

Many of the features listed here are available in other digital sequencer packages, though they may have different names and appearances. Consider this section as a list of features currently available in most programs on this level and use it to begin a list of features you would like in the software you eventually purchase.

Notation and Printing

All of the MIDI/digital audio software mentioned in this chapter, including Cakewalk Pro Audio, Digital Performer, Cubase VST, and Logic Platinum, can print notation from MIDI. The programs convert the MIDI information to musical notation. Generally, the more pricey the program, the more staves are available, usually eight staves and up. Audio tracks cannot be easily be notated and printed with software. However, some programs can convert mono digital signals to MIDI and from MIDI to notation.

Another option for creating printed parts and scores is to purchase a dedicated notation program that can work in concert with MIDI/digital audio software. There are several excellent programs that are designed specifically to print notation, including Finale (by Coda), Sibelius (by Sibelius), and Overture (by Cakewalk).

It is possible to transfer MIDI files to a notation program by first saving it as a MIDI Sequencer File or Standard MIDI File. Once the MIDI file is in Standard MIDI File format (SMF), it can be read by notation programs, such as Finale, to print out notation scores and parts.

Figure 8.13. Finale Notation Software

Selecting a High-End Digital Audio Card

If you purchase one of the MIDI/digital audio programs such as Digital Performer, Cakewalk Pro Audio, Cubase VST, or Logic Platinum, you have the choice of purchasing a wide variety of digital audio cards. Mid-level audio cards and external interfaces were discussed in chapter 7. Cards are available that can be used with any high-end MIDI/digital audio program including the Midiman Delta DiO 2496, Yamaha SW1000 XG, Yamaha DSP Factory, Korg 1212 I/0 and Oasys, Sonorus STUDI/O, Alesis PRC, Lucid PCI 24, Digital Audio Labs CardDeluxe and others. Expect to spend $1,000 or more for a high-end card.

When selecting high-end MIDI/digital audio program, consider the following criteria items:

• computer platform (Macintosh and/or Windows)
• cost
• number of MIDI tracks
• number of audio tracks
• mixing features
• plug-ins
• unique features
• notation and printing options
• interface options

Digital Audio Packages

In chapter 7, several all-in-one packages were reviewed that include all of the necessary parts: software, audio card, and interface. There are also all-in-one packages for high-end applications. Digital-audio packages such as Pro Tools by Digidesign and Paris by Ensoniq put all of the parts together in one package. The advantage of these is that all of the components, software, hardware and interface, are purchased together. The advantage of the MIDI/digital audio programs mentioned previously is that they can be used with a variety of audio cards. Following is a brief overview of Pro Tools and Paris. These packages are highly priced, but depending upon your needs they can be a good value. Paris has a list price around $4,000, while Pro Tools systems range from $4,000 to $10,000.

Integrated Hardware and Software Systems

Digidesign and their Pro Tools products have pioneered many advances in hard-disk recording. Pro Tools is available for the Macintosh and Windows NT and is compatible with the Pro Tools and ADAT interfaces described below.

Pro Tools is the Swiss Army Knife of digital hard-disk recording. For openers, it's a 16-bit or 24-bit recording system. Version 5 and later supports 128 MIDI tracks. Once your audio is recorded in Pro Tools, non-destructive editing features provide the flexibility to slice, dice, and generally rearrange audio. The software has a digital patch bay and a wide variety of effects. The software also includes a digital mixer with dynamic automation (see chapter 10) for mixdown functions. What does it do for and encore? Well, it can bounce your final mix to a stereo file on the hard drive so you don't need a mixdown deck. The stereo file is ready to be burned to CD.

Pro Tools Basics

When you open Pro Tools, the Edit window is the first thing you see. Here you can create, record, and edit tracks. Along the top of the Edit window are the tools and controls for editing audio. Along the left side are lists of group names assigned to grouped tracks. When you move one track of a group all the tracks move. Along the right side are lists of audio files and MIDI tracks in the current file.

Audio files can be brought into Pro Tools in a variety of formats and can also be imported directly from an audio CD. You can preview the selection and set the start and end times that you require.

Running your recording session is easy with the transport window and its tape-deck-like controls. Computer keyboard keystroke equivalents are available for the transport commands (such as pressing the space bar to start and stop playback).

Moving over to the mixing window, you'll

Figure 8.14. Pro Tools Edit Window

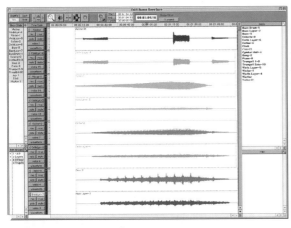

Figure 8.15. Pro Tools transport

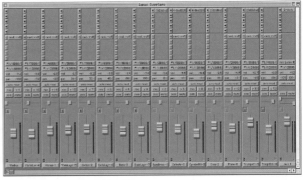

Figure 8.16. Pro Tools Mixing Window

find a fully functional digital mixer. It is possible to combine tracks together using virtual faders, making it easier to add effects to the entire mix rather than applying them to every channel, one at a time. There are sixteen separate faders in the following graphic.

Each channel has five inserts and five bus options to route signals. Assigning a signal to a bus is as simple as clicking the bus location on the channel strip and selecting the desired route from the popup menu.

Pro Tools Effects Plug-Ins

Pro Tools effects options come in two types: Audio Suite and TDM. Audio Suite effects are written to a file. Since this type of editing is non-destructive, when an Audio Suite effect is applied, the audio file is copied and the effect is applied to the copy of the track. It is possible to audition the effect before writing the file.

Audio Suite plug-ins are accessed from the edit window. TDM plug-ins are assigned from inserts in the channel strip and then following the pop-up menu to the desired plug-in.

TDM plug-ins offer the same instant feedback as using separate outboard effects units,

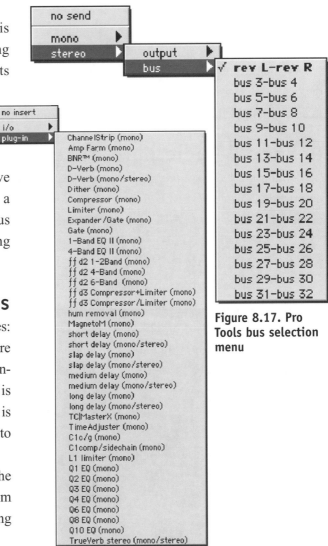

Figure 8.17. Pro Tools bus selection menu

Figure 8.18. Pro Tools 4.3.1 Plug-Ins

also called outboard gear. Changes in the settings can be auditioned and heard instantly. TDM plug-ins do not have the same hardware limits as outboard units. The only limit is in the DSP (digital signal processing) card and the number of effects you are using in a session.

Audio Suite and TDM plug-ins come in a wide range of functions from a growing number of companies. Hardware effects manufacturers such as Lexicon, Focusrite, and TC Electronics offer software plug-ins based on their hardware products. These software effects plug-ins will be dealt with in more detail in chapter 17.

In chapter 14, the process of making a digital recording using Pro Tools will be explained in detail, along with more information about plug-ins, digital editing, and other features in the software.

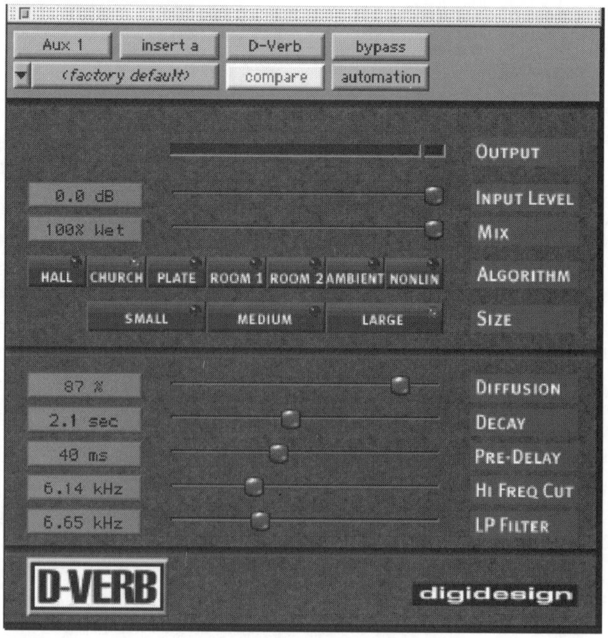

Figure 8.19. Pro Tools Effects Window

Pro Tools Audio Card/Interface Options

Digidesign has a variety of cards and external interfaces, beginning with the mid-level Digi001 described in chapter 7. Some of the Pro Tools interfaces designed for the high-end studio are described in the following section. All Digidesign products come with Macintosh and Windows NT drivers.

Pro Tools 882 | 20

The 882|20 is Pro Tools' entry-level interface. The single-rack-space unit has eight switchable quarter-inch jacks for a choice of balanced and unbalanced connections. For output to a DAT deck, or other digital device, there are two RCA S/PDIF connectors. The converters are 20-bit, but the S/PDIF ports can handle 24-bit files. In addition to working with Digidesign's Pro Tools software, the 882|20 can function as an independent two-channel A/D D/A converter. The unit can also work with the 888|24 interface to provide additional ins and outs.

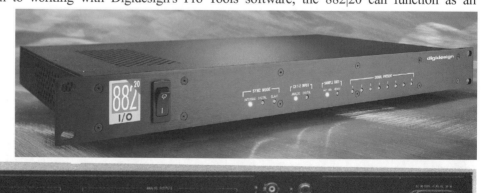

Figure 8.20. Pro Tools 882|20

Pro Tools 888 | 24

The 888|24 is Digidesign's top of the line interface, offering 24-bit digital I/O. The eight analog ins and outs are balanced XLR connectors. AES/EBU is also supported with four stereo ins and outs.

Two RCA S/PDIF connectors are provided for digital connections to DAT or other digital devices. The unit can work at either 44.1-kHz or 48-kHz sampling rates. The choice of sampling rates is made from Pro Tools software in the hardware-setup dialog box.

For sync, two BNC connectors allow linking to a sync device or tape deck. The 888|24 can also function as a stand

Figure 8.21. Pro Tools 888 | 24

alone A/D D/A converter. Multiple units can be connected to the computer for up to seventy-two channels of analog or digital I/O. The unit comes with drivers for Macintosh and Windows NT.

Pro Tools 1622

The Pro Tools 1622 provides sixteen channels of quarter-inch input jacks. This is ideal if you want to patch in a lot of MIDI gear or external effects. The jacks are switchable between balanced and unbalanced connections. Gain for the analog inputs is set by the software but stored internally. Gain settings are retained even when power is turned off, which allows for instant routing of any piece connected to

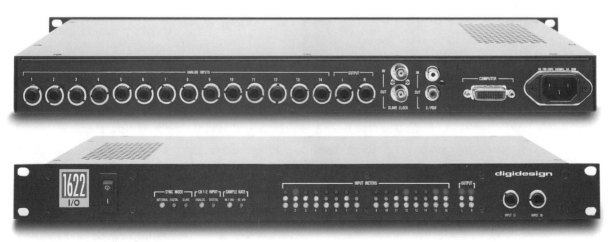

Figure 8.22. Pro Tools 1622

Figure 8.23. ADAT Bridge

the interface without recalibrating the gain. There are two quarter-inch output jacks for analog output. Provided are two RCA connectors for S/PDIF digital I/O and BNC connectors for sync. The Pro Tools 1622 has drivers available for Macintosh and Windows NT.

ADAT Bridge

For ADAT owners, the ADAT Bridge provides lightpipe connectors for sixteen discrete channels of digital audio. This allows you to record in 16-bit or 20-bit resolution on an ADAT system and transfer the tracks digitally to the computer for editing and DSP processing. Tracks can be mixed in the computer or transferred back to the ADATs for final mixdown. Multiple units can be combined to provide seventy-two channels of I/O. For monitoring and output there are XLR connectors for AES/EBU connections and RCA connectors for S/PDIF signals. BNC connectors are provided for word clock sync. The ADAT Bridge comes with drivers for Macintosh and Windows NT.

Combinations

It is possible to combine any of the four interfaces just described within a single system. However, each requires its own PCI card and slot inside the computer. Most computers only have two or three PCI slots. You can get around the limited number of slots by adding them externally. For instance, Magman makes an expansion PCI chassis for both Macintosh and Windows PCs.

Paris by Ensoniq

Paris is another option in the high-end digital audio line. Like Pro Tools, it is a complete digital audio system that includes hardware and software in one package. It supports both Windows wav and Macintosh Sound Designer II (sdii) file formats. Paris' operations are organized into thirteen different windows that control basic session information, transport, mixing, editing, automation, a patch bay, and more. The windows are accessible via a single keystroke so moving from place to place in Paris is never difficult.

The Edit window contains a wealth of editing tools grouped on to several different toolbars at the top of the window. The toolbars can be alternately hidden or shown by clicking the appropriate button in the top left of the window. The editor, automation, and mix windows can be customized, saved, and recalled.

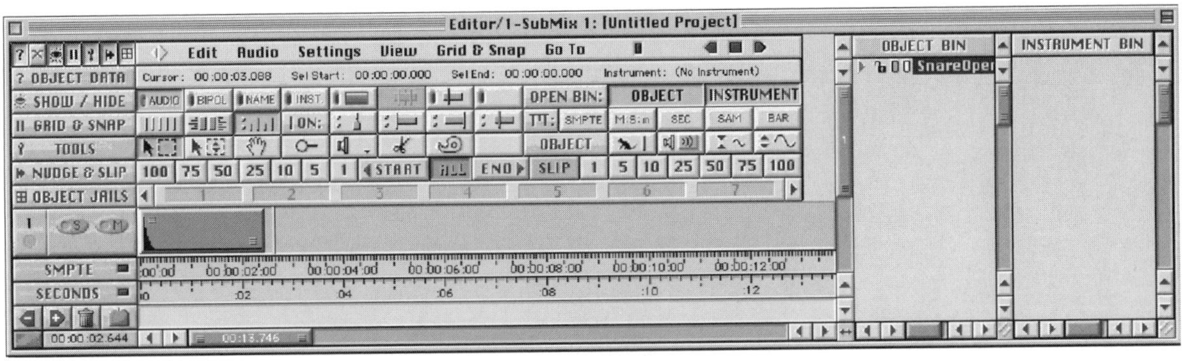

Figure 8.24. Paris' Edit Window

Paris has its own set of effects plug-ins as well as an extensive patch bay window for graphic signal routing. Paris features an ADAT module, making it possible to transfer files between it and ADAT recorders.

The Paris system includes a PCI card that plugs into the PCI slot inside the computer. There are two choices for external interface boxes. The 442 model provides 20-bit converters and has four analog ins and outs, a digital I/O and a sync in and out. The Modular Expansion Chassis (MEC) is designed for studios that require more expansion cards and input/output options. It has nine card slots for your choice of input cards and eight analog ins, eight analog outs, or ADAT interface card.

Paris also comes with piece of hardware called the Control 16. It resembles a small mixer and allows you to control the software using faders, buttons, and knobs instead of a mouse or trackball.

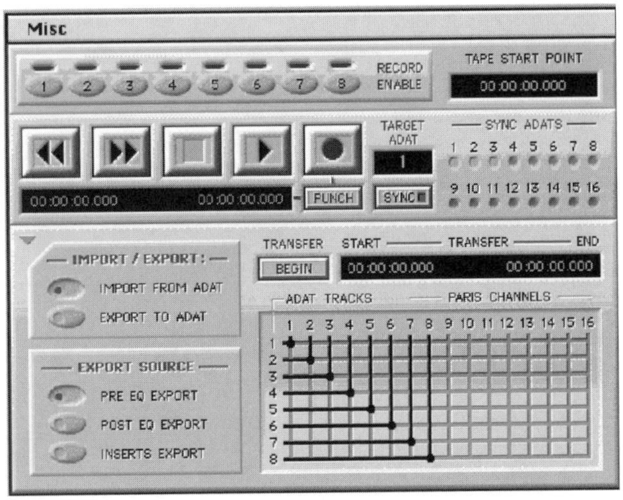

Figure 8.25. Paris ADAT Optical Interface Module

Summary

This chapter explored some of the options for the professional, high-end, computer-based digital recording studio. The choices include selecting an all-in-one package such as Pro Tools or piecing together a custom setup by choosing the MIDI/digital audio software and then the audio card and interface.

Figure 8.26. Ensonig Paris Hardware

Chapter 9.

File Management and Backup

When using any form of hard disk recording it is helpful to have a basic understanding of how computer storage media function. The purpose of this chapter is to provide an overview of the basics of disk management and of the various options for archiving and storing files available on the market today.

Inside of every computer and hard-disk based digital audio system is a hard drive. (The terms *hard disk* and *hard drive* are used interchangeably.) The term hard drive refers to a type of hard magnetic surface that is used to store files and programs, hence the term hard disk. The term hard disk was used initially to differentiate between floppy (insertable) and hard drives.

Again, every computer-based or hard disk-based digital audio system uses some type of computer drive to store the digital files. No matter what medium or type of hard disk is used, it will degrade over time and is, after a while, prone to crash. A crash is when a disk is no longer readable and cannot be used. Crashes occur without warning. Therefore, when working with digital files of any kind, be it on a computer or any other hard drive-based system, it is extremely important to have a means to copy, or back up, the digital files. It is extremely important to have a basic understanding of how digital files are stored and precisely how to copy or to back up the files in case they are lost or damaged.

So, on to technicalities: There are two basic types of drives: internal and external. The internal drive is located inside the computer or hard disk recorder while the external is connected to the device via a cable.

Floppy Disks

The floppy disk is a disk in a 3.5-inch case that is used to transfer and copy relatively small files from computer to computer. A floppy disk can hold approximately 1 megabyte (MB) of information. Since digital audio files are frequently much larger than 1 megabyte, a floppy disk is not a viable storage option. Floppy disks are still commonly used in computers and some keyboard workstations. In recent years, due to the ever-increasing size of computer files, the floppy is being replaced by other drives, described in the following section.

Hard Drives and SCSI

A hard drive is the heart of any digital audio workstation or computer-based digital recording setup. The hard drives used in today's computers and hard disk-based digital audio recorders are small units that use a hard magnetic surface. A head floats above the surface to encode and store the information. Hard-drive storage is measured in megabytes or gigabytes. One gigabyte (GB) is equal to 1,000 megabytes of information. To put this in perspective, a gigabyte is roughly equal to one thousand 1-megabyte floppy disks. So the bigger the hard drive, the higher the cost.

Computer drives are frequently identified by the amount of storage and how they connect to the computer. For example, let's look at the phrase, "6 GB IDE hard drive." IDE stands for Integrated Drive Electronics, which is a type of hard drive that entered the market in 1988. This drive technology is one of the most popular types used in hard disks. In order to take advantage of better performance the enhanced IDE or EIDE drive was introduced. The basic difference is the EIDE drive can transfer data at a faster rate and this is quite important when recording digital audio.

The next advance in hard-disk technology was the SCSI (pronounced "scuzzy") or Small Computer Systems Interface. A SCSI interface allows for a faster transfer rate than IDE. In addition, SCSI is able to support up to seven devices, which may include hard drives, but also scanners, printers, and other devices that are SCSI-compatible.

SCSI Accelerator Card

Some of the digital audio software mentioned in chapters 7 and 8 requires a faster data-transfer rate from the computer to the hard-drive system than SCSI can handle. Transferring chunks of 24-bit audio requires a fast transfer rate. This requires a SCSI accelerator card that plugs into one of the computer's internal slots. An accelerator card provides the increased transfer rate and adds verification to make sure the data is transferred accurately.

USB Hard Drives

USB or Uniform Serial Bus is the newest standard for computer components. The advantage of USB is that the data transfer rate is significantly faster than that found with SCSI. A single USB port connects up to 127 devices, such as modems, scanners, printers, and hard drives. In 1998 USB became very popular with the introduction of the iMac. Both Mac and Windows computers now offer USB as a standard feature.

Currently, USB hard drives are not as ubiquitous as SCSI drives. Most computers that offer USB also offer SCSI. SCSI drives are currently the best option for digital recording.

Hard Disk Space

When purchasing computer and self-contained hard disk digital recording units, purchase the largest drive you can afford. No matter what, the space on the drive will fill up quickly, especially since every new module introduced to the market seems to demand more drive space. So get the most storage possible.

Backing Up

A hard drive is a powerful, fragile device. The drive surface can become corrupted and crash. Often times this happens without any warning. For example, hard drive has a floating head and if jarred while in operation it can become damaged. Also, because of the large size of digital audio files, it is often necessary to have a way to continuously copy and store files. For example, each session may be recorded using the unit's built-in hard drive. Then the file is copied to another disk medium and erased from the original to make room for the next recording project.

So, given the reality of hard drive technology, the question is not *if* you are going to back up data, but *how*. Many computers today come with several different drives such as a floppy, hard disk, CD-ROM, or DVD-ROM. With multiple drives, it is possible to copy files from the hard drive to another, removable medium such as a floppy or CD-ROM. It is also possible to add an additional external drive for backups.

Removable Drives

There are several types of drives that use a removable disk to store files. These are similar to the 3.5-inch floppy drives, but the storage capacity is much larger. Removable disk formats include Zip, Jaz, and Superdisk.

Superdisk Drives

One of the latest entries into the removable disk area is the Superdisk. This drive uses a disk that resembles the size and shape of the 3.5-inch floppy disk but Superdisks can store approximately 100 MB of data. The other advantage of using a Superdisk is that it can also read and write to a standard 3.5-inch floppy disk. These units are available as both internal and external devices and are a good way to make backups of files. Superdisk drives can also read standard 3.5-inch floppy disks. They are only good for backups.

Zip Drives

Zip is the brand name of an external or internal drive produced by Iomega that uses a magnetic media called a Zip disk. A Zip drive can be thought of as an expanded 3.5-inch floppy drive. Zip drives are available in 100-MB and 250-MB versions. The original Zip drives can only read 100 MB of information.

Zip drives are relatively inexpensive, costing under $200, with disks costing approximately $10. The biggest drawback of a Zip drive is its speed. It is relatively slow, which means for digital audio recording it is functional only as a backup storage medium, either for transfer to another computer or for storage. It is too slow to be used as a drive for direct digital recording.

Jaz Drives

Like a Zip drive, Iomega's Jaz drive uses a removable disk. But a Jaz drive is significantly faster than a Zip and can be used to support multimedia and digital audio recording and playback. Jaz drives are a bit more expensive, about $250. Each disk stores approximately 1 gigabyte of information. The Jaz drive is superior to the Zip drive.

Magnetic Media Storage Considerations

No matter which medium is used, Zip, Jaz, Superdisk, or some other, it must be carefully handled and stored to insure longevity. Every type of storage media has its problems. Back in the days when reel-to-reel tapes were used in the studio, the tapes had to be stored in a specific way or the information on the tapes would degrade. The same is true for disks. Follow these guidelines to ensure that disks will not degrade over time:

- Use an indelible marker on the disk label. Do not use a pencil or eraser as particles can damage the drive.
- Store disks in a dry and cool place.
- Don't touch the exposed part of the disk.
- Keep disks away from magnets and magnetic fields.

Optical Drives

Optical drives use laser technology to store information. Optical storage is less volatile than the magnetic media used in hard drives and removable tape drives. With the advance of inexpensive optical disc burners this technology is now an affordable option for backing up and archiving files. Like the Zip drive, optical drives are not fast to record digital audio. One interesting note on the spelling of the word disk (disc). Magnetic media are usually spelled with a *k* and optical media with a *c*.

CD-ROM and CD-ROM Drives

CD technology for computers began with CD-ROM, or CD read-only, drives. CD-ROM drives can only read, but not record, CD audio and CD-ROM discs. CD-ROMs can store much larger amounts of information than 3.5-inch, Superdisk, Zip, and Jaz drives. The CD-ROM format has become the common medium for distribution of software. Every computer made today has a CD-ROM drive.

The performance of a CD-ROM drive is rated in terms of X speed. The X speed of the drive refers to the number of times it spins in comparison to a standard audio CD. For example, a 1X drive spins at the same time as an audio CD. Speeds currently range from 1X to 24X and more. The higher the spin rate, the faster the information access.

CD Writers (Burners)

The next evolution was to CD-R or CD-Recordable drives. These drives, called CD burners or writers, could read CDs and CD-ROMs and also write once to blank CDs. Once a CD was burned it could not be erased. Now, we have the CD-RW or CD-rewritable. A CD-RW drive can burn a standard CD or CD-ROM. It can also write to rewritable discs that can be erased and overwritten multiple times. Write-once CDs can be purchased for approximately $1 each. CD-rewritable discs cost more, about $10, but can be rewritten up to twenty-five times.

A CD-RW (rewritable) drive can be very helpful in the digital studio as a means for backing up and archiving digital audio files. CD burners can be used with computers and some hard-disk recorders, such as the Roland VS-1680 portable hard-disk recorder.

One drawback of the CD-RW rewritable disc is that it can only be read on data CD drives. In the studio the primary use of this technology is to copy and archive files. For this purpose the incompatibility with audio CD players is not a major concern. Another of the many advantages of using a CD burner is that the discs can be read by CD-ROM drives in both Macintosh and Windows PCs so file exchange with other computer users is easy.

CD-RW discs can be extremely useful in the studio during the recording process. Digital files can repeatedly be copied and backed up using one rewritable disc. When the session is complete and you are ready to share the files with other users, burn a CD-R disc that is compatible with other CD and CD-ROM players. A CD-RW drive can be purchased for under $500.

DVD

DVD, which originally stood for Digital Versatile Disc, is the latest generation of optical disc storage technology. It can be thought of as the big brother or sister of CD-ROM and CD audio. It is the same size disc as a CD, but can hold many times the amount of information including video, audio, and computer files.

The goal of DVD is to be the standard digital format for all uses—CD, videotape, and CD-ROM. There are two types of DVD in use today: DVD-Video and DVD-ROM. DVD-Video is an enhanced videocassette format offering higher quality picture resolution and better quality sound. DVD-ROM discs hold computer information and can be read by DVD drives. Some computers are including DVD-ROM drives as standard equipment. One advantage to DVD-ROM is that it can also read CD-ROM discs.

Like CD-ROM drives, DVD-ROM drives come in several formats. DVD-R drives can write once to a DVD disc. DVD-RW drives can write several thousand times to a single disc. In the studio, a DVD-RW drive can be an excellent unit for backup and archiving of digital audio files.

File Compression

Digital audio files tend to be quite large. File compression is used with computers to reduce the size of large files for storage. There are several computer formats for compressing files. These include Stuffit for Macintosh and Zip for Windows. It is important to realize that these formats cannot be used with digital audio files. If you are using extremely large files in the studio, consider using a removable media, such as Jaz, or burning rewritable CD, or DVD discs, for backup.

Summary

Disk storage and backup is a critical matter when dealing with hard disk and computer-based hard disk recording. Consistent backup of data is crucial. There are several options for backing up data. Begin by reviewing the specs of your hard disk recorder and the manufacturer's recommendations. The choice of backup media should then be selected according to your budget and needs.

Chapter 10.
Digital Mixers

One of the hottest growth areas in the digital recording world is digital mixers. If you are primarily a composer or performing musician, most of your money has been spent on equipment for making sound or organizing your musical thoughts. The role of a mixer, if you owned one at all, was to control volume on your MIDI rig and maybe add an effect or two. However, a recording studio is built around the mixer. Walk into any large studio and what dominates the control room? The mixing console (or desk, as it is referred to in England). For example, the Sony OXF-R3 Oxford digital mixing console costs around a half-million dollars and is beyond the scope of this text. Consoles like this dominate not only a room but also the dreams of several of my engineering friends. For this book, however, I'm going to limit our dreaming to consoles costing less than a house.

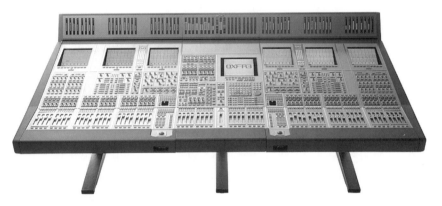

Figure 10.1. Sony OXF-R3 (Oxford) Digital Mixing Console

The mixer is the heart of every recording studio, no matter how large or small. All signals pass through it at some point. Therefore, any noise or coloration a mixer has will be printed on every signal that passes through. The term coloration describes the audio signature of the mixer. Analog mixers are prone to including noise and coloration but digital mixers are not. For this and other reasons detailed in this chapter, you will surely want to add a digital mixer to your studio.

Mixer Overview

If you are not familiar with the functions of a mixer, a quick overview follows. Audio signals enter the mixer through inputs. Analog mixers usually have separate inputs for microphone and line level signals. The mic inputs are usually equipped with phantom power to provide current for condenser mics.

Digital mixers have options for digital inputs either from an MDM or via the AES/EBU protocol. The digital signals sent by the recording device are patched directly to the digital mixer without going through digital to analog (D/A) conversion. This is good because the digital signal is not altered in any way. The signal is then assigned to a channel, according to where it is plugged in, that allows you to control the gain and to add EQ. Next the signal is routed to its destination through a connection called a bus. The more flexibility a mixer has in signal routing, the more space on the console for buttons and knobs, all of which drives up the cost.

On a professional level mixer there are four bus types. The stereo master bus is the main output for the signal. This output will go to the mixdown deck and to the control room loud speakers. The cue and monitor bus send the signals to the headphones or monitors in the studio. The group, sub group, or recording bus sends the audio to the multitrack recorder. The aux (auxiliary) bus sends audio to the effects units, referred to as outboard effects, for signal processing.

On an analog console, each one of these bus types requires a hardware connection. That is a major contributor to the size and cost of an analog mixer. With a digital mixer, the bus connections occur in software, not hardware. This not only brings down the size of the physical unit but also provides more flexibility in signal routing. For example, if you want to send ten channels of drums to two tracks of an MDM. On an analog mixer this requires bussing the ten channels to a stereo bus to send to the recorder, tying up twelve channel strips. The channel strip is the vertical column of controls on the mixer's front panel that control effects assignment, volume or gain, and signal routing for a specific channel. On a digital mixer, those ten inputs can be grouped to a single fader once the individual channel levels are set.

Digital consoles make the most out of the available faders by being able to reassign them to a second, third, or fourth set of tracks, or sends. With the addition of onboard, or built-in effects, the number of external connections is minimized even further. Effects devices can be routed internally as well as adding a digital to the other goodies in the digital mixer. Every external connection adds unwanted distortion or noise to the signal, as does each pass through A/D and D/A converters. So, fewer A/D and D/A conversions means a cleaner signal and better overall sound quality. Because of the many advantages, a digital mixer is surely worth the cost.

Benefits of Using a Digital Mixer

Digital mixers excel in many ways. Consider the following:

• They maintain a clean digital signal. Unlike analog mixers, no sound coloration or distortion is added to the signal.

• They all have some type of mix automation. There are two basic types of mixer automation. First is snapshot automation, also called scene automation by some manufacturers, means the mixer can save a single setting for all the parameters of the mixer. The second type of automation is called dynamic automation. This means the mixer can control parameters over time. The difference between scene and dynamic automation can be best illustrated in a simple fader move. Snapshot automation would require a series of snapshots to step the fader from one position to another. Dynamic automation can move the fader from point A to point B in a smooth continuous motion, as if controlled manually.

• Most digital mixers have some kind of built-in effects beyond standard EQ. The Yamaha series have reverb circuitry from their popular reverb units. Mackie's Digital 8 Bus console has software plug-ins similar to some of the popular computer-based software packages, including Antare's pitch correction software. These may or may not eliminate your need for external or outboard effects. How many built-in effects each mixer has will be a determining factor, as well as how much you like the sound of the effects themselves.

Digital Mixers and Computer Sequencers

Digital mixers are equipped with MIDI connections for a reason. Combining a digital mixer with a computer running a MIDI sequencer program can enhance the functions of a digital mixer. Many of the mixer's controls, the faders and knobs on the front panel, can be transmitted via MIDI data. The MIDI data can be recorded by the sequencer software and played back during the mix. For mixers with snapshot automation, MIDI can advance the mixer from snapshot to snapshot. Some mixers can receive continuous data and be dynamically automated with MIDI data or MIDI Time Code transmitted from the sequencer. Alternate mixes can easily be created and compared, and editing is a breeze. Keeping a record of the mix in a sequencer is a great way to back up the mixer and to save and store mixes. This is especially helpful if you are simultaneously working on a number of different songs or projects.

Selecting a Digital Mixer

Physical size is not always the most important element in digital mixer design. The front panels of digital mixers are simply interfaces designed to resemble analog mixers. It is important to select the best model for a studio based on the specific features. Digital mixers range from those designed to handle one or two 8-track recorders to mixers that can handle thirty-two tracks or more. Take time to match features and capabilities for your setup.

When you read the specs of a digital mixer, be aware of the internal resolution. Internal resolution is the rate used by the internal circuitry of the mixer. For example, the Yamaha 01v has 20-bit AD/DA converters but 32-bit internal processing. Don't confuse these numbers, you only have to concern yourself with the I/O or AD/DA resolution.

An overview of several mixers in the entry, mid-level, and high-end price ranges follows. This is not a comprehensive survey, but will serve as a guide to the key digital mixer features to consider.

Entry-Level Digital Mixers ($200 to $3,500)

One of the biggest areas of advancement is the availability of relatively low-cost digital mixers designed for the entry-level studio. Features that a few years ago cost several thousand dollars are now available at quite reasonable prices.

Fostex VM04

The Fostex VM04 digital mixer is as far removed as possible from the Sony Oxford mentioned at the beginning of this chapter. It is limited to four inputs and was designed as an add-on unit for the Fostex FD-4 and FD-8 multitrack recorders to increase the number of simultaneous recording tracks. However, the unit can be used for recording live to 2-track.

The Fostex VM04 includes 20-mix scene or snapshot memory, and has the ability to add effects. A small PA system or keyboard rig could be controlled by a VM04. In a setup with several synths, the VM04 can be used to control the volume of each unit by setting up a mix scene. It can even be used as a headphone mixer.

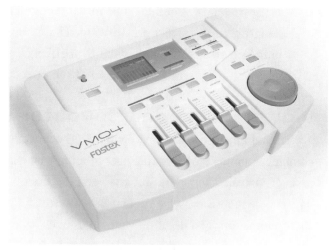

Figure 10.2. Fostex VM04 Digital Mixer

TASCAM TM-1000

The TASCAM TM-1000 is a 16-channel mixer that bears the most resemblance to its analog predecessors. It has sixteen channel faders and four aux send faders along with a stereo master fader. Only the buttons in the shaded control section and the MIDI Machine Control section have more than one function. Default values in preprogrammed areas can be customized according to your preferences. The TM-1000 has snapshot automation and memory for 128 shots that store data from every function. You can automate a mix by moving from snapshot to snapshot using the onboard control, sending the advance commands via MIDI program change. Alternatively, you can control a mix dynamically by recording and replaying the mix from your MIDI sequencer. There is one expansion slot in the unit for a card that adds two additional AES/EBU and SPDIF inputs.

Figure 10.3. TASCAM TM-1000 Digital Mixer

The TM-1000 has two stereo effects processors that can be routed in several ways. For example you can assign one effect to specific tracks using the auxiliary (aux) bus while applying reverb to all tracks by assigning the second effect to the stereo bus. Effects can even be reconfigured as four mono effects.

The TM-1000 is configured with a TDIF port for connection to any of the TASCAM DA-series MDM multitrack recorders. ADAT owners must purchase an IF-TAD converter box to convert the signal from TDIF to the ADAT lightpipe protocol. A videotape tutorial is included to help you get up and running with the TASCAM TM-1000.

Figure 10.4. IF-TAD Converter

Yamaha 01v

The Yamaha O1v is a descendent of the O2R and O3D digital mixers. The O1v has common hardware and features usually found on top-of-the line mixers and is in a relatively small case. The O1v is designed for a single MDM, or 8-track modular hard disk system. It also incorporates effects from Yamaha's ProR3 and REV500 effects processors. The display window is large enough to include graphics and text.

Figure 10.5. The Yamaha Olv Digital Mixer

Digital Mixer Math

The O1v is listed as a 24-channel mixer but a quick scan of the unit reveals fourteen channels and a master fader. To access the other ten channels you need to understand the world of digital mixer mathematics. First of all, there are twelve XLR/line inputs for channels 1 through 12. Channels 13, 14, 15, and 16 are combined as two stereo channels, ideally for stereo synthesizers. The pan positions for each of these four channels can be changed, but fader moves effect both channels. Channels 17 through 24 are reserved for digital inputs from an expander card. Cards are available for ADAT lightpipe, TASCAM TDIF, and AES/EBU formats. There is a place for one add-on card that provides four more analog outputs. All eight digital outputs on the expansion card are assignable, as are the four analog outs.

Digital Mixer Geography

After digital mixer math there is digital mixer geography. With an analog mixer, one would find rows of buttons and knobs on each of a number of channel strips. In the typical digital mixer, all the information is displayed in a graphic display screen. To the right of the display are the pan, frequency, and gain knobs, and the EQ band selection buttons for all channels. No more scanning channel strips, or adjusting the next one over by mistake. Now the trick is to make sure the correct channel is selected before you make any adjustments.

The O1v has a 99-scene, or snapshot, memory for automation and can be controlled or automated via MIDI. The O1v also has a To Host port which can be used to connect two Olv units together for a 48-input system. The To Host connection can also be used as a serial port to connect it to a Macintosh or Windows PC.

Mid-Level Digital Mixers ($3,500 to $7,000)

In this price range there is more design diversity. Each manufacturer takes a slightly different approach while trying to offer unique features.

Yamaha 03D

The Yamaha O3D builds on the Yamaha O1v's features by adding full automation by syncing to an external MIDI Time Code source. The larger graphic display has enough display size to warrant an optional mouse for navigation. The O3D also has surround-sound mixing capability.

Spirit Digital 328

If you are using two or more MDM recorders you are going to need more digital-tape returns. The Spirit Digital 328 comes equipped for the task. It has two built-in sets of TDIF and ADAT lightpipe connectors. There is also a separate ADAT lightpipe aux output that can function as a digital group out or a digital replacement for the four analog aux sends. A floating S/PDIF and AES/EBU I/O, and MIDI ports are also built in. A link port is also available for cascading two consoles if you want to drive a 32-track recording setup. There are no expansion slots on this board, but some external modules available that attach to TDIF ports. One module converts the TDIF output to eight RCA analog ins/outs, another converts the TDIF

Figure 10.6. Yamaha 03D Digital Mixer

signal to AES/EBU with four XLR ins/outs and a mic preamp interface with eight XLR connectors.

Each channel has its own peak hold LED meter and indicator light when the channel is armed for recording to a multitrack recorder. There is a separate area for controlling the transport of the recorders. It reads SMPTE and reads and writes MTC. As on many other digital boards, the faders have several functions: controlling the input channels (1–16), the tape returns (17–32), the groups (1–8), the aux sends (1–4), and the two internal effects sends. Effects for the Spirit 328 are by Lexicon. Parameters can be controlled via MIDI.

The Digital 328 is not a graphic interface board. The E-Strip uses a horizontal row of knobs with sixteen lighted positions. It can function as a horizontal channel strip for any of the input or output channels or it can control the same parameter across all sixteen channels. A row of buttons across the top of the strip selects the mode of operation and the parameter selection. It can also serve as the volume control for the sixteen channels not assigned to the faders, allowing you to control thirty-two channels simultaneously.

Figure 10.7. Spirit Digital 328 Digital Mixer

Settings can be copied and pasted from one channel to another.

Automation on the Spirit 328 is snapshot with full automation available via MIDI. One hundred snapshots can be stored, named, and given a time code position.

Panasonic WR-DA 7

The Panasonic WR-DA7 console takes us into the realm of 24-bit converters for input and output. With the addition of expander cards there are thirty-eight inputs, broken down into sixteen mic/line inputs for channels 1–16, channels 17–32 come from two of the three expansion card slots. Add to this four analog and two digital aux sends and you get a 38 x 8 mixer.

The third expansion card slot can be used to replace the analog inputs for channels 9–16 with digital inputs from the card. The expansion cards support the standard recorders: ADAT lightpipe, TDIF, AES/EBU, and analog. A video sync card is available for working in a postproduction environment. A variant of the mixer, the DA7V, is available when the video sync card is installed. There is also a card for syncing two DA7s together for 76-channel studios.

Figure 10.8. Panasonic WR-DA 7

The functions of the DA7's fader section are similar to other digital mixers. The automation is dynamic and onboard. Fader moves are not transmitted via MIDI, but most of the board's other controllers do send and receive MIDI data. The DA7 offers a serial port and software for both Macintosh and Windows PCs to display the mixer's data on a computer screen.

Roland VM-C7200

Roland's VM 7000 series uses a modular approach to digital mixers. The digital I/O is separate from the desktop control surface. The I/O model designation is VM-7200. This unit contains forty analog input channels, twenty balanced quarter-inch TRS, and twenty balanced XLR connectors with phantom power on all channels. For output there are eight assignable analog quarter-inch TRS connectors and two channels of AES/EBU. The converters are 24-bit on both input and output. If you need more from your I/O you can cascade a second unit with the VM-24C Cascade Kit.

Figure 10.9. Roland VM-C7200

For connecting ADATs or DA series MDM recorders there is a 1/3-rack-space unit DIF-AT interface box, that converts the MDMs digital signal to and from the Roland's R-Bus format. If you have a large studio or work live and need even more inputs, the VM-24E I/O expansion board can add twenty-four additional ins and outs with three of Roland's ADA-7000 AD/DA converters. The AE-7000 provides eight channels of AES/EBU connectors and can also use the VM-24E connection. The VM-7000 houses the onboard effects. Two stereo multi-effects processors are included but there are slots for three additional effects cards. The effects can be used as stereo or mono effects.

With this I/O flexibility the mixer has a lot to handle. Not to worry, the VM-C7200 can handle up to ninety-four channels of digital automated mixing. Digital mixers are not only mixers and effects units, they are also patch bays. With Roland's FlexBus design, routing possibilities are many and can be saved and stored with the EZ Routing feature. Options for this system also include the VM-7100, a smaller I/O, and the VMC-7100 mixer. The I/Os work with both mixers and as does the expander modules and cards.

MAX Digital Mixing Software

Panasonic's MAX Software, short for Mixing Automation Expansion Software, allows total system control from a Macintosh or Windows PC. In addition to controlling the mix, you can easily save your mix to your computer hard drive for easy archiving and recall.

The main screen offers an overview of the mixer including recorder transport control, thirty-two channel faders, aux channel faders, and the stereo master fader.

A menu selection can change the view to EQ settings. There are several other view presets and you can also customize a few of your own.

Popup menus can be accessed at the bottom of the channel strips for realigning and grouping tracks, or using the faders to send MIDI controller data. There are many options for editing fader moves. There is a graphic display where fader moves can be hand drawn, cut, copied, pasted, or cleared. In the Create Fader Moves window, fader moves can be created based on db level and time for smooth and precise positioning. There is also a Cue List where all the mix events are displayed in SMPTE order and the list scrolls in real time during playback. Data can be cut copied, pasted, moved, offset scaled, and cropped. Surround panning for surround mixes can be accomplished with the Panning Module. The popup menu allows for selection of individual channels or groups.

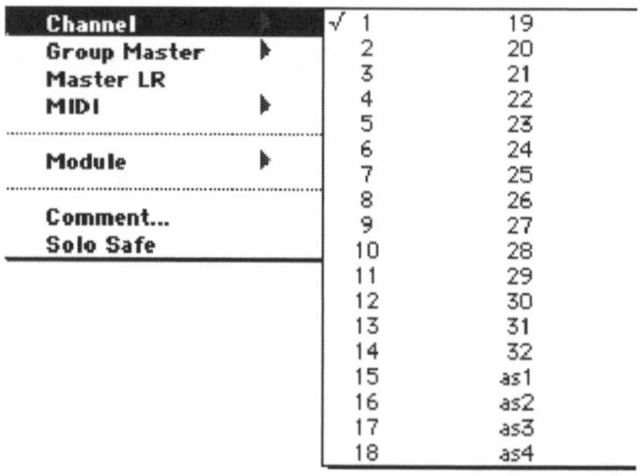

Figure 10.10. Max Software

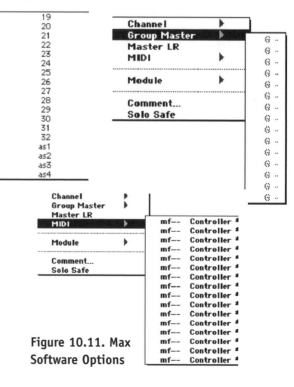

Figure 10.11. Max Software Options

High-End Digital Mixers ($7,000 to $10,000)

The saying "you get what you pay for" is true in the world of digital mixers. The high-end as defined in this chapter does not include the mixers that can cost as much as a car or small house. The high-end is defined as approximately $7,000 to $10,000. These mixers can handle just about anything you throw at them, metaphorically speaking, of course.

Yamaha 02R

The Yamaha O2R is the current state-of-the-art for digital mixers. The basic architecture and most features have been mentioned previously in this chapter since they are present in the Yamaha 01v and 03D mixers. The Yamaha O2R has four expansion slots for I/Os in multitrack formats along with AES/EBU and analog.

There is an easy to read graphic display that shows waveforms and curves. Three surround-sound panning modes are represented visually. The faders are touch sensitive so editing and automated mixing is simple. For fine-tuning mix automation, events can be moved back or forward relative to the time code. The O2R allows copying and pasting of fader, channel, pan, EQ and all mix events.

The O2R transmits MIDI data and has control pages for other Yamaha mixers, effects processors, and tone generators that can be controlled from the O2R. Mix settings can also be controlled from other MIDI devices. Multiple O2Rs can be cascaded with an expansion card on each unit.

Figure 10.12. The Yamaha 02R

Mackie Digital 8 Bus

Mackie analog mixers are found in many studios, so, when Mackie announced a digital console, it became one of the most eagerly anticipated pieces of gear. The Mackie Digital 8 Bus is a mid-size console in pro studio circles that has many full size console capabilities. This is the largest mixer mentioned in this chapter and it has more dedicated controls and buttons than the previously mentioned models.

It has a built-in meter bridge, the row of LEDs at the top of the mixer for monitoring signal levels for whatever signals the faders are assigned to control. Other digital mixers display this in the screen on the front panel. The O2R, Panasonic, and Roland mixers offer a meter bridge as an add-on that must be purchased separately. An optional S-VGA monitor, ASCII keyboard, and mouse provides a visual interface to the mixer's controls.

The Digital 8 Bus contains many of the same digital mixer conventions as the mixers mentioned previously. The twenty-four channel faders can be assigned to four different banks. Bank 1, Mic Line, covers channels 1–24 and is the bank used for tracking. Bank 2 covers channels 25–48 and is used for tape monitoring. Bank 3, is for effects returns and eight optional returns that require an optional digital card. Bank 4, called Masters, contains eight virtual groups, eight MIDI controllers, and eight bus masters. Switches for each

Figure 10.13. Mackie Digital 8 Bus

bank are conveniently located on the front panel, not in the software.

Also located on each channel strip are buttons for muting and soloing each channel. Above those buttons is the select button for accessing the DSP parameters for the channel. Along the bottom is a scribble strip for labeling the channels.

At the top of the strip are the LED indicators, which show whatever information is passing though the active layer assigned to the faders. The Trim control is for the analog preamp for the mic and line inputs on channels 1–24. It is always active on those inputs regardless of what signals are routed to the faders.

Channels 1–12 have a *MIC* button. When pressed, it activates the high headroom, low noise discreet preamp circuitry for microphone signals. The *REC/RDY* button is for recording tracks on a multitrack recorder so you can control the deck from the mixing console. The Assign button sends the channel's signal to a bus or output. The write button enables the track for automation.

To keep the length of the channel strip small enough for the unit to fit on a table top, all the knob controls are condensed into a single strip of controllers called V-Pots. The V-Pot is a knob with an 11-segment LED to indicate the setting for each of the seventeen functions the V-Pots performs. Assigning V-Pots is done from the Master V-Pot section to the right of the V-Pot strip.

This section controls the DSP power of the console, which now includes third party plug-ins. The values for the current option chosen and channel selected are displayed above the Master Controls. Here it is possible to load and save settings for effects, allowing you to create libraries that you can recall instantly when recording or mixing.

Figure 10.14. Mackie Digital 8-Bus Channel Strip

Figure 10.15. Mackie Digital 8-Bus Trim Control Strip

Underneath the Fat Channel section are the solo and headphone mixes. Mackie digital mixers always include a traditional "Rude Solo Light" that decorates their mixer line. In the Solo section there are options for how solo channels are routed and heard. It also handles the controls for the talk back mic.

With the Digital 8 Bus it is possible to have two separate cue mixes. It is possible to copy the main mix to the cue mix section, which can be tweaked further at the performer's request. To make playback of a take easier, with the push of the Control Room button you can instantly run the control room mix to the headphones so the musicians can hear what you are hearing.

In the Control Room section there are options for selecting three different analog 2-track sources, two different digital sources, or the master for control room listening.

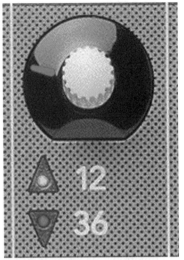

Figure 10.16. Mackie Digital 8-Bus V-Pots

There are separate buttons for selecting mains or near field monitors with a V-Pot to set levels for each. The

Dim button lowers the volume of whatever source is currently being listened to in the control room by 20 dB for situations when conversation becomes inevitable, e.g. answering the phone or telling the client how big to make the number on the check. The Talk Back button also dims control room monitor volume by 20 dB and also routes the Talk Back mic into both Phones/Cue mixes and studio outputs. Full

Figure 10.17. Mackie Digital 8-Bus Fat Channel

transport and autolocate control is available for multitrack recorders with MIDI Machine Control. The LED display can be set for SMPTE or MIDI time code.

The back panel of the mixer shows a large number of jacks and expansion slots. All I/Os use 24-bit converters and the internal processing is 32-bit. The card slots are for digital I/O to accommodate whatever digital recorders are in your studio.

The large connector on the left of the back panel connects to the remote CPU and power supply. The CPU is rack mountable and connects via a 15-foot, 25-pin cable.

The CPU is a Pentium compatible computer with 16 MB of RAM and an internal hard drive. There is a floppy drive on the front of the unit

Figure 10.18. Mackie Digital 8-Bus Selecting Monitor Sources

for adding additional software or saving sessions in DOS format. This is a dedicated computer and cannot be substituted with any other computer, nor can it be used for running other software.

The rear of the CPU contains connections for the monitor, mouse, and SVGA monitor. MIDI in and out connectors are included since the faders can transmit and receive MIDI data.

The computer monitor gives a slightly more traditional view of the console's functions. Most of the front panel controls are accessible via the software interface.

DSP settings are accessed via a plug-in interface and third party plug-ins are beginning to appear for this platform including the popular Antares Auto-Tune software that provides control over pitch inaccuracies that occur on various tracks.

In addition to output in several digital 2-track formats, the Mackie Digital 8 Bus also supports mixing in 5.1 and 7.1 surround formats, along with quad- and left-right-center surround modes. With the console's Morph mode, it is possible to specify a start point and an end point for a pan, give the computer a start and end time for the move and have the computer perform a perfectly timed pan.

Summary

This chapter presented an overview of digital mixers and how they can enhance the digital audio recording studios. Several mixers were described in a variety of price ranges, including entry-level, mid-level, and high-level. The basic features of digital mixers were reviewed in general and several specific models were reviewed in particular.

Figure 10.19. Mackie Digital 8-Bus Rear Panel

Figure 10.20. Mackie Digital 8-Bus CPU Rear Panel

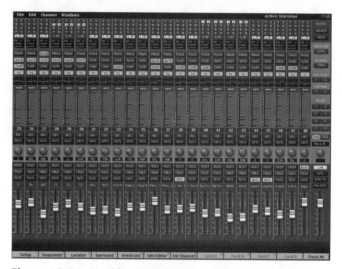

Figure 10.21. Mackie Digital 8-Bus Software Display

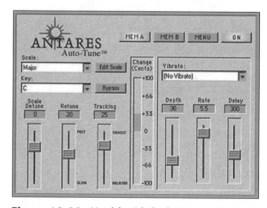

Figure 10.22. Mackie Digital 8-Bus Plug-In, Auto-Tune

Chapter 11.

Microphone Overview and Techniques

Every recording begins with a sound source or signal, and the warning "garbage in, garbage out" applies. The cleanest digital gear cannot compensate for a sound that has been poorly recorded. This chapter focuses on the various microphone concepts and techniques for recording acoustic instruments and vocals.

Microphone Basics

The microphone is a *transducer*. A transducer is a device that converts one type of energy to another. Microphones convert acoustic signals to electrical signals. The electrical energy flows through the system as voltage. As voltage flows through a circuit it encounters resistance, called impedance. There are two kinds of impedance, high and low. Most microphones used for recording are low impedance. Low impedance is less susceptible to hum and electric noise and can use long cables.

There are various types of microphones, so carefully select models that best suit your needs in the studio. Generally, microphones are categorized in two ways. First, by the components, or element, used to capture sound, and then by the pickup pattern.

Microphones have one of three types of elements:
• moving coil microphones, commonly called dynamic microphones
• ribbon microphones
• capacitor microphones, commonly referred to as condenser microphones

Each element reacts to sound waves in a slightly different way and therefore can serve different purposes in the recording studio.

Microphone Pickup Patterns

Microphones "hear" sound in different ways. Some listen to sounds produced directly in front, some listen to sounds produced from various directions. There are five basic pickup patterns that microphones use: cardioid, super cardiod, hyper cardioid, omnidirectional, and bidirectional (also called figure eight). The one-dimensional focus of the pickup patterns keeps unwanted noise or room reflections to a minimum. Cardiod,

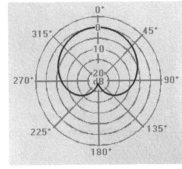

Figure 11.1. Cardioid

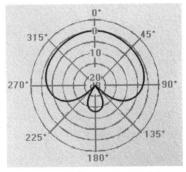

Figure 11.2. Super Cardioid

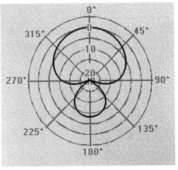

Fig. 11.3. Hyper Cardioid

super cardiod, and hyper cardiod mics are used for directional recording when the goal is to focus on a specific instrument or area of them room.

The omnidirectional and figure-8 bidirectional patterns are better suited for recording large choral and instrumental ensembles with one or two microphones.

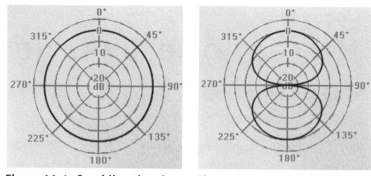

Figure 11.4. Omnidirectional   **Figure 11.5. Bidirectional**

Dynamic Mics

Dynamic, or moving coil, microphones are rugged and capable of handling loud sounds such as drums and amplifiers used for electric guitars. Dynamic mics are not as sensitive to soft sounds, such as vocals and string instruments, making them less than ideal for capturing sounds with a wide dynamic range and subtle nuances. They are the least expensive to purchase with a price range of $100 to $600 depending on the make and model.

Ribbon Mics

Ribbon microphones are the opposite of dynamic microphones. They are among the most expensive, from $500 to $5,000. Many of the classic models of ribbon microphones, such as the RCA 77, are still used but no longer manufactured. Ribbon mics are delicate instruments and must be handled with care. Do not use them for sharp, loud sounds like drums. They have a warm mellow sound but a low output level. Ribbon microphones are most often used on wind instruments.

Condenser Mics

Condenser microphones are an excellent choice for studio recording. Sound reproduction is clear and detailed, exactly what is needed for a noiseless digital recording. Condenser mics cost from $200 to $5,000. They are not as fragile as ribbon microphones but not as rugged as dynamic microphones. They can distort with sharp loud sounds like drums but are excellent for most other uses. Condenser mics are fragile, so be sure to handle them with care.

The growth of the project studio market in recent years has driven development of high quality, low priced condenser microphones. These microphones also retain their value well, with the some models even growing in value. The pictures in this section are of a Neumann U-87 condenser mic, the Rolls Royce of microphones. (Neumann is a German company, so it might prefer to be called the Mercedes of microphones.)

Figure 11.6. Neumann U-87 Cut-Away Full View

Condenser microphones require power to operate. Older condenser microphones had a separate power supply but today power is usually supplied by the mixer through the mic cable itself, called phantom power. Most mixers have phantom power capability.

Additional Condenser Features

In addition to excellent pickup quality, condenser mics can have a number of additional features that make them even more versatile—for

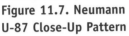

Figure 11.7. Neumann U-87 Close-Up Pattern

Figure 11.8. Neumann U-87 Pad Switch

Figure 11.9. Neumann U-87 Close-Up Roll Off

example, selectable pickup patterns. When selecting a mic it is important to note if it has one pickup pattern, or a choice of several. There are microphones that can switch between omni, bidirectional, or cardioid patterns. When using condenser microphones, be sure to check that the proper pickup pattern is selected.

There are also microphones, such as the AKG C-480, that have interchangeable parts called capsules for different pickup patterns. If your budget will only allow a few microphones, this feature can be an

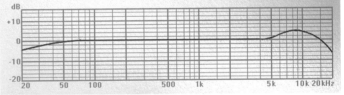

Figure 11.10. Neumann U-87 Full Response Graph

important consideration. Some mics also include a pad switch that is used when miking a loud sound source. The microphone's sensitivity is reduced by the indicated amount on the mic. In Figure 11.8, the Neumann U-87's sensitivity is reduced by 10 dB. This allows the mic to be used with louder sound sources such as tom-toms on a drum set or a guitar amp. Remember to check the mic setting before recording.

Another feature of many studio microphones is bass cutoff, or roll-off. When recording in close

proximity to a source, there is an unavoidable boost of bass frequency called the proximity effect. To counter this effect, some microphones have a switch that cuts off bass frequencies in the low end of its pickup range.

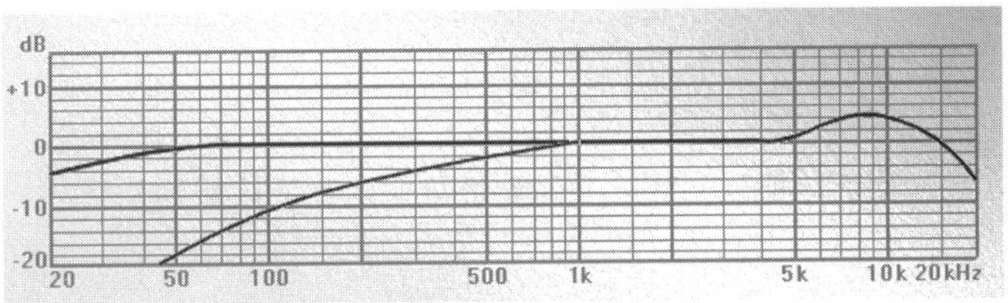

Figure 11.11. Neumann U-87 Full and Pad Graph

Figure 11.10 that follows shows the Neumann U-87 normal frequency response, which normal begins to trail off at 50 Hz.

With the bass cutoff switch engaged, the pickup of the mic begins to fall off more rapidly, beginning at 1 k and is almost gone at 50 Hz.

Low to Middle Budget Studio Microphones

In today's market, inexpensive doesn't necessarily mean poor quality. Quality condenser microphones no longer require a major chunk of your bank account. The Marshall Labs MX200XL is an inexpensive, quality mic and can be purchased for approximately $200. Moving up towards the $500 mark brings more choices from RØDE, Groove Tubes, Audio Technica, and Shure. In the $700 to $900 range, there are some top quality microphones from AKG, RØDE, G Prime, and Neumann.

If you are planning to record a single source in stereo, such as an acoustic piano, you will need two microphones. They should be the same model so the sound quality matches. The ideal setup is a matched pair of microphones so identified by the manufacturer. This insures that both mics have been tested at the factory and found to have similar and complementary characteristics. If purchased at separate times, the electronics may be slightly altered by updates or the materials used may be slightly different.

If you are purchasing only one mic for vocals and the occasional acoustic instrument, I suggest purchasing the best quality mic you can afford. When investing in a microphone, remember—they rarely become obsolete. Stick with the top manufacturers. It is also advisable to hear the mic live if possible. This can be done by visiting a local music dealer.

**Figure 11.12.
Byerdynamic MCD100**

High-End Digital Microphones

Digital microphones are still relatively rare. As of this writing only the Beyerdynamic MCD100 and MCD101 are on the market. The MCD100 is a cardioid mic and the MCD101 is an omnidirectional mic.

A digital microphone has its own D/A converter and external power supply that also handles sync when the mic is the slave mode. Slave mode is used when the sync code necessary for digital recording is coming from another source such as a computer-based recording system. The digitized signal from the mic uses the AES/EBU protocol and 3-pin XLR connectors. The software used by the converters in the mic eliminates digital clipping without using compression or limiting. Digital clipping is the distortion that results from peaking the dB meter. This allows the gain from the input signal to max out without creating digital clipping noise.

Virtual Mics

Every microphone has its own characteristic sound. There are products available today, including those from Roland and Antares, that simulate the characteristics of existing microphones. These products allow you to emulate microphones you don't own. Roland's COSM microphone emulation technology is built into the CM 7000 series digital mixers. Antares' Microphone Modeler is a software plug-in for digital recording computer software mentioned in chapters 7 and 8. In order to simulate the sounds of various types of microphones the signal must be clean or transparent. A digital microphone is the best mic to use when simulating other mics as it does not add any color of its own to the sound.

Choosing the Right Microphone

The hallmark of many major studios is their substantial and varied microphone collection. Many top audio engineers bring along their favorite microphones to every recording session in every studio. The microphone is the key to delivering quality sound to the recording media, no matter if the recording is analog or digital. Currently, many recording studios are using vintage analog microphones, some of which are more than 30 years old. One of the criticisms of early digital recording was that the sound was harsh and brittle. The solution to this problem was to use older tube mics, with their natural warmth.

The mere act of choosing from the wide variety of mics can be a bit daunting. There are so many shapes, sizes, and unique characteristics to consider. For some sage advice on the subject of microphone selection, I have turned to the chief engineer at 3 IPS Studios and Temple University digital audio instructor, Jack Klotz Jr.

Jack suggests you never buy a mic until you hear it. Ideally it should be auditioned with the instrument(s) you will be recording. When you are in recording studios or music stores, listen to and take notes on the brands and types of microphones used. Time spent in other studios can be your prime chance to hear different mics in action and to observe how recording engineers use them.

Microphone Placement Techniques in the Digital World

Rule number one when tight miking for pop music is that there are no rules. (This is not the case for distant miking as used in classical music, for example.) There are some general guidelines based on each microphone's characteristics. The rest is knowing which instruments you'll be recording and how much of a budget you'll have. The following section includes a review of the popular instruments in pop recording and advice on how to select the mic that best suits your needs. (Some of Jack's favorites are vintage microphones that are no longer manufactured, so a few have been updated with new model designations.) Use the mic positioning tips that follow as a place to begin your own experimentation.

Miking Drums

The kick (or bass) drum sounds best with a large diaphragm dynamic mic. As mentioned previously, dynamic microphones handle the high pressure of loud sounds without distorting them the way a condenser mic would. The large diaphragm responds better to the low frequencies in the bass drum. Some choices include the AKG D112, Sennheiser 421, or the EV RE20. Jack's favorite is the AKG D12, the older version of the 112.

Recording a drum set takes preparation. First, make sure the drums are properly tuned. It is helpful to tune a bit tighter and deader than sounds good in the room. Next, lubricate the pedal to prevent unwanted squeaking. It is a good idea to keep a drum key

Figure 11.13. AKG D112 Microphone

and a can of WD-40 around the studio, just in case. To control the ring of the bass drum put a blanket, pillow, or foam rubber inside the drum. It is also common to remove the front head or use a head with a hole cut in the

Figure 11.14. Shure SM 57 Microphone

center to allow a mic to be positioned inside the drum.

For snare drum, a small diaphragm dynamic mic is a good choice because it is well suited to pick up the higher frequencies of the snare drum. It will also be subject to a fair amount of spill from the other drums and cymbals. Jack's choice here is the all-round workhorse mic, the Shure SM57.

The safe choice for miking tom-toms is large diaphragm dynamic mics. The large diaphragm can capture the full body of the tom's sound and has a moving coil to handle both the volume from the toms and the spill from the rest of the kit. Find a position that suits your taste. For the more adventurous, try a medium diaphragm condenser mic. Make sure the mic has a pad so that it can handle the loudness of the drum sound and the spill. The Sennheiser MD 421 is a good choice. Jack prefers the Neumann KM 84.

Miking Cymbals

Hi-hats can be handled with a bright condenser mic. If you are recording music with an overall loud volume, like rock and roll, be sure the mic has a pad. The pad will also help control spill from the

Figure 11.15. Sennheiser MD 421

snare and bass drums. A good model in this category is the Shure SM81.

Over the drum kit, place a pair of microphones, strangely enough called the *overheads*. Overhead microphones can be any general purpose condenser microphone. Quality high-frequency response is a must, since these microphones will be primarily responsible for picking up the ride and crash cymbals. The mics should also have a wide flat response since they will also pick up the whole kit. The overheads should be a few feet above the highest cymbal and positioned to get a good stereo image of the entire kit. The microphones will usually be high off the floor, so invest in some sturdy boom stands that can handle the height. The Shure SM81 or the AKG C460 are good choices for this role.

General Placement Tips for Tight-Miking Drums

There are two approaches to mixing the overall drum set sound. For a tight, isolated sound, the individual drum mics will be the main sound source for the drums, with the overheads providing the cymbals to the mix and a little fill to the overall sound. Using this approach, Jack offers the following tips.

Figure 11.16. Shure SM 81 Microphone

Kick—Place the mic inside the drum, if possible. Avoid positioning the mic in the center of the drum even though that is often the spot where the beater strikes the head. The center of the drum is the point at which the greatest degree of phase cancellation occurs, and therefore, the sound will be pretty awful if you put the mic there. Place the mic off to one side, aimed toward the beater. The closer you place the mic to the drum's back head, the crisper and punchier the sound will be; the farther away, the more boomy and ringy.

Snare and Toms—Aiming toward the rim will provide a crisper, brighter sound while aiming more toward the center of the drum will provide a fatter, rounder tone. Try a hybrid approach. Position the mic near the rim of the drum and aim in toward the center to get the best of both worlds.

Cymbals—A brighter sound is found toward the center of the cymbal, at the bell, and a wider, fuller sound is found more toward the edge. However, beware; placing the mic too close to the edge of a cymbal will produce a flanging sound after the cymbal has been struck as it swings up and down— closer to and farther away from the mic.

For a more acoustic, open sound, treat the drums as a single instrument and use a "distant pair" approach. This will work exceptionally well if you are recording in a great sounding room. Place the mics a couple of feet above the center of the kit. An X-Y or coincident array in which two matched mics are positioned so that their diaphragms are directly on axis with each other or a "near-coincident" array in which the mics are spaced just a few inches apart from each other can provide excellent results.

In this case, the overhead mics will become the main mics for the whole drum kit and the tight mics will act more like accent or fill mics to add definition to the sound of each drum and aid in stereo positioning. The cymbals will be the dominant sound since they are part of the kit that is closest to the mics, especially if the mics you use for your overheads have a sufficiently bright frequency response.

Electric Bass

Usually electric bass is recorded directly into the mixer through a direct box. This brings the bass signal down to mic level. Direct boxes are available from Countryman, Beringer, and Whirlwind. The prices range from $30 to $155.

Electric Guitar

A guitar amp is another loud sound source so dynamic microphones are a good choice. Some of the same microphones used with kick and snare drum will also work effectively on a guitar amp. Be sure to use a pad if the volume will be loud. The Shure SM57 and EV RE 20 are good choices, depending on the amount of bass response desired. Jack will occasionally break out a Neumann U-87, depending on the sound he's looking for. Be sure to use a pad on every condenser mic if the volume is going to be loud.

When miking an amplifier, experiment with the distance of the mic from the amp. Moving it closer produces a tighter sound. Moving it away from the amp means more of the room sound is heard. Try between 6 and 12 inches and experiment with everything in between. Aim the mic directly at the center of the speaker for a bright tone. If the sound is too bright, move the mic off the center of the speaker and angle it so the mic is not directly facing the amp. This produces a more mellow sound with more bass emphasis. Moving the mic off axis in this manner prevents it from picking up some of the high frequencies of the sound.

It is also possible to record the guitar through a direct box. To alter the sound, use outboard gear such as a multi-effects unit, or a computer-based effects processor such as Amp Farm (more on Amp Farm in chapter 17).

Figure 11.17. EV RE 20 Microphone

Acoustic Guitar

Acoustic guitars have a very delicate sound that can be even more challenging if the musician is both singing and playing. Jack's preference is to record acoustic guitar with a matched pair of small diaphragm condenser microphones. The Shure SM81 is a good choice. Jack owns a matched pair of AKG C460s, and, just as important, an excellent Taylor acoustic guitar. The better the instrument, the more detail there is to be captured. If spill is a problem with singer/guitarists, try mounting a wood or Plexiglas board horizontally between the guitar microphone and the vocal mic to act as a baffle. Jack generally prefers to mic guitars in stereo but it can be done with a single mic in mono.

The desired sound will have a lot to do with the style of music and the type of guitar being used. Mic positions can range from 4 inches to a few feet depending on the sound desired and where the mic is aimed. Higher frequencies come from around the bridge of the guitar and lower frequencies come from the sound-hole area. To reduce fret noise, angle the mic towards the body. It is usually best to avoid aiming the mic directly at the sound hole.

Consider how much detail there is in the music. If isolation is a consideration, try placing the mic 4 to 8 inches away from the instrument. Be sure to listen to the instrument, the room, and the music and adjust the mic placement accordingly.

Acoustic Piano

Acoustic piano is one of the most challenging instruments to record. For the best quality recording the instrument must be well maintained and tuned. Jack has achieved good recording results using the Microtech Gefel. Microtech was part Neumann until the Berlin Wall went up. When available, Jack uses the Neumann U-87 for pop or jazz styles and the DPA 4006 (formerly the B&K 4006) for classical music.

Because the piano is a complex instrument, it is difficult to make a miking generalization. Sometimes the job might entail compensating for the sounds of an inferior instrument. For upright pianos, open the top and place one mic above the opening. Point another directly at the middle of the soundboard on the back. For a stereo sound use four mics with a pair above and a pair on the soundboard. For baby grand and full-size grand pianos, position mics just above the hammers to cover the full width of the strings. Positioning close to the hammers will produce a crisp, punching tone, great for

Figure 11.18. DPA4006 Microphone

rock and roll. Another approach is to mic along the length of the piano to achieve an audience perspective. Raise the lid of the piano to the maximum height to reduce reflections inside the piano. Experiment with distance if you have a good room. Acoustic instruments are designed to project sound, so pulling back the mics can often allow an instrument to blend more naturally, producing a smoother sound.

Vocals

Vocals are the most common and most critical mic placement in the studio. A good vocal mic is worth every penny you can possibly spend. I'm assuming that all the instrumentalists have skipped to the next paragraph when I say the vocal mic will be way out in front of every mix. A large diaphragm condenser mic is the type to consider in order to capture every nuance and detail of a performance. When working with a vocalist who records a lot, you may find that he or she has a preference for a certain mic. The mic of choice at 3 IPS Studio is the Microtech Gefel UM70. Jack's classic picks are the legendary Neumann U-47 or AKG's C-12.

Most pop vocalists prefer singing within a few inches to a foot of the mic. Only the pop filter keeps many singers from physically touching the mic. If they have some recording experience they may have learned to pull back a little during extremely loud passages. The singer should not move too far away from the mic because the signal to the compressor changes resulting in a dramatic shift in the sound going to tape. Position singers who have been trained to project—especially theater and opera singers—farther back from the mic. Opera singers can be a few feet away from the mic and still make the compressor

Figure 11.19. The Next Generation Tube C12VR

work overtime. Position the mic slightly above mouth level to keep the singer's head up and throat open.

Saxophone

For the saxophone, a medium or large diaphragm ribbon mic is ideal and gives a warm overall sound to the instrument. Large diaphragm dynamic microphones also work well and are less expensive and more durable than diaphragm ribbon mics. Position the mic above the bell but pointed at the keys. Don't place the mic close to the instrument, as it will add some unwanted brightness, and it could also pick up key and pad noise. The Electro Voice EV RE20 is a good choice. Jack's preference is the RCA 77 ribbon mic or the Neumann U-87 condenser mic.

Trumpet

There is no confusing where the sound is coming from when miking a trumpet. Keep at least a foot of distance between the bell of the horn and the mic. Moving back will round out the sound and keep valve sounds from being recorded. For a more mellow sound, move the mic at an angle to the bell. Small diaphragm ribbon microphones provide a warm sound for trumpets and flugelhorns. The other option is to use a medium diaphragm dynamic mic. The Beyerdynamic M160 or Neumann U-87 are Jack's preferred trumpet microphones.

French Horn and Trombone

Mic positioning should be the same as with the trumpet mentioned previously. For large bore brass instruments a large diaphragm condenser works well. The Microtech Gefel UM 70 is good versatile mic that has served very well in a lot of different settings. Jack's picks are the Neumann U47 or the RCA 44.

Violin

Violin requires a mic that can match the instrument's brightness without getting brittle in the upper register. Position the mic a few feet over the face of the violin for the best sound. Once again, let the instrument project. The closer the mic is to the strings, the coarser the sound. Close miking works as an effect to produce a country fiddle sound. The Shure SM81 is a good basic mic for this instrument. Jack's selection here is the AKG 414.

Figure 11.21. AKG C414 Microphone

Cello and Acoustic Bass

The rich warm tones of a cello are ideally captured by a large diaphragm condenser. For cellos and basses

Figure 11.20. Beyerdynamic M 160

position the mic two to three feet away from the instrument, directly in front. Place the mic off the bridge for a bright sound. Aim the mic toward the F-hole for a fuller sound. The Microtech Gefel UM70 works well as does Jack's favorite mic for cello and bass, the Neumann U-87.

General Purpose Mics

For those people keeping score, there are a few microphones that keep coming up in a variety of applications. The good news is that a quality mic can be used in a number of different situations and the price of these mics continues to drop. New models, built with the entry and mid-level studio in mind, are appearing from companies with long standing reputations as well as new entrants to the market place. For example, the Microtech Gefel UM 70 has become the workhorse of my studio. For home studio use, consider a cardioid pickup pattern for all microphones. This will eliminate a lot of unwanted room sounds and reflections. Do some research both in the studio and in stores to see what fits your style and your budget. If you review the overall microphone suggestions mentioned in this chapter, the small

Figure 11.22. Microtech Geffel UMT70

diaphragm microphones are best used for high sounds, and large diaphragm mics are used for low sounds. This is correct but it is also a generalization. Always listen first to judge the characteristics of a particular microphone. Unconventional mic techniques often provide the sound that makes a track unique. Remember, there are no hard and fast rules. Read through magazines like *EQ*, *Recording*, *Electronic Musician*, and *Keyboard* for miking hardware and placement advice. They often contain interviews or columns dealing with miking techniques and possibilities.

Professor Jack's Lecture Notes

Jack gives his audio production students this advice about using mics.

- Never mount a mic on a stand until after attaching the cable. Once the cable is connected, should the mic fall out of the clip, the cable will prevent the mic from falling to the floor, or hitting anything along the way. This is also why the mic cable is wrapped around the stand, along with keeping the excess cable out of the way of the musician.
- Use care in handling mic cables. When wrapping them up, cup your hand and drape the cable over it. Coil it carefully so it falls in a uniform loop. Make sure the cable is not twisted. Twists increase the stress on the cable, which will cause shorts and eventually, cable failure.
- Once they are coiled, hold the cables together with a Velcro or plastic cable tie.
- Store mic cables in a neat and orderly fashion.

Pop Goes the Plosive

Ever since the *We Are The World* video appeared, people have been buying one of those little round things to put in front of the microphone. Those round things are called pop filters. Their purpose is to diffuse the high pressure sound waves, smoothing them out for the microphone's element. The plosive "P" or "B" is the best example. Pop filters also serve as a barrier to keep the vocalist from getting too close to the mic. It is usually positioned somewhere from 1 to 3 inches in front of the mic.

The filter is sheer fabric. Filters can be purchased or easily replicated using a woman's sheer stocking stretched over an embroidery hoop or a wire clothes hanger. Some models available for purchase have a clamp assembly that will fit on the same stand as the microphone. Otherwise you will need another stand on which to mount the filter.

Microphone Preamplifiers

A mic preamp is a separate device that allows the signal from the mic to be routed through the pre-amp box directly to the recorder. Since this signal is still in the analog domain, more connections means greater potential for noise and signal loss. The preamp typically provides phantom power and EQ, some-times including compression, limiting, expansion, and gating. This minimizes the number of external patches required to get the signal to tape. Not all features are available on every make and model of pre-amp so check the specs first.

Mic preamps have two basic types of circuitry: solid state and vacuum tubes. Prices range from several hundred to several thousand dollars depending on the type and quality of the circuitry used.

Vacuum tube construction is the most expensive. It is also the most desirable sound for many engineers. In the digital studio, the return to vacuum tube circuitry adds coloration reminiscent of analog recording, and can warm up the harsh "edge" found in many digital recordings.

Preamp Basics

The first function of an external mic preamp is to amplify the incoming signal to line level. This will be either –10 dB or +4 dB depending on the machine. This process alone will color the sound. It is important to test the microphone and preamp and listen to the sound the combination produces. Some microphones and preamp combinations are more transparent than others and will sound a little different. If the mic has already been purchased, take it with you when shopping for a preamp. If both are being purchased together, try several combinations.

Since the preamp is intended to replace the mixer's input, phantom power is a must for connecting condenser microphones. A preamp may also have a –10 or –20 dB pad feature for high output microphones

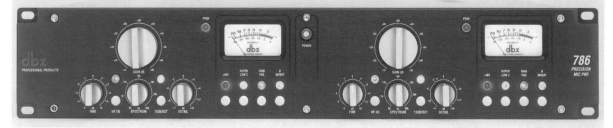

Figure 11.23. Dbx 786 Microphone Preamp

that do not have this feature built-in. A low cut filter is another preamp feature that is similar to a microphone's bass roll off switch. It can eliminate unwanted low frequency noise and is also helpful when using microphones not equipped with this feature. One last preamp feature is a phase reversal switch for changing the phase, or polarity, of the signal 180 degrees. This can be used to reverse polarity of mis-wired equipment, cancel leakage from adjacent mics, or as a special effect.

Some mic preamps also have an instrument input to act as a DI (direct input) box. These jacks are usually located on the front panel of the unit for connecting electric guitar, electric bass, or other electronic instruments. Direct box inputs are needed as the signal produced by electronic instruments is less than microphones. Electric instruments range between –30 dB to –20 dB as opposed to –30 dB to –60 dB for microphones. These features compose the basics of preamp function for getting a signal to tape. The next step would be to process or alter the signal in some way before it gets to the recorder.

Preamp Processing

If you are trying to get a level on a vocal or other signal and find that it often peaks the meter, chances are it would benefit from some compression. The first stop for most vocal signals in the external processing world is the compressor. Compression is used on signals whose dynamic range exceeds the capability of the recorder. Standard compressor controls include the threshold level, which is the decibel level the incoming signal has to reach for the compressor to kick in.

Hard knee and soft knee are the two most interesting parameter names and control how suddenly the compression begins. The ratio setting determines the level of the output in relationship to the incoming signal. For example, 2:1 ratio indicates that for every 2 dB input change above the threshold level there will be a 1 dB change in output. After being compressed, the signal is now softer than when it entered the compressor, softer than it needs to be for the recorder. To compensate, the compressor has an output control to boost the compressed signal as it leaves the unit or module.

The extreme form of compression is called limiting. Limiting is when the compression ratio is 10:1 or above. When a signal is compressed, it still rises dynamically but not as rapidly as an uncompressed signal. When a signal is limited, once it reaches that decibel level it is not allowed to go above it.

Compression can be a necessity when recording dynamic sounds, as an effect used on an instrument, or on the mix as a whole. Compression is commonly used on drum tracks both to control dynamic microphones and to give it a little more punch in the mix. Adding some compression to a final mix will give it added punch that is especially noticeable when listening to tracks and commercials on the radio. More about this in chapter 18.

An expander works at the opposite end of the dynamic range from the compressor. It is used to eliminate unwanted noise from the recording. Here the threshold determines the level below which sounds will be softened by the selected ratio. This can be used to eliminate headphone bleed, lip smacks, or faint noises if your studio is not completely soundproofed.

Gating is the expander equivalent of limiting, a set decibel level below which all sound is shut off completely. This can be used to eliminate a constant, unwanted sound like guitar amp noise or air conditioner and ventilation system noise. This is also used as an effect, most popularly on drums, most notably on Phil Collins' drums. The gate cuts off the instrument's natural decay giving it a fat, punchy sound.

Try to avoid using EQ on vocals, if possible. However, if tone is a problem, EQ can be your friend. Essentially, the EQ acts as volume controls for selected frequencies and those around them. Turning the EQ up amplifies those frequencies, turning it down reduces their volume. On the top end this can add brightness to a dull sound or reduce the shrillness of a piercing sound. It can add body or reduce a nasal quality in the mid range. In the low end it can add bottom or reduce the rumble or muddiness of unwanted frequencies.

Filters generally operate on the extreme ends of the EQ spectrum. The trick is to remember that the high-pass filter handles the low end and the low-pass filter handles the high end. (Hey, don't e-mail me, I didn't make this up!) The high-pass filter controls everything below a certain frequency, usually around 75 Hz, since the human voice doesn't go below 80 Hz. This is useful for eliminating any mic handling noise or rumble from other equipment or sources that you can't control. The low-pass filter, conversely, controls everything above a certain frequency and is great for eliminating high frequency noise such as hiss.

Another word I didn't just make up is de-esser. A de-esser was designed to deal with the nasty sibilant sounds produced by the letter "s" and its frequent partner in crime, the "sh." The process of

Figure 11.24. Aphex Tubessence Mic Preamp

de-essing actually involves applying compression and EQ on a selective basis. The EQ boosts the frequencies where the offending sibilant sounds are concentrated, usually between 3 kHz and 8 kHz. This makes a compressor more sensitive to them and they are compressed in line with the rest of the vocal track.

The Basic Preamp

The Aphex Tubessence is a basic mic preamp. It has no internal effects processing other than it attempts to replicate the sound of a tube preamp as it amplifies the signal from the mic. Microphones are connected to the front panel of the unit but most others have connections on the rear. There are switches for a 20 dB pad and bass roll-offs in case the mic itself does not have these features. This is also handy for live recording when it may not be possible or practical to reset the switches on the microphone body. All preamps are capable of supplying phantom power to condenser microphones, a requirement in bypassing the mixer.

Figure 11.25. Focusrite Red 1

Preamps are available in several configurations. The Aphex handles two microphones, the Focusrite Red 1 handles four microphones. The current crop of preamps contains units that handle from one to eight microphones. The Focusrite uses vacuum tubes and Class A circuitry, making it more expensive.

These products still require patching through other effects devices if processing is required. Focusrite, for example, has two lines of modular units designed to work together for complete processing of any signal. The dbx 386 combines a basic preamp with an A/D converter. Sampling rates of 44.1 kHz, 48 kHz, 88.2 kHz, and 96 kHz are available by AES/EBU or S/PDIF connections. Using the dbx 386 for instruments is easy as there

Figure 11.26. Dbx 386 Microphone Preamp

are two quarter-inch jacks located on the front panel. The "two units in one" approach can save you money, a few rack spaces in the studio, and weight in a portable recording setup.

Mic preamps are also located in interface units supplied with mid-level and high-end digital audio products that were introduced in chapters 7 and 8. For example, the Digi 001 unit contains two mic preamps. Any additional signal processing must be handled in Pro Tools LE with the use of plug-ins. This begins to bring up the possibility of not needing a mixer, or at least not as big a mixer for a computer-based system like Pro Tools.

Full Featured Preamps

The Focusrite Green Series Channel Strip combines a mic preamp, 4-band variable frequency EQ, and a compressor for controlling loud sounds or sounds with a wide dynamic range. This unit handles a single input so the downside is more features means less inputs.

Figure 11.27. Focusrite Green Series Channel Strip

Figure 11.28. Focusrite Platinum Series

It is possible to purchase full feature units. The Focusrite Platinum is a solid state unit with mixer features like EQ, compression, expander, gate, and de-esser.

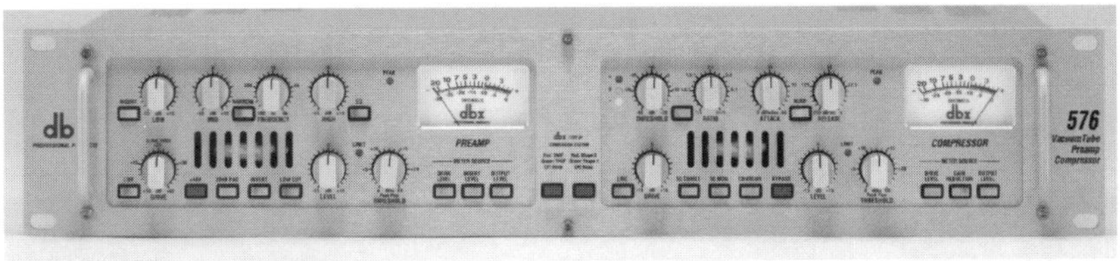

The dbx 576 is a vacuum tube unit with built-in 3-band EQ, compression, and limiting. This unit handles two

Figure 11.29. DBX 576

signals with balanced XLR and quarter-inch connectors. The dbx 576 has an option to add an A/D converter for AES/EBU or S/PDIF connections at 16-bit, 20-bit, or 24-bit resolution.

Summary

This chapter introduced the basic microphone concepts and listed several that should be considered for the digital studio. The chapter also included specific mic placement and models for the most common instruments. The equipment needed for microphone input and processing includes preamps.

Chapter 12.
The Studio Environment

The recording equipment described in the previous chapters has become small enough to fit into almost any size room. However, before putting equipment into any room there are several concepts to be carefully considered. This chapter focuses on entry-level and mid-level studios with specific recommendations for treating existing rooms to get the most out of the area for digital recording.

The Nature of Sound

Once a sound is set loose in a room it will interact with everything in its path until it dissipates or is absorbed. The sound quality is dependent upon the shape of the room and the materials on the walls, floor, and ceiling. Professional recording studios often have nonstandard-shaped rooms. The design of the room addresses proper control and handling of sound waves.

Every room has its own sound, referred to as *room tone*. Room tone is the result of many factors. For an exaggerated example, sit in a living room and listen to sounds, and then go to your bathroom (assuming its walls are tiled) or shower stall and listen there. Ever wonder *why* you sound so great singing in the shower? The sound waves bounce off the hard surface of the ceramic tiles gradually decaying and producing an effect called *reverberation*, or reverb. Even without a sound being made, you should be able to hear the difference in the size and construction of the living room and bathroom.

Next, clap your hands in each room and listen to the results. The sound waves reflect off the walls, ceiling, and floor until their energy, or sound, dissipates. In a small room, sound waves bounce back and forth rapidly because the distance they have to travel is small. In a tiled bathroom, the waves reflect off the hard surfaces so the sound lasts longer. Sound reflects rapidly off of many hard surfaces in the space and is not absorbed.

In addition to the initial sound wave reflection, you also hear the wave continue to reflect off the opposing walls over and over until the sound wave dissipates. Diffusion is the term given to the decay of a sound wave.

In some large spaces, you may hear a strange sound called a flutter echo. Flutter echo sounds like the flutter of a bird's wings as it takes flight.

Another way to experiment with various reverberation types is to sample them using your digital audio software plug-ins or outboard effects devices. Try different size room settings and listen to the difference in the quality.

Professional Studio Design

Professional recording studios typically comprise two separate spaces. One room is the control room. The recording equipment is housed there and the recording engineer sits there during the recording. There is also a separate space where the performers play or sing into microphones. If there is enough room, the recording space can be divided into a main recording area and in an isolation booth, frequently used for recording vocals.

In a typical control room, the walls and ceiling narrow at the front of the room and angle up and out toward the back. The concept of this design is to permit the sound waves to move through the space and diffuse equally, with no specific frequency range remaining to fool the listener's ear.

Each recording space is specially designed with acoustic properties to fit the room's function. Rooms are typically separated with soundproof walls and double glass windows for complete isolation. This is to prevent noise in one room from leaking or spilling into the other and interfering with recording and/or monitoring.

Home Studio Options

Simulating the acoustic environment of a professional studio is a difficult task. For most project or home studios, it comes down to making the best of the space at hand. The goal is to create a space that does not create acoustic problems that haunt every recording. Some of the options for the various budgets include:

- Entry-level: modifications might range from nothing to such temporary treatments as baffles acoustic tiles attached to ceiling and wall surfaces.
- Mid-level: modifications might consist of permanent construction of soundproof areas or temporary soundproof structures to create a quality recording environment.
- High-end: modifications might include complete conversion of an existing space or creation of a studio designed from the ground up as a dedicated recording facility. This can be either an addition to a home or a complete self-contained building.

Ultimately the goal is to isolate each track being recorded from any and all unwanted sounds. The key is creating a room that is devoid of excess reverb. If the room is overly live, meaning there is a lot of natural reverb, this will also be recorded through the microphone. If you increase the volume of the track being recorded, it will also increase the volume of any unwanted sound such as room reverb. This makes it difficult to control overall blend and volume when mixing.

Construction Options

Construction and design of recording studios is a specialized field. It requires experience in a variety of areas including architecture, construction techniques, building materials, and acoustics. For a high-end studio, or if you are building an addition onto your house, consider hiring a contractor who has experience designing and installing studios. An experienced designer can analyze your needs and is aware of the appropriate materials and techniques. It will cost you a little more money but you can sleep securely knowing you did it right the first time. For example, the Wenger Corporation, in Owatana, Minnesota, will develop specifications for studios and will supply the necessary materials. Another option is to contact local construction companies to see if any have experience building recording studios.

Preparing a recording space in your home can range from a major building renovation to simply hanging some sound absorbing materials. It all depends on your requirements, your budget, and how much your family will tolerate before requesting an intervention by Gear Sluts Anonymous.

Outside Noise

An important part of studio design is to remove as much outside noise from the room as possible. In your studio, you are likely to notice outside noise. Consider how much traffic is on your street, how close you are to a major airport, and the noise made by your kids, your neighbor's kids, lawn mowers, leaf blowers, air conditioners, household appliances, even birds and thunderstorms. We often take these sounds for granted, but they can ruin a recording session or that killer take you've worked hours to produce. You will remember to shut off the ringer on your telephone, won't you?

The studio equipment itself also produces noise. Because of this equipment noise, many professional studios have a separate room for tape decks, hard drives, and other devices. It is not possible to screen out every extraneous sound but it is important to control as much as possible.

There is also the issue of containing the sound in the studio and keeping it from interfering with others in your home or apartment who might actually want to sleep, or neighbors who might have the local police on speed dial.

Entry Level: Discovering the Studio Space

Rooms come in two varieties: wet and dry. Wet rooms have walls and floors that are hard and therefore highly reflective of sound. This creates an overabundance of room reverberation. Rooms that typically have a high level of reverb include the bathroom, kitchen, basement, garage, and hallway with a stairwell. Basically, all rooms with hardwood floors or stone walls will be wet or ambient. These rooms usually have little in the way of natural sound absorbing materials such as carpets, drapes, or upholstered furniture.

Dry rooms usually have a minimum of natural room reverb and echo because the have surfaces that absorbs sound waves such as carpets and drapes. Dry rooms usually include the bedroom, living room, dining room, and clothes closet.

Ceiling height is also an important factor. You may have more height in the living room or first floor space than in a bedroom or second floor room. A higher ceiling will add to the reverberation time of the sound.

Keep in mind that it is easy to add reverb to a recorded track. However, live room ambiance is difficult to remove. If you are not sure how it is going to fit in the final mix, err on the side of dryness. Early recording studios used to be constructed with wet rooms until the 1970s, when dry rooms and isolation booths became popular. In a home studio, it is usually best to record in a dry space and add reverb during the mixdown.

Sometimes using different recording space can be an advantage. For example, if you want to add natural room ambience or reverb to a vocal track, try setting up the mic in the bathroom or hallway. Placing a guitar amplifier in an ambient stairwell and fiddling with an EQ might be a stroke of genius when you can't quite find the right sound in a dry recording room.

Acoustic Materials

If you are designing a studio in your home or apartment, it is a good idea to consider making minor alterations to the room to enhance the sound quality for recordings. This can be done at a minimal to moderate expense depending on the materials you use. In many cases, materials can be used that are not permanently affixed to the room. Merely adding or removing furniture can affect the sound in a room. If a room with a bare floor is a little too wet, try placing area rugs or blankets to dampen the sound. If a room is a little too dry, try removing furniture, drapes, or any other absorptive materials in the room.

Everything in a room absorbs sound to some degree. However, every type of material has its own rate of absorption. The measure of how much sound a particular material absorbs is called the sound absorption coefficient. Materials are rated on a scale from 1.0, total absorption, to 0.0, completely reflective. For example, the absorption rate of carpet changes if it has padding underneath. A padded carpet has a rating of 0.08 for signals in the 125 Hz range and a healthy 0.73 rate of absorption at 4 kHz. Concrete block absorption changes if it is sealed and painted.

The absorption rate varies with different frequencies. One common characteristic of most acoustic room treatments is that they absorb high-range and mid-range frequencies better than low-range frequencies. For the low frequencies a diaphragmatic absorber, more commonly known as a bass trap, is recommended. A bass trap is usually made of a panel of wood mounted over an air space that resembles a rectangular box attached to the wall. When it is struck by a sound wave, the panel resonates at frequencies determined by the rigidity of the wood panel and the size of the air space behind the panel. This dampens sound waves of the same frequency as they strike the trap. Acoustic tiles and foam can be positioned on walls and ceiling to absorb sound waves and eliminate unwanted first reflections.

Analyzing a room to determine the correct treatment for sound recording requires some knowledge of acoustics. If you want to explore the technical side of acoustical treatments read F. Alton Everest's book, *Acoustic Techniques for Home & Studio*, published by Tab Books.

Mid-Level: Building a Room Within a Room

If you can spread out and use several rooms for various recording needs, it may provide some isolation, both for musicians and the recording engineer. To completely isolate a room for recording, you must build a room within a room. This is expensive. Some options to consider include installing a drop ceiling and/or adding a layer of insulation to all of the walls. You will also need an insulated door and stripping around the doorjamb to seal it. If you are considering this type of setup, remember to consider cable runs, electrical outlets, and proper ventilation. Before you undertake building a room within a room, think for a moment about how long you plan to remain in your current location. These modifications may not enhance the resale value, unless you find someone else who wants a home recording studio. If you are not going to reap the long-term benefits from creating a room within a room, consider some of the less permanent options mentioned in the following section.

Room Treatments for the Do-It-Yourselfer

As mentioned previously, isolation gives you more control when mixing. This is important if you are blending tracks from several different sources or locations. If you plan to record vocals, consider constructing a separate vocal booth. There are prefabricated units you can buy from Wenger Corporation and other companies, or you can adapt the space using room treatments. For other construction ideas, visit other recording studios in your area.

Baffles can also be helpful. You can use Plexiglas or other materials to baffle off the area around the pickup pattern of a particular microphone. Baffles can be made at home using materials from your local hardware store. For example, purchase a door or dressing screen. Glue some foam or carpet on one side. If you use a door, construct a base so it will stand securely. You could also build a wood frame, fill it with fiberglass insulation, and then cover the frame with bed sheets. (Be sure to follow safety procedures for handling all construction materials.) You also can contract a carpenter if you don't have the tools or if you tend to cut off body parts when you try to be handy.

In addition to the do-it-yourself option, consider purchasing prefabricated materials from companies including Acoustical Solutions or Acoustic Sciences Corporation (ASC).

Setting Up the Control Room

It is ideal to use multiple rooms, one where the musicians will perform and one for the recording engineer. It is possible to have the recording equipment and microphones all in one room, but it may be difficult to monitor the sound as it is being recorded. Either the engineer must use headphones or the control room monitors must be turned down to a very low level to avoid re-recording too much of the track with the vocal.

In order to produce a quality product, the listening environment for recording and mixing is crucial. If you can use two different rooms, it is best to locate the main recording area, or control room, in a separate room from the main recording area.

Once you have decided where your control room will be located, proper positioning of the audio monitors is a priority. Monitors should be placed at least 18 inches away from back or side walls. This is to avoid unwanted reflections. Make sure the wall behind both speakers is of the same construction. Try to place the speakers in the middle of the room (avoid placing them in a corner). An ideal placement is 6 feet between your listening position and the speaker, with the speakers 6 feet apart, forming an equilateral triangle.

If you are in a small space such as a spare bedroom, there may be unwanted reflections from the opposite wall. Adding some acoustical foam on the opposite wall will absorb or diffuse the unwanted sound. You may also need to add some treatment to the ceiling and side walls as well.

Spend time tuning your room. Start by playing a familiar CD recording at different volume levels and carefully listen to the room sound. Move around the room and see if there are any places that have a buildup of bass frequencies, especially in corners or coves. To address this, add room treatments to specific areas.

Ventilation

On a less technical note, give some consideration to proper room ventilation. If you are in an unventilated room, heat buildup can be a problem. Some equipment may malfunction if the temperature gets too high. Make sure air can circulate around the rear of the recording gear and amplifiers.

A room air conditioner or central air can be a good investment. Try to find a model that runs quietly. You will have to turn it off for critical listening or when recording live tracks. Ceiling fans can also be an option as they tend to operate more quietly than air conditioning units.

The Economics of Ergonomics

After your studio space has been defined, you will need furniture to complete the setup. If you are particularly handy, you can make your own, but given the price of materials, some prefabricated units can actually be cheaper. A small studio setup may fit on stock office furniture or a computer desk with a library top. For more complex setups you may want to investigate units built specifically for recording by companies including Raxxess, Omnirax, and Argosy.

Figure 12.1. Omnirax Studio furniture   Figure 12.2. Argosy Studio furniture

These products are designed for audio and video hardware gear. Each company offers a variety of options so it is a good idea to review each company's catalog offerings.

The Seat of Power

Before you sit down and get to work, consider the chair you will be sitting in while recording, editing, and mixing. You will be spending a lot of time working in the studio, and it is essential that you are comfortable for long periods of time. Visit the local office supply store and look for a quality office chair. It may be several hundred dollars or more, but when you add up the hours you will be spending in it, you will get your money's worth. Physical problems, especially back ailments, can be exacerbated by using an inferior chair. This is especially true if you've already abused your back hauling equipment around to gigs and recording sessions.

Summary

The recording space environment has a significant impact on the recording quality. There are several options from which to choose with regard to room construction. Entry- and mid-level studios are usually located in a room in the home or apartment. High-end studios are typically custom designed. It is possible to make alterations to an existing room to enhance sound quality.

Chapter 13.

Connecting Your Studio Equipment

Once you have selected the equipment for your studio, you will need to connect it. This chapter explores some of the challenges you will face and some possible solutions.

Placing the Furniture

Once you have purchased furniture, the next step is to place it in the best location in the studio. First, put the equipment you will use most often where it is most accessible. If you're a composer or keyboard player you'll probably want your synths and modules front and center. If you're an engineer, the mixer will most likely take center stage. If you use a computer-based system the computer keyboard and monitor should be placed where they are easily accessed.

Next, position the supporting cast of equipment. Again, anything you use frequently should be placed as close to you as possible. The front panels of equipment you adjust most often should be easily viewable and within arm's length. Studio lighting should not produce glare on the front panels. Group equipment so your synths are together and your effects are together in the rack.

Before you get too far along in planning your layout, take time to review the equipment connections and cables. For computer equipment the length of the cable is a factor, especially for SCSI connections (see chapter 9). Bear in mind that for audio cables, extra length can mean more noise or degradation of signal. So plan carefully where each component will be placed to minimize the length of cable.

Equipment Isolation

If you use a computer in your setup, be aware that the computer itself can generate noise. Many computers have built-in fans that make noise. The noise made by an external CD burner and/or a hard drive or two can interfere with audio editing and recording. The best way to control this equipment noise is to isolate the equipment in a separate room, often referred to as an isolated machine room. In a home studio you can convert a closet to hold the equipment, but be sure it is well ventilated because extreme heat can be deadly to your equipment.

Computer Cables

Isolating computer equipment brings up another problem: the monitor, keyboard, and mouse cables supplied with the equipment will not reach more than a few feet. Extending the distance between components will require additional equipment. The Gefen TSE100 allows a computer monitor to be up to 500 feet from the CPU, and the keyboard, mouse, or trackball can be up to 1000 feet away. The TSE100S is connected to the CPU. It amplifies the signal coming from the computer and sends it over cables to the TSE100R positioned near the monitor and keyboard locations. From there you plug in the normal monitor, keyboard, and mouse or trackball cables into the TSE100R and you are set.

Gefen offers other products for supporting two monitors from the same CPU and controlling two computers from the same monitor, keyboard, and mouse or trackball. It is possible to have both a Macintosh and Windows machine run from that type of setup.

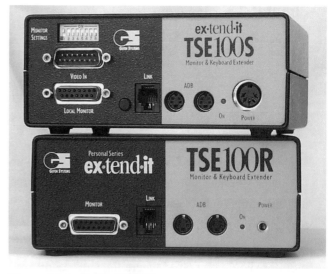

Label Your Cable

One piece of advice about cables: Label your wires on both ends with a piece of white or light-colored tape and a felt tip pen. There will inevitably come a day when a cable or a connection will become suspect and you'll have to do battle with the dust bunnies behind

Figure 13.1. Gefen TSE100

your equipment to find the culprit. In poor light, back panels are hard to read and the tangle of wires will make it difficult to find the exact connection you need to check.

If you are using individual cables for connections to multitrack recorders, use plastic binders or Velcro cable wraps to group cables together as a makeshift snake. This will make handling the connections easier and keep the cable paths a little more organized.

Quality Cable

Be sure to purchase high quality cables for your studio. Cables aren't likely to wow people, but they sure make a big difference in sound quality. On more than one occasion I have had an otherwise perfect mix ruined because a cable shorted out.

There are different brands of cable and the best come at a higher price. Monster Cable is the premium cable brand in the audio world. It is available for car stereo, home stereo/theater, MIDI, musical instruments, speakers, and pro audio applications. Monster Cable comes in three grades: good, better, and best. I recommend going with the best quality cable.

If you already have a setup, budget to replace your cables on a regular basis. Begin with the connections to and from the mixer. The most often-used signal paths are output to the power amp and monitors and to any outboard gear. Continue to upgrade your cables throughout your entire system.

Sittin' on the Dock of the Patch Bay

In this chapter you'll frequently see the word patch bay. A patch bay is a junction box for routing signals. All signals flow into it from the source, then back out again to the destination. If you have done any flying you most likely have found yourself in Chicago or Atlanta. Think of the Chicago or Atlanta airports as a patch bay. Frequently, you can't get anywhere without going through one of these airports. In the studio the patch bay serves as the central location to connect MIDI, audio, and digital audio signals.

Patch bays date back to the beginnings of the telephone system. They are the central hub of a wiring system, where any incoming signal can be routed to any outgoing location in the system. Patch bays are used to route signals from the point of origin to a number of different destinations without unplugging and re-plugging. For example, large mixing consoles have so many possible connections that it would be inefficient to manually re-patch each connection during a session, or set up a specific route for using reverbs, compressors, and other outboard effects. The answer is to connect all the ins and outs of the mixer to a central point, the patch bay. All inputs in the studio are wired into the patch bay as well so that any microphone or line input can be routed to any channel on the mixer. The outboard effects are also wired so the signal from any channel or bus can be sent to any effects device. Large mixing consoles usually have a large patch bay.

If you are just beginning to assemble an entry-level studio, chances are your connections will be fairly simple. By simple I mean you have all your equipment hooked up to your mixer without the need for regular re-patching.

Your equipment should help, not get in the way of your creativity. With a constant setup, and enough practice with it, working in your recording setup should be second nature. In order for this to take place, some additional equipment may be needed.

Audio Patch Bay

Sooner or later you may require more audio connections. For example, a complex MIDI sequence may require using a synth's aux outputs, or you may add an additional piece of outboard equipment to add capability to your mixer. One solution to deal with the connection of equipment is to add an audio patch bay to your studio. Audio patch bays come in three basic configurations: normalled, half-normalled, and de-normalled.

Figure 13.2. Fostex Audio Patch Bay with RCA Connectors

The typical patch bay is designed so the incoming signal into patched into the top row of jacks and the outputs along the bottom row (see Figure 13.2). When using a patch bay the top input and bottom output comprise a route that the signal would normally take if connected directly, hence the term *normalled*. In a *half-normalled* connection, a patch cable is inserted into the input jack and the incoming signal is sent both to the patched output as well as the normalled output connection below the signal's input. In a *de-normalled* configuration, all of the patch bay's connections are independent. Input signals can only be routed to a destination by manually patching them to an output.

In a normalled patch bay, a signal coming in on the top row of the patch bay is automatically routed to the out that is beneath it (see figure 13.2). Of course, signals can be re-routed by inserting a cable in the top jack and sending it to another output.

Patch bays are available in a variety of wiring options. Rear panels can be RCA jacks or quarter-inch patch chords. Some require soldering the wires to terminals. Front panel connections are usually RCA or quarter-inch or a mix of the two. There are also patch bays offering unbalanced and balanced connections. XLR patch bays are used for connecting mic cables in a studio's recording space or stage rig but are not used in the control room racks because the connectors take up too much physical space on the front panel. Tiny-Tel or Bantam connectors are another connector type used with larger format consoles. They resemble quarter-inch plugs but are thinner and shorter, allowing for more connections per rack space. This is essential when there are a large number of connections required and space is at a premium.

You should select a patch bay with a single type of connector for the front panel to standardize the connections in your studio. You'll also need to purchase some short patch cables for making the connections. Begin with a diagram to lay out your connections and determine your cabling needs.

Figure 13.3. Fostex Audio Patch Bay with Quarter-Inch Connectors

Signal Converters

If you have to mix balanced and unbalanced equipment (see chapter 3) in your studio, there is a solution. The TASCAM LA-80 converter takes eight unbalanced line inputs and amplifies them to balanced line levels. The LA-81 takes eight balanced line inputs and converts the signal to unbalanced levels.

Figure 13.4. TASCAM LA-80 ANO LA-81 Signal Converters

Multitrack Connections

For ADAT users there is an ELCO connector on the back of every ADAT that can be used for routing analog balanced connections to a mixer or patch bay. The ELCO routes sixteen cables (eight in and eight out) into a single connector that plugs into the back of the ADAT. There are also patch bays with ELCO connections allowing you to patch your ADATs directly into a balanced patch bay with one connection per ADAT.

Homemade Wiring

If you are handy with a soldering iron and electronically inclined, you can make your own wires. Connectors and wire can be purchased from an electronics supply company. The advantages of making your own cables include saving money and being able to customize the length of your wires to reduce excess. Remember to leave some slack on connections to allow for routine expansion and contraction, and to allow for movement of the rack for access without stressing the connections.

Digital Audio Patch Bays

Digital audio patch bays bring the same signal routing flexibility to digital equipment. Using re-patching equipment is never pleasant; with optical cables, each time a cable is connected and re-connected it is an invitation for dirt to creep into the jack. Dirt can have a negative impact on the signal.

The Midiman Digipatch 12 x 6 handles digital S/PDIF connections. There are twelve input connections: six RCA and six optical. Signals can be converted from one format to another using this unit. The optical connections can accommodate ADAT optical format as well as TOSlink stereo signals. The unit is able to translate RCA to optical and optical to RCA format S/PDIF.

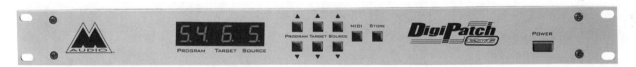

Figure 13.5. Midiman Digital Audio Patch Bay

The Digipatch can be programmed from the front panel, or by using software for Mac or Windows that is included with the unit. Two or more units can be connected for more I/Os and routing options.

The Fostex DP-8 has six optical S/PDIF I/Os that accept TOSlink or ADAT optical connections and two RCA S/PDIF I/Os. One optical I/O is located on the format panel for temporary connections. The DP-8 can convert to and from optical and RCA formats.

Figure 13.6. Fostex DP-8 Digital Audio Patch Bay

Digital Signal Converters

To be compatible with one another, different digital formats must be converted. The TASCAM IF-AE8 converts between the DA-88 series' TDIF format and AES/EBU format. The unit also performs sample rate conversion and has Word Clock built in for locking both decks together.

Figure 13.7. TASCAM IF-AE8 Digital Signal Converter

Multitrack Format Converters

Since the DA-88 and ADAT use different size tapes it is difficult to work between the two types of recorders. Of course, you could purchase one of each. Now, however, using the TASCAM IF-TAD converter, it is easy to accommodate both formats in the same setup or to digitally transfer tracks. The IF-TAD converter handles a connection between a single ADAT and a DA-88 series machine. Data can be transferred in both directions. Word Clock is included to provide syncing when the TASCAM deck is the master in the setup.

The MOTU 2404 Digital Interface discussed in chapter 8 also functions as a format converter between ADAT optical and TDIF formats and is capable of simultaneously handling three machines of each format.

Figure 13.8. TASCAM IF-TAD Converter

Computer Configuration for Digital Audio

If you are using a computer to serve as the center of your studio for MIDI and/or audio production it will need to be correctly configured. If you have purchased an audio card that plugs inside the computer (see chapters 7 and 8) first install it in the computer. If you are nervous about making the card installation yourself, take it to a local computer store or computer service company along with the documentation and installation software. Some audio cards must be placed into a specific slot in your computer, especially if you have other cards installed.

After the audio card is installed, load the MIDI/digital audio software that you own or the software that came with it. After the card and software have been installed, the next step is to configure your computer's operating system. There are two steps involved: making the appropriate settings for digital audio and, if you also have MIDI devices, setting the MIDI configuration.

Configuring Digital Audio

To set the configuration for digital audio go to the control panels settings in your computer. The Macintosh has a Sound control panel that allows you to select the hardware for digital input and output. It also controls the system sounds and output volumes. If you have installed a digital audio card inside the computer and installed the software or drivers that came with the card, it will be listed as one of the options for digital audio sound input and output.

In Windows, there is a Multimedia Properties control panel that is used to set the recording (input) and playback (output) options. This will allow you to configure the digital audio options from the sound card or digital audio card installed in the computer.

Specific audio settings can be set for the sound card or other installed digital audio cards by selecting the Customize option from the Multimedia Properties control panel.

Managing Multiple MIDI Devices

If you are using digital audio and MIDI, it is helpful to install a MIDI management program to give access to all of your MIDI devices. For the Macintosh

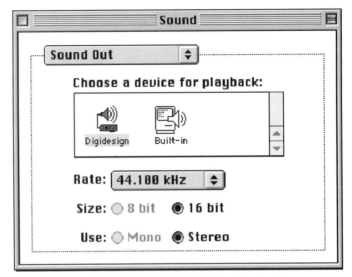

Figure 13.9. Macintosh OS Sound Control Panel

Figure 13.10. Windows Multimedia Control Panel

there are two options: OMS, or Open Music System developed by Opcode, and FreeMIDI, developed by MOTU. For Windows, OMS (Open Music System) is currently the only option. These MIDI operating systems usually come with the software or drivers packaged with the MIDI interface or MIDI software you buy. Always read the manual for proper installation procedures.

The first step is to run the configuration program, OMS or FreeMIDI. This will allow you to configure the MIDI interface and equipment connected to it in your system. Both FreeMIDI and OMS will scan the various computer ports for equipment and devices.

Once OMS or FreeMIDI is properly configured, you will see the overall setup of your system.

Once OMS or FreeMIDI installed, it will be easy to select specific MIDI devices and channels from the

Figure. 13.11. FreeMIDI and OMS Setup Screens

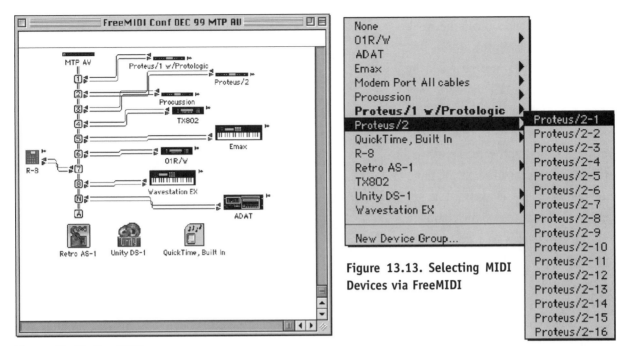

Figure 13.12. FreeMIDI

Figure 13.13. Selecting MIDI Devices via FreeMIDI

MIDI/Digital Audio software you are using. For example, the following screen shows the device selection options from Digital Performer.

One of the main advantages of using OMS or FreeMIDI is the patch list feature. The word *patch* refers to the various sounds available in a piece of MIDI gear. Patch is synonymous with program and voice. OMS and FreeMIDI allow access to different banks of sounds or equipment in the system. For example, in my system, all the Korg O1WR patch lists are available from one menu in the MIDI/Digital audio software.

This patch list makes selecting sounds a breeze and setting up patch changes easier as well. I can use Digital Performer's Default Patch fea-

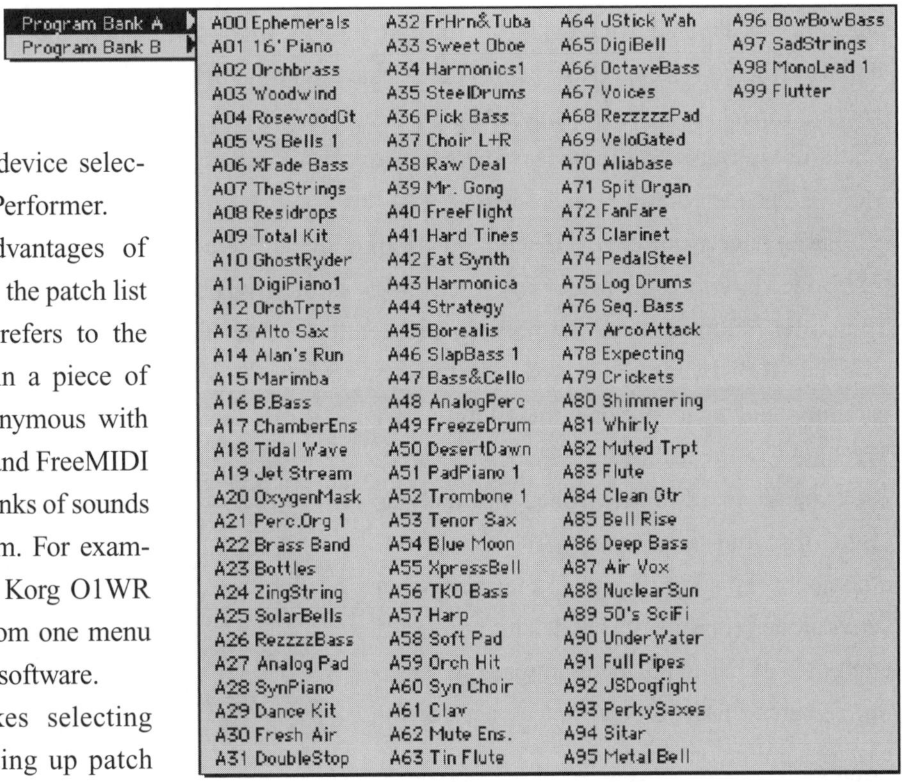

Figure 13.14. Accessing Multi-Banks of Sounds Using Digital Performer

ture so that each time I play the sequence a patch change is sent to the instrument changing it to the patch I've selected. This is especially helpful if you are using sequences in live performance or moving back and fourth between different projects in the studio.

These features are provided by FreeMIDI and OMS but how they are accessed depends on the application. For example, when using Finale music notation software, FreeMIDI or OMS allows me to select the input and output device. However, I do not have the same access to my complete rack of MIDI gear as I do in using my digital audio software.

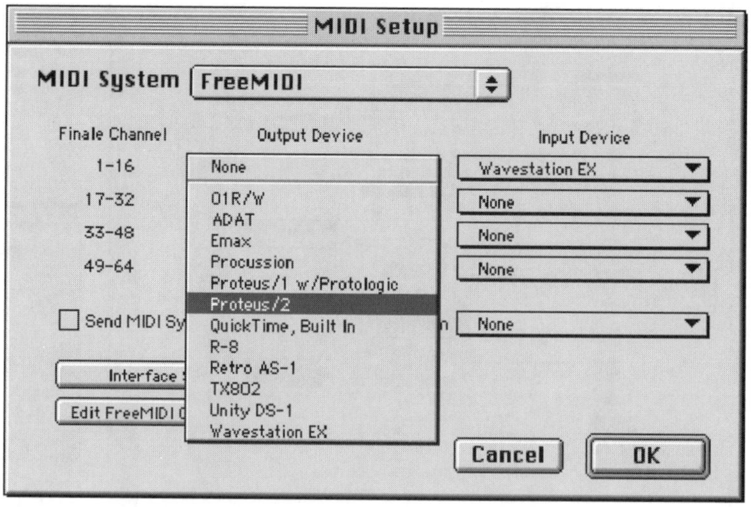

Figure 13.15. FreeMIDI Setup in Finale by Coda

MIDI

Just as audio setups become more complex, your MIDI setup can quickly grow beyond the abilities of a simple MIDI interface, discussed in Chapter 2. In the early days of MIDI a simple interface was sufficient but with the introduction of multitimbral synths and modules, setups have become more complex. The first MIDI interface routed MIDI data from the master keyboard or computer to the synths and modules attached and also filtered selected data such as patch changes and other MIDI controller data. Today's MIDI patch bays are capable of independently addressing each output on all sixteen channels, providing flexible use of multitimbral synths and modules. There are several different models of MIDI patch bays available from MOTU, Opcode, Midiman, and others.

If you have a simple MIDI setup but require SMPTE sync for video work you will need to purchase the proper interface. Consider interfaces such as the MOTU Pocket Express or the Midiman BiPort. They offer multiple in and out ports in addition to the SMPTE capability.

The MOTU Micro Express has four ins and six outs, handles up to 96 MIDI channels, and adds more patching and sync options including MIDI Machine Control. The MOTU Micro Express XT expands to a full rack space unit and has eight ins and nine outs for 128 MIDI channels. This unit can function as a stand-alone patch bay sync device without a computer. It has MIDI patching and processing features that can be saved as presets for easy system reconfiguration.

My current studio is configured with FreeMIDI and the MTP AV MIDI patch bay.

Figure 13.16. Midiman BiPort MIDI Interface

It is a MIDI interface with eight ins and eight outs, and a 128-MIDI-channel patch bay with added synchronization power.

Figure 13.17. MOTU MIDI Timepiece

The MOTU MIDI Timepiece can be configured from the front panel or the MTP/Express Console software that is included. The unit will confirm the connection of the interface to the computer in the Network Configuration window.

It is possible to chain two MTP AVs together. Two MTPs networked together provide a whopping 256 MIDI channels allowing control of a large synth or sampler rig, or a combination of synths, effects devices, digital mixers, tape decks, or any MIDI capable devices.

If you've configured your system with FreeMIDI, the Cable Routing window will display the names of all your supported devices in two columns for input and output routings. Making the software connections is as easy as clicking on the output device and dragging to the input device. A line, or virtual cable, is drawn in the window and you can specify one or more MIDI channels for communicating between the two devices. The default selection is to have all channels selected.

One problem with having so many devices connected is that making a simple patch change somewhere in the setup gets broadcast to the rest of your gear. In the Event Muting window (see Figure 13.20) you can control what MIDI data is received and transmitted

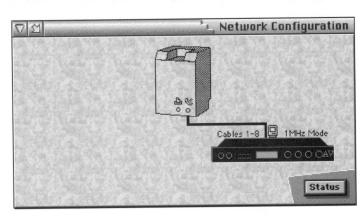

Figure 13.18. MIDI Timepiece Network Configuration

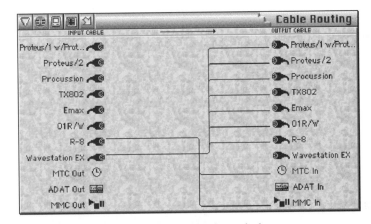

Figure 13.19. Free MIDI Cable Routing window

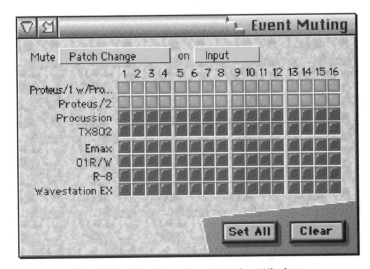

Figure 13.20. Digital Perform Event Muting Window

by each device in your setup. The popup menu provides a list of MIDI events that can be muted.

Think of the event muting channel map (see Figure 13.21) as a patch bay within a patch bay. The channel map makes it possible to reroute signals from channel to channel within a device or between two devices.

Settings can be combined into base setups. The MTP contains eight base setups that can be modified. Each setup includes information for all the settings in the unit.

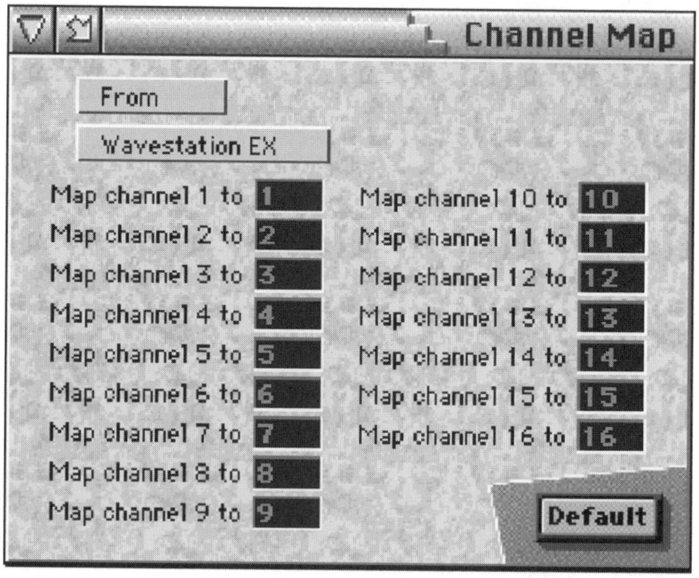

Figure 13.21. Digital Performer Channel Map Window

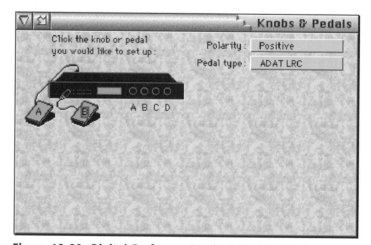

Figure 13.22. Digital Performer MIDI Machine Control

MIDI Machine Control allows tape transport commands to be sent via MIDI to and from external devices such as tape recorders, drum machines, or external sequencers. The MIDI Machine Control window in Digital Performer and AudioDesk gives me control of the ADAT in my studio from the controls in either software application or from the Controls window in the FreeMIDI application.

The ADAT's LRC remote control can be used for transport control as well

Figure 13.23. Digital Performer Knobs & Pedals Window

by connecting it the Pedal B jack on the front of the MTP AV.

The MTP AV also reads and generates SMPTE Time Code for syncing to external tape decks or sync devices.

Synchronization: SMPTE and MTC

Some devices in the studio will need to be connected and synced together—for example, if you are syncing tape decks with MIDI sequencers or working with sound and video. The most common sync format is SMPTE time code. SMPTE is an acronym for Society of Motion Picture and Television Engineers. SMPTE time code consists of a series of binary impulses that indicate the location of each frame on film, video, or audio tape in hours, minutes, seconds, and frames. It was developed in the 1970s for film and video. Its accuracy and widespread acceptance has lead SMPTE to be adopted by the audio world. There are two kinds of SMPTE: Longitudinal Time Code or LTC and Vertical Interval Time Code, or VITC (pronounced VIT-see).

LTC is the audio form of SMPTE. It is a signal that oscillates between 2 kHz and 4 kHz to form an 80-bit word (1s and 0s) for each frame on a tape. That word describes the location of each frame in hours, minutes, and seconds. VITC is the video form of SMPTE. An analog video signal consists of 525 scan lines. At the edge of each frame are a few dozen blank scan lines. The VITC signal is recorded on several of these blank scan lines.

Figure 13.24. Digital Performer Selecting the SMPTE format

In both forms of SMPTE there are several formats for counting the number of frames per second. Those formats are 24, 25, 29.97 non-drop, 29.97 drop-frame, and 30.24. The U.S. standard for film and audio is 30.24, video uses 29.97 non-drop and 29.97 drop-frame. The European film standard is 25 frames. The 30.24 format is usually shortened to 30.

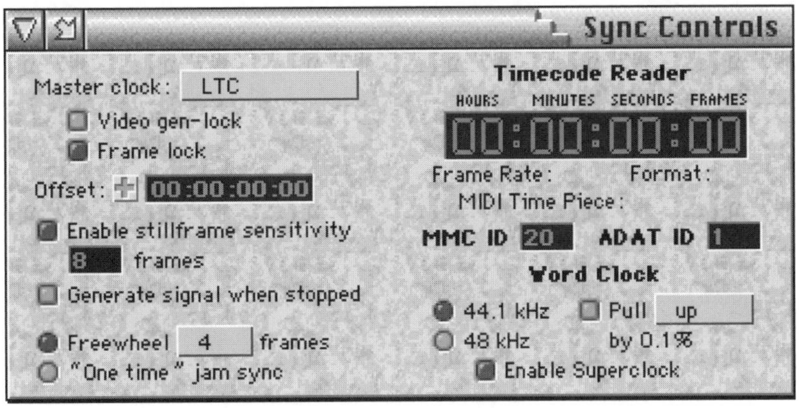

The drop-frame (see Figure 13.24) was developed for color video's frame rate is not exactly 30 frames per second. In order that SMPTE time always matches the clock time, the drop-frame code drops two frames every minute except for the tenth minute.

Figure 13.25. Digital Performer Sync Controls

If your unit can generate SMPTE, be sure to check that the proper format is selected. Failure to choose the correct format can cost time. In video productions, music is usually the last thing to be produced so there is barely enough time to do it once.

MIDI Time Code, or MTC, is LTC code that has been translated for communication over MIDI cables. This allows MIDI devices to sync operations to an external device, independent of the tempo of the music. In figure 13.26 the top number shows the bars and beats display. Underneath the bars and beats display is the elapsed time in minutes and

Figure 13.26. Digital Performer SMPTE Counter

seconds. Below that is the SMPTE or MTC counter. There are two differences however, SMPTE displays an hour number at all times. The last number in each box is also different. The Time Elapsed window displays fractions of seconds. The SMPTE or MTC window displays frames, which is a part of SMPTE Code.

The bottom number in the display (see Figure 13.26) is the number of samples. This is important digital audio data for proper placement of audio data. In the digital domain, bouncing or copying signals can effect the timing of the signal. With each transfer the signal can drift further and further out of time with the original track. The alignment of signals is measured in samples. When samples are properly aligned they are phase-coherent. When two signals are phase-coherent, they have the same frequency and the peaks and valleys of their respective waveforms are aligned in time with one other. Throw two waves of the same frequency out of alignment, or phase, and the result is that they cancel each other out and you will be left with silence. Chances are you will not get total silence because the two waveforms will not be 100 percent identical but you will end up with a comb filtering effect that destroys the final mix. If you move or transfer audio files between tracks or devices and something is not right when you play them back, the answer is almost always drift in the starting point of the sample.

Word Clock

It may be a bit confusing that several so-called syncing formats are available on the same device. Not every form of sync is truly a SMPTE type time code. Word clock deals with the timing of audio samples being transferred over S/PDIF, AES/EBU, ADAT Optical, and TDIF connections. Some of the conventions are the same as other forms of sync. One unit has to be the master, sending the clock signal to all other devices. Word clock is transmitted by a BNC cable or over the digital connection itself.

ADAT Sync

ADAT Sync uses a 9-pin connector to connect multiple ADATs together to work as a single unit with or without a BRC (big remote control). The BRC can translate between SMPTE and ADAT Sync allowing ADATs to be synced to SMPTE time code. An ADAT Sync cable carries transport commands from the master deck or BRC, a 48-kHz square wave clock, and the ADAT time code. ADAT Sync provides for a more accurate sample placement of digital events for playback and transfers. ADAT Sync is also supported by a number of third party digital audio devices. This allows ADATs to sync with other multitrack recorders, computer-based audio editors, and MIDI sequencers.

Connecting External Devices to Your Computer

As discussed in chapter 9, computers can be connected to a variety of equipment including printers, hard disks, CD-ROM drives and burners, scanners, modems, and MIDI devices. Whenever you connect devices like an external hard drive or CD-ROM burner be sure to consult the manufacturer's installation recommendations. Also check the manual and Read Me document for known conflicts with other devices and software. Be sure your computer is turned off whenever you connect or disconnect any external device.

Lessons From the School of Hard Knocks

Some of the best lessons are learned from experience. For example, in my current studio I've learned that my CD-ROM burner does not function properly when it is more than one SCSI device (see chapter 9) away from the files it is writing. Failure to observe this results in the burn stopping somewhere in process and destroying the CD I am burning (of course they do make nice drink coasters!).

Most mid- and high-end digital audio software such as Digital Performer are able to communicate with hardware samplers connected to the SCSI Network and transfer sounds to and from the unit. I was anxious to try this feature out with an AKAI S5000 sampler. Before hooking up the sampler to the SCSI chain I read the AKAI manual addendum which stopped me cold. The manual warns of a potential problem should two devices try to access the same hard drive at the same time. The result could be disastrous to the computer internal hard drive! AKAI warns of this in the manual and clearly states that they are not responsible for any data lost if there is a problem. I had to make the necessary changes to my system in order to get the hardware working.

Pro Tools recommends using a SCSI accelerator card when using external hard drives. This speeds data to and from the drive(s) so that there are no problems with recording or playing back audio data. Playing back data over a poor SCSI connection will result in clicks or pops.

These examples show how important it is to carefully consider equipment and connections in the digital studio.

Connecting a Digital Tape Deck to a Computer

With so many studios already using MDMs (see chapter 4), it is very popular to connect these decks to a computer for editing and mastering. When transferring digital audio from an MDM, DAT deck, or other digital source to a computer it is important to remember to select the computer to be either the master or the slave for the transfer. Failure to do this can result in inaccurate data transfers. For example, in my studio I have a TASCAM DA-30 DAT machine that is connected to my computer via an RCA S/PDIF connection. If I want to transfer something from a DAT tape into the computer I must set the computer to receive the data and sync the computer to the clock in the DAT machine.

When using a mid- to high-end digital audio software program there are typically several synch choices when importing audio data.

In Pro Tools II the settings must be made in the Hardware dialog box in the Setup menu. Once the data has been transferred the Sync Mode must be set to Digital so the system will use its own clock for playing back the data properly. For transferring back to the DA-30 the system will already be properly configured.

When transferring information from one digital source to another be sure to investigate how to make the proper selections in the software you are using.

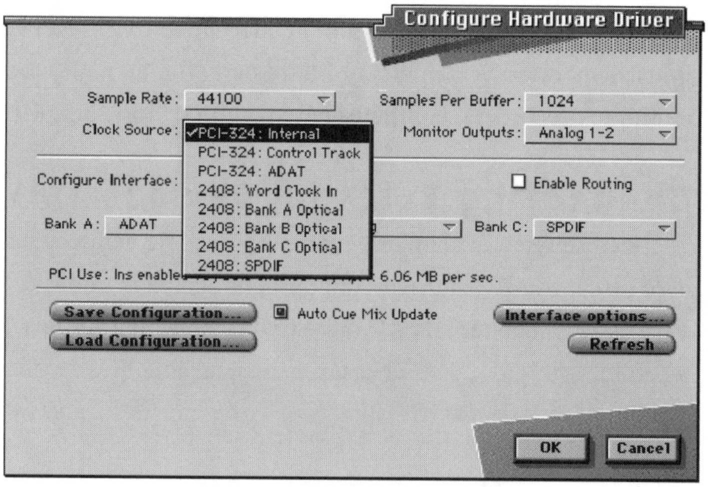

How to Use the Manual

Yes, those books that came with the equipment or software are usually sitting in pristine condition over in the corner of the room. OK, so you may have used them to locate the telephone number for technical support. Big deal! The truth is, most of those initial calls are easily avoided with a little time spent with the manual. The trick is to stay calm even though you've spent

Figure 13.27. Digital Performer Configuring the Hardware Driver

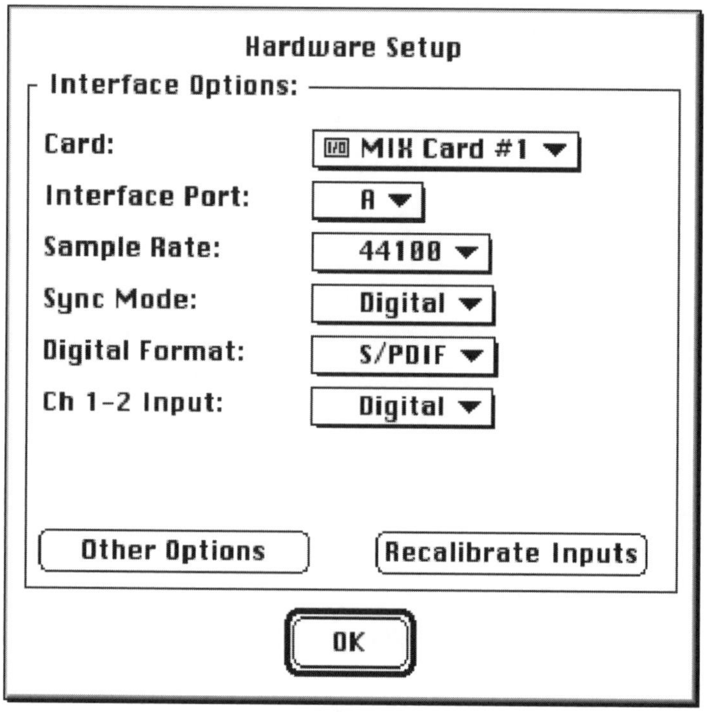

Figure 13.28. Pro Tools Hardware Setup Dialog Box

a pile of cash on a pile of gear that doesn't seem to like you very much.

Manuals can be well written and informative or they can be disorganized and confusing. No matter which type of manual you are reading, chances are the information you need is in there, but it is up to you to find it.

Manuals are not meant to be read cover to cover. The first thing you should look for is a list of included parts and cables then check to see if everything is in the box. You may find that equipment that requires audio cables may not be included and will have to be purchased separately. Once you have all the parts together, look for the installation guide. This is usually at the front of the book. Follow the directions for initial installation. This is critically important when installing PCI cards and software.

After completing the installation, look for a troubleshooting area, usually in the back of the manual. The troubleshooting guide can help you solve many common problems. For specific topics, refer to the index in the back of the manual. Many manuals also include a helpful glossary of unfamiliar terminology and acronyms.

Once your new toy, excuse me, new tax deductible piece of professional digital audio equipment, is up and running, it's time to take on the tutorials. It takes time to commit all operations to memory, so be patient. Explore a little bit at a time and read new sections. Go back and review areas as needed. Don't be afraid to explore. Most of all, if you don't know what it does, look it up.

When you can't solve a problem, the next step is to call customer support. The number is usually printed in the front of the manual. Another option is to go to the company Web site and send an email message. Many times this is an efficient method and is much less expensive than a long distance phone call.

Summary

The first step in connecting the gear in the studio is to place the equipment in the best location. It is important to consider both digital and analog patch bays to facilitate these connections. In the computer world, special connections need to be made in order to be able to use the installed equipment and software. The proper interface must also be selected. Special synchronization issues must be dealt with including SMPTE and others. Computers are frequently used to connect to various types of digital equipment and recording decks and again, important settings must be considered. Using the manual effectively is also helpful to gaining knowledge and confidence with your gear.

Chapter 14.
Setting Up and Tracking a Digital Recording Session

Once all the equipment has been purchased, placed into the studio, wired up, and powered on (whew!) it is time to start making music. A recording session is much more than twiddling knobs or clicking mouse buttons. It is an event that calls for the skills of a manager, roadie, technician, artist, diplomat, accountant, and collection agent. Running a well-managed recording session will go a long way toward a successful end product.

For a recording session to run smoothly, a fair amount of setup and preparation is required. This begins with the recording space, and placing items such as chairs, music stands, baffles, microphones, and other studio gear. The next step is to check that all equipment is in good working condition and the necessary recording materials are on hand. Other considerations include preparing the session paperwork, and including track sheets and log sheets. Any blank media used will require a label. Computer-based hard disk systems should be organized in clearly labeled folders. Once the basic setup is completed, you will need to spend time configuring your software and hardware for the session. We'll begin by reviewing an overall checklist and then conclude by reviewing the various software and hardware setup considerations.

The Pre-Session Checklist

Ideally, recording surprises will be limited to the music. Remember that the devil is in the details so if there are a hundred details on your list, check them all in advance and don't stop at 99 because the last one will be the one that sinks you. Always spend time in preproduction working out the technical requirements. Make sure all the details are checked and any repairs or changes are made before the musicians arrive.

Chasing down technical problems is frustrating and time consuming. Your clients pay for your expertise in recording them, not troubleshooting your gear. That's why I recommend getting everything up and running before anyone arrives. This doesn't mean every session will go off without a hitch, but it will minimize the things that can go wrong. Of course, once the musicians have loaded in and set up, other needs arise.

Airline pilots have checklists for every phase of a flight. Every system is checked to make sure it is active and properly set before it is needed. This is done on every flight so that no detail is ever overlooked. The same philosophy can be applied in the recording studio. Make a checklist you can run before each session to verify that every detail is ready. Here are some suggestions to start with: customize them for your own studio and use them in the planning stage for every session.

Some of these tips are not exactly high-end digital technology, but all of them are very smart. Since you are obviously smart enough to purchase the latest in recording technology, being on top of the details will only make you look even more like a genius.

• *Is the main recorder in optimal condition?* To make the best possible recording, the recording device must be in excellent working order. For analog recorders this means cleaning the recording and playback heads and checking the alignment. In digital recording it translates into several paths depending on the media you are using.

For MDMs, follow the manufacturer's suggested guidelines regarding regular cleaning of recording heads and of the transport mechanism. Be sure to use a tape brand recommended by the manufacturer. It is not necessary to clean the heads before every session, but keep a log of the time the deck has been running and follow the manufacturer's suggested guidelines for cleaning. This information is in the owner's manual.

For removable media, make sure there is plenty of room on the disk so the session is not interrupted by the disk filling to capacity. Keep a fresh disk available just in case the disk you are using fills up during a long session.

For the computer's hard disk, clear as much storage space a possible. Back up or delete any old files left from previous sessions that are not needed for the current session.

• *Which microphones will be needed for the session?* Select the microphones for whatever instruments or vocals you are planning to record. Make sure they are clean and in good working order. Test each mic before setting up for the session. Make sure selector switches on the mic such as pad, roll off, or pickup patterns are in the proper position. If the microphone requires an internal battery, be sure to have a spare on hand.

• *How many microphone stands are required?* The mic stands need to be sturdy so they will not fall over if accidentally bumped. Boom stands must also be secure so they do not fall down, or completely off, whenever they are adjusted. Make sure any extensions used are securely tightened at the proper height and are firmly held. Nothing is more annoying to a musician than a perpetually sinking mic stand. If all you'll ever do is record one musician at a time then get one quality stand. If your studio is large enough for several musicians, have a stand for every mic you own.

• *How many microphone cables are required and which lengths should be used?* Check the mic cables to make sure they are working properly. Always try to make the cable runs as short as possible, but not at the risk of creating safety hazards that could cause someone to trip and fall. Remember to secure the excess cord around the microphone stand.

• *Will any other cables be required?* Keep a stock of quarter-inch cables in varying lengths on hand. It may be better to use your own cables in the studio with visiting musicians since their cables may have been in the back of their van too long and may be a bit worn and thus prone to be noisy.

• *How many power cords will need to be plugged in?* Here's one of the often forgotten details of setting up, especially if recording on location. Get into the habit of having a power strip or two on hand at all times, and don't leave home without them! A few long, heavy duty extension cords are also recommended.

• *Are there any other materials needed?* For all long cable runs it helps to have plenty of duct tape to secure the cables wherever there may be foot traffic. Duct tape is like The Force in *Star Wars*: It has a light and a dark side, and it binds the universe together. Even better than duct tape is *gaffers* tape, which won't leave a sticky residue on your cables or damage your floor.

• *How many music stands are needed?* As with mic stands, quality equipment will help make the session run smoothly. A quality metal music stand will not fall over easily in the middle of a take. To reduce noise, place a piece of felt, a towel, or a piece of carpet on the stand to quiet the shuffling of papers and the natural ring of the metal stand. This material can be glued to the stand or secured by other means such as butterfly clamps.

• *How many chairs are needed?* Even if a musician stands for playing or singing, it's nice to have a chair to rest in during playbacks. If the musician is going to play while seated, make sure the chair does not squeak. Office chairs with casters are a bad idea for the studio. Proper mic placement in relation to the instrument is essential for maintaining proximity to the mic. If the musician can easily move the sound will change making overdubs difficult. A basic, padded armless chair, similar to those used in hotel conference rooms, will do nicely. Having a stool available is also a good idea since it is often the best thing for acoustic guitarists.

• *What additional equipment belonging to the studio will be required for the session?* This can include musical instruments, specific pieces of outboard gear or a PlayStation™. Whatever it is, make sure it is in good working order before the client arrives.

• *Did you remember to clean the bathroom?* 'Nuff said!

• *I forgot my tuner, do you have one?* Portable tuners are a staple for electric guitar and bass players. Occasionally a player may arrive without one. Having an electronic tuner on hand will help speed the session along. Some digital recorders can generate an A 440, which will do in a pinch. If overdubs of acoustic instruments are planned, record some tuning notes from a keyboard or tuner so the instrumentalist can tune to the notes on the tape. Drums need tuning too! Have a drum key on hand for drum tweaking.

• *Do you have any water?* Singers and voice-over readers need to keep their throats from drying out during the session. Many bring a supply of bottled water with them, but have a glass or bottle of water handy for them just in case. Keep it at room temperature, do not chill it. Warm water is better for the throat than cold. Some performers may request hot water. Fill a mug and heat it in the microwave as you would water for a cup of tea.

• *Can I write on this? Oh, can I borrow your pencil?* If sheet music, lead sheets, or lyric sheets are being used make sure every musician has a copy he can write on and provide each musician with a pencil. Even if you've given the musicians copies in advance, have extra copies ready for the session just in case someone forgot his copy. After all, these are musicians we are talking about. Pick up a box of No. 2 pencils so time is not wasted while one pencil, usually yours, makes the rounds every time notes are given.

• *How many instruments and vocals will be needed on the song?* Musical preproduction can take place long before the musicians arrive or while they are setting up, but it is a good idea to review the requirements for each song. The most important consideration is the number of available tracks in a small studio. It is usually limited so it is very easy to end up painted into a corner once the ideas begin flowing.

In a 24-track or 48-track environment the drum set alone can take up to ten tracks. Even with 24-tracks, a complex song can still cause some problems with track space before recording is complete. Be sure to ask about solos, additional guitar tracks, vocals, double lead vocals, background vocals, and any effects. There is always the chance someone will want to "try something" without erasing a previous track. With virtual tracks on most hard disk systems this is very easy. On tape-based systems it may not be possible to keep both tracks. Allocating tracks in advance will prevent a lot of frustration. Send a stereo mix of the drum set to tape instead of a track for each mic. "Virtual track" any MIDI tracks. Virtual tracking is the process of syncing a MIDI sequencer to the recorder so that it plays in time with tracks recorded on the tape. This frees up tracks on the tape for live instruments and vocals. Instead of recording an instrument in stereo, try recording it on one track, panning it to one side and routing it to a digital delay set for a 10-millisecond delay. Pan the return from the delay to the opposite side of the mix. Part of the challenge of the project studio is finding ways around limits. Be creative!

If budget is a consideration, determining the number of hours required and the number of musicians to be paid should also be worked out up front.

• *What additional keyboard sounds will be needed?* Keyboard players with large collections of sounds need to organize before a session so the exact sounds required are easily located and loaded. The keyboard player should prepare a list of required sounds and which disks, cards, or cartridges are needed. It may also be helpful to keep a list of favorite sounds such as leads, pads, and keyboards in case a new sound is requested during the session.

• *What samples will be needed?* If samples or loops are being used for the session, ready them in the same way as the keyboard sounds. If it is possible to edit or process them in advance, do it. If there is a question about obtaining legal clearance for use of a copyrighted sound sample, this should also be done well in advance of the session.

• *Will a click or click track be needed?* This can be a touchy subject unless the musicians are experienced in playing to a click. If you are recording an ensemble or rhythm section together, there may not be as great a need for a click track unless the musicians are having difficulty keeping time. If the recording is being constructed by overdubbing each instrument, then a click track is usually necessary to keep the tempo constant while each track is added.

A click track will be necessary if MIDI tracks are to be combined with live performance. MIDI sequences can be programmed for small fluctuations in the tempo to make the overall speed more natural, but they still require that the musicians play in a strict and perfect time to sound correct. A click track will also be necessary if the material will be performed live with a taped accompaniment. The click can come from a metronome, drum machine, MIDI sequencer, or digital audio software. In most cases only the drummer will need to play to the click; everyone else will play to the drum recording.

Remember to always record a count off, whether or not you are using a click. Without one, any overdubbing instrumentalist will be guessing where the first beat of the track is, and the tempo will most likely be tentative for the first few bars. Use the 1-2-3-4-1-2 count where the last two numbers are silent, so there is no extraneous noise on the track. Be careful with the volume of the click, because if it is too loud it will bleed from the headphones back into the mics, and on to all live tracks.

Session Paperwork

One point I can't stress enough is to accurately log your session. This begins with a track sheet for the multitrack recorder. At the top of the track sheet there is a lot of basic information like the date, name of the song, tempo, project, studio, client, producer, engineer, and assistant engineer. This information can be very helpful later on in assembling accurate album credits. Also logged are the number or name of the

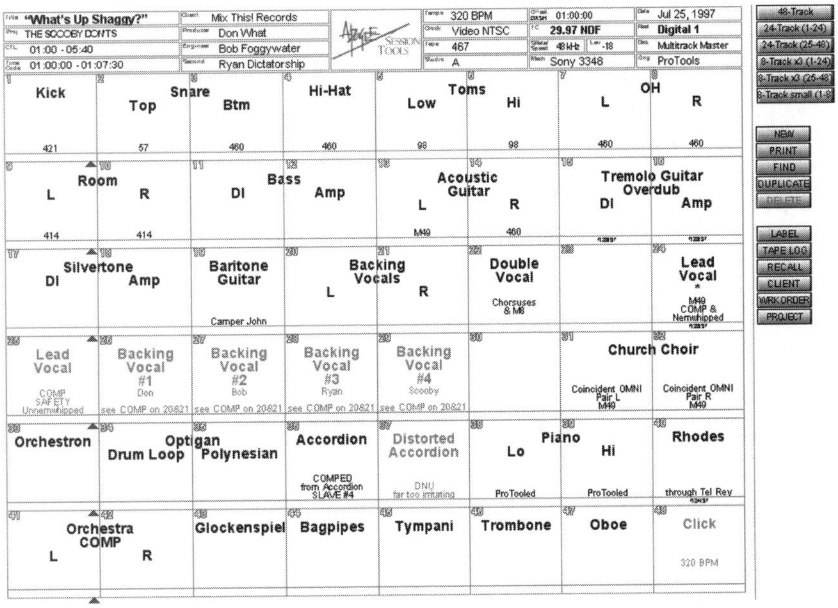

Figure 14.1. Track Sheet from Session Tools Software

tape the song is on, its counter location and any time code or clock information. For digital recordings the sample rate is listed. For analog recordings the tape speed would be logged.

Figure 14.1 shows a sample track sheet. This one is from Apogee's Session Tools software. Each box on the track sheet corresponds to a track on the multitrack recorder. In each box, fill in the name of the instrument being recorded on that track. This way you will be able to manage your tracks and instantly know how many are available for use. The track sheet is also a place to log other information relevant to the recording, like the mics or external effects used, and any tracks that have been edited or composited. Musicians' names can be indicated, as can additional recording dates for overdub sessions. If you have multiple takes of a track, say a vocal, indicate which track is to be used. Mark any tracks that will definitely not be used with the indication TBE (for "to be erased") so they can be wiped and used for something else if necessary.

Keeping all this information may seem unnecessary in a small studio, but let me assure you, it will save you a lot of time and spare you frustration. The more things you are trying to do yourself, the less focused you are on each one. All it takes is selecting the wrong track and accidentally erasing something once to learn that the hard way. A well-kept track sheet is a must if you work with another person on the project, take the project to another studio, or go back to it after it's left your short-term memory.

Let's take a closer look at Apogee's Session Tools software. This package is designed for professional recording studios and not only tracks session information like track sheets and effects logging, but also handles tape labeling, tape logging, billing, client contact information, and equipment repair. Storing records in the computer will help cut down on the paper pile in your studio but remember to regularly back up these files.

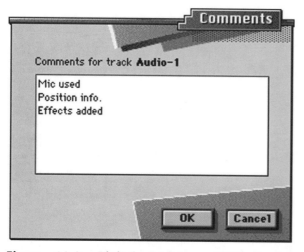

Figure 14.2. Digital Performer MIDI Track Comments Window

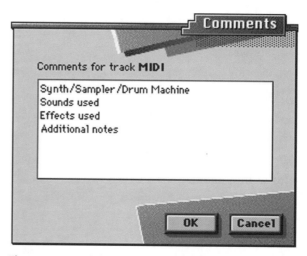

Figure 14.3. Digital Performer Audio Track Comments Window

Figure 14.4. Digital Performer Tracks Window

If you are working with a computer-based system, you will be able to manage your tracks by naming them on screen. MIDI/digital audio sequencers allow you to enter comments for each audio or MIDI track so that information on each track may be logged.

Figure 14.4 shows how the information is displayed in the tracks window of Digital Performer.

I recently went back to a project I had completed six years ago to update a tape for a client. The sequencer files were a mess of chunks, rehearsal tracks, discarded tracks, and final tracks. The musical director I originally worked with on the project had left and was working on a cruise ship, so I was on my own in reconstructing the song files. Fortunately, I had made detailed notes on the MIDI setup used for the recording so I knew which synths and sounds were used and what MIDI track was used for which data. So, I was able to quickly reassign tracks for the sounds I am currently using without too much trouble.

When recording multiple takes in a session, a take sheet is used to log information about each take. A take sheet, not to be confused with a track sheet, can be a specially printed form or simply a sheet of notepaper. First log the take number and start times of the take as it appears on the tape counter. If there is any start ID or memory locator information, log that as well. Then list what is being recorded, followed by any comments on the take made by the producer. Comments would mention any obvious mistakes as well as sections that are usable. Sometimes a performer makes a mistake at the beginning and starts over rather than waiting for the tape to stop and be rewound. This is logged as a false start. Once a take has been chosen, indicate clearly which take is to be used.

A time-log sheet would only be necessary if you were doing work for a paying client and needed to track the session time and any other billing related information, such as the amount of blank media used.

Start labeling tapes at the beginning of their use and add new information as you begin each new song. The same goes for Zip or Jaz disks or any other devices that you use to save data to removable media.

Setting Up the Mixer

The first thing to do when you sit down at your mixer is to make sure all input signals are routed to the proper channel strips. Check the gain level on the mixer to ensure your cables are providing a clean signal. Next, label your channels. Use a piece of white removable tape to create a scribble strip if your mixer does not have one. I use 3M 6-Line Correction and Cover-up Tape in my studio. It's large enough to write on and is not hard to remove after the session. I've also seen artist's tape and removable masking tape used. Boards with scribble strips use a china marker to write in the names; the markings can be removed with a cloth or paper towel.

This section contains screen shots from Digital Performer and Pro Tools Software. This is partly to demonstrate the features of these packages and partially to provide visual examples. However the concepts are the same, regardless of which software or hardware you may be using.

For most computer-based systems, you will need

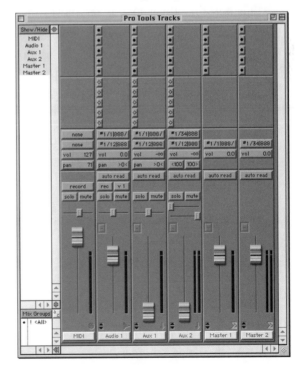

Figure 14.5. Pro Tools Mix Window Channel types

159

to create and name the proper number of tracks. Figure 14.5 shows the type of tracks available in Pro Tools. You can create MIDI tracks, audio tracks, mono and stereo aux tracks, and mono and stereo master tracks. Build your mixer first, including aux and master faders, so that you have all the flexibility of a large console right from the start. You can add any type of channel as you go, so you'll never paint yourself into a corner.

If you are using a MIDI/digital audio sequencer there are similar options. Figure 14.6 shows Digital Performer's mixer view. In addition to MIDI tracks it also has mono and stereo audio file tracks, mono and stereo aux

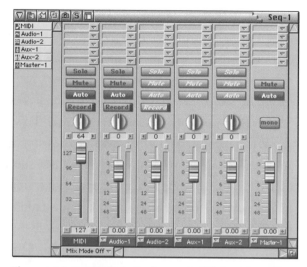

Figure 14.6. Digital Performer's Mixing Console Channel Types

send tracks, and a stereo master track with a mono button for checking mono compatibility. After creating your channels, check the cable routings to make sure the signal is reaching the proper channel and that the gain level is acceptable.

Software offers the option to create templates and save them for future use. Once the number of tracks is set up and labeled, save the document with an easily identifiable name. Lock the files so they cannot be accidentally overwritten. Then, at the start of each new session or song, call up the template and immediately save the file.

Getting the proper tone is the most time consuming part of a recording session. It takes time and critical listening to tweak EQs and get the right level of compression for a good sound. Take advantage of being able to save that information in your mixer so that you have a starting point for each new session.

Once you've confirmed the signal path into your mixer, it will need to be routed to the proper recorder track. You will have to look at the signal level going to the tape or hard disk. Digital has a lot of recording and editing flexibility but it is totally unforgiving when it comes to peaking the meters while recording. This may mean relearning some habits when it comes to setting the levels going to the recorder. Read on for the laws, loopholes, and penalties of digital zero.

Digital Zero

When setting the gain for digital recording there is one absolute barrier that cannot be broken: the top indicator on a digital recorder, 0 dB. With analog recorders, wandering into the

Figure 14.7. ADAT LED Display

red zone means analog tape compression or some distortion. Both have been used as effects in many pop and rock recordings. However, pinning the meters on a digital recorder results in an unpleasant noise sounding like a combination of static and feedback. Unlike loud analog signals that can be brought down by compressors and fader controls, there is no way of fixing this once it is on tape. The digital rule of thumb is to err on the conservative side with your levels when recording someone live. The same goes for mixing to a digital 2-track machine unless the mix is automated. Tracking sequenced sounds provides the safety net of backing up and trying again if you peak.

The relative accuracy of your meters is something you'll become aware of using your equipment. In my experience there are certain sounds that will occasionally light up the red LED on my ADAT that do not result in digital noise. These sounds contain a lot of high frequencies, like cymbals, or low frequencies, like synth basses. There is a small amount of headroom built-in to many recorders. Think of it as the extra few gallons in your car's gas tank after the indicator hits E. You can survive an occasional peak but don't make a habit of living on the edge because sooner or later it will get you. During mixdown I've experienced DAT decks that have metered a perfectly safe level during a trial mix but peaked during the actual mixdown with no change in volume. Playing back the DAT usually indicates the recording is fine. Once again, don't assume. Listen carefully, and maybe back the level down a hair.

Main and Monitor Mixes

While recording the basic tracks, you will need to create a basic mix to listen to in the control room while other tracks are being recorded. If you are tracking live musicians you will need to create a monitor, or headphone mix. This allows the musicians to hear each other and the track as they record.

Digital recording consoles and software make it easy to copy the main mix to use as a basis for the monitor mix. The levels of the monitor mix may vary from musician to musician. A drummer might need a lot of bass to keep the feel tight, while singers need more keyboard or guitar for better pitch. Always make sure that the singer hears plenty of the vocal. If they are struggling with pitch or diction take that as a sign to

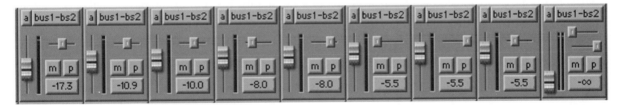

Figure 14.8. Pro Tools Headphone Mix Window

boost the vocal a little in the headphones. Some mixers can simultaneously output several monitor mixes, each of which can be adjusted according to the preferences of the musician. Other systems are limited to a single mix for everyone. Check the specifications before purchasing if this is a priority for your studio.

Getting the monitor mix to the musicians in the studio can take several routes. If the mixer has a dedicated headphone output, this can be routed directly to a single performer. For recording more than one person at a time, the signal will need to be split. The simple solution is a headphone amplifier. This takes the signal from the mixer and feeds it into a number of outputs, each with its own volume control. With this setup only one monitor mix can be used for all musicians.

If more aux sends are available it is possible to send the mix out in sub groups to smaller mixers in the studio that the musicians themselves control. Using a small 4-channel mixer, it is possible to separate drums, bass, and vocals off onto separate tracks so the players can adjust levels themselves.

The Tracking (Recording) Session

Now that the engineer is ready and the musicians are ready, it's time to start recording. Have the musicians play down the song while fine tuning the gain for each input. The goal is to get the strongest, clearest signal possible to the recorder without distortion. As the musicians get warmed up chances are the decibel level will go up a little. Watch for this and make adjustments as needed.

At each level there are challenges to overcome and techniques to help you get the most out of your system. Following is an overview of each level as well as the process of tracking a recording.

Tracking with Entry-Level Systems

Working with entry level gear means working around limits. This can cause frustration and help foster creativity all in the same session. Remember that the Beatles set the standard for pop studio production with 4-track machines. We've become very spoiled with technology in the studio but don't let the focus shift from the product we are recording.

Portable Hard Disk Recording

Obviously, the number of tracks is a big concern. Plan in advance as much as possible: I can't stress that enough. It is no fun to be trapped by poor or inadequate planning and that's very easy to do. Here are some ways around this limitation.

The process of overdubbing originally meant recording extra parts over an existing track. It has expanded to include pop recording begun with a click track and built from the drum track up, one or two parts at a time. I recommend keeping overdubs to a minimum. Recording the basic rhythm section all together helps with groove and can be done on as few as two tracks. Even if there are some minor flaws, that "in the pocket" feel can do more for the track than the pristine perfection of each part, as long as there are no major train wrecks or obvious clams. Overdub the vocals, background vocals, and any prominent instrumental solos. These will be the performances that are most noticeable and the tracks you'll need to control in the final mix.

If there is a MIDI sequencer in the studio, do not record the keyboard parts onto the multitrack recorder. Instead, use a technique called virtual tracks: sync the sequencer to the recorder so live players can play with the sequencer's tracks. This increases the track capacity of your studio by adding the MIDI tracks to the number of tracks on the recorder. The only limit would then be the number of input channels on the mixer. Live instruments or vocals can be recorded in perfect sync with the MIDI tracks allowing more recorder tracks for live performances. The keyboard parts are then mixed with the live performances during the mixdown to stereo. Keeping the keyboards separate allows greater control of levels for blending and for adding any processing or effects in the final mix.

Multiple Takes

The final performance of any part does not have to be a perfect performance, or take, from beginning to end. Let's say that you have a take that is generally acceptable except for a few portions. There are two ways of dealing with these flaws, punching or compositing.

In the punching process the flawed section of the track is recorded over while the performer plays or sings the part again. This process can be repeated until the performance is good enough. There are two concerns with this process, one technical and one artistic. The technical concern is in finding a space in the performance to begin the new recording and a place to stop recording. The punch needs to begin where there is a significant pause or rest in the material. Before punching the vocal, listen for the vocalist's breathing. When performing a punch, or any kind of editing, it is important to remember that you are editing sound, not just a musical performance. That sound includes noises made by the performer, such as lip smacks and breaths that sometimes fill up the space between musical phrases. Clipping off a breath or any other noise when going into, or out of record may be the number one reason some punches do not work. I'll give some tips on how to avoid this, and the punching process overall, in the next section. On the artistic side, repeating a part over and over can result in a mechanical performance. The quest for technical perfection can often leave the proper musical feeling in second place. The challenge to the performer is to maintain the proper feeling, while working on delivery, pitch, timing, or whatever else made the take unacceptable.

Punching Practices—Not the Marquis du Queensbury Rules

The following tips apply to punching on any recorder format. Hard disk recorders are a bit different since the punch will be assembled as a composite. However, the tips listed below still apply since they deal with getting the best musical and technical performance to edit.

1. Work with the performer on the amount of pre-roll before recording. Pre-roll is the amount of the track played before punching in. Too long of a pre-roll can cause the performer to lose focus before the recording starts; too little can catch the performer off guard, or not allow them to get into the proper feel. Determine what feels best before starting to record each section.

2. Make sure the performer maintains the same distance and proximity to the microphone as in the original recording so that the sound of the performance will match the existing track.

3. Have the performer sing or play along with the track during the pre-roll and post-roll to preserve the phrasing or breathing at the in and out points. This gives a more natural feel and helps match the dynamic, or volume, of the existing track.

4. If the performer is struggling with a particular phrase, frustration may set in. If you recognize this, take a break. Taking five minutes at the right time can save hours of studio time.

5. Both engineer and performer should rehearse punches when there is little space at the in-and-out points. The performer may have to pay particular attention to cutting off notes to match the existing track and to allow the engineer time to punch out before the next phrase.

6. Tell the performer to always keep playing or singing until the music stops! Occasionally the engineer will miss-hit a button and remain in record. If the performer keeps going the punch can be saved and the engineer will get out at the next logical break in the performance. Dinner is usually on the engineer at this point.

Assembling Composites

The second method of constructing a final performance is called compositing. In this method the performer will record the track from beginning to end several times on different tracks. The exact number of tracks recorded is arbitrary. The goal is to assemble the final performance by choosing the best sections of each take and copying it to a new track. Having a large number of tracks aids this process since the physical limitation of track numbers will dictate how many performances can be recorded. A digital recorder's virtual tracks are excellent for this process since the unused audio can be discarded in the end.

My only rule for this process, and it's an important one, is to make all determinations concerning the final performance before touching the microphone, mixer, or effects settings. This is a precaution in case another performance is needed. It is essential that the technical settings be the same for each section of the performance to match the audio quality.

The reason for using a composite approach instead of punching in is to preserve the intensity and emotion of a whole performance. Those feelings can get lost when repeatedly working over a single section or line as with a punch.

Tracking with Mid-Level Gear

On this level I'll assume that MDMs, modular hard disk, or a mid-level computer-based system is being used for recording. A limited track count is still an issue but there are more ways for working around it. If you are upgrading from entry-level equipment, the skills I've mentioned in the previous section will serve you well in any situation. I've been in sessions where having twenty-four tracks was limiting. Necessity is always the mother of invention, so don't restrict your creative thinking to the music.

MDM Systems

Modular recorders are straightforward to use, no different from their analog predecessors. As long as the machine is kept in good working order, the session will go without a hitch.

The total number of tracks available will dictate a lot of your decisions. Having eight tracks usually means that the drums get mixed to two tracks, but if you're overdubbing, they can be recorded to six tracks, then bounced to two tracks later. TASCAM machines with internal mixing features can do this internally. Combining an ADAT with a lightpipe equipped multi-effects device such as the Alesis Q2 allows digital bouncing while effects are added in the same process. This leaves one fewer track to be processed when mixing. If the setup includes a sequencer and keyboards, it is possible to use the virtual track technique described earlier in this chapter, and sync the recorder to the sequencer. This allows all of the recorders tracks to be used for live performers. In my studio this is accomplished by using a J. L. Cooper Data Sync that receives the ADAT's clock data and converts it to MIDI Time Code. This signal is carried by MIDI cable to the computer sequencer through the MTP AV. Digital Performer is set to receive sync, and is then controlled by the ADAT's transport controls throughout the recording process.

Locate Points

On the front panel of all Alesis and TASCAM machines are buttons for locate points. These buttons can be assigned to any time on the tape. After the point has been assigned, pressing the button will cause the transport to wind the tape to that point, or time, on the tape. Using locate points at the beginning of a song or just before the section being worked on can save a lot of time finding the correct place on the tape. Hard disk based systems have spoiled us regarding rewind time. Though it will never be instantly accessible, locate points can help take some of the drudge out of tape-based recording.

Portable Studios

The studio-in-a box approach is not just for entry level any more. Some of latest units, such as the Yamaha AW4416 and the AKAI DPS16I offer substantial recording and mixing power in a single, portable unit.

The Yamaha AW4416 can be expanded to handle sixteen tracks of simultaneous recording on internal hard disks of up to 64 GB. Available bit rates for recording are 16 and 24, at either 44.1-kHz or 48-kHz sampling rates. There's even 90 seconds of sampling memory and eight trigger pads for adding beats or effects. The mixer section is the equivalent of an O2R digital mixer complete with motorized faders. Mixdown can be handled internally and there is an option for an internal CD-RW drive to burn the results without ever connecting anything but the power cord. Optional expansions include digital connections to MDMs so the portable studio can be used as field units for everything from cutting basic tracks to final mixing on the road.

Computer-Based Hard Disk Recording

At the entry-level (see chapter 6) it is possible to use the computer's built-in sound capabilities. In this case you will be limited to one or two tracks, stereo or mono, of sound. There is no way to monitor a previously recorded track while recording a new one without adding a sound card with full-duplex capability.

Mid-level hard disk systems are the hottest thing on the market as of this writing. The MOTU

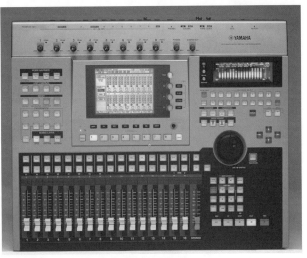

Figure 14.9 Yamaha AW4416 DAW

1208 system and the Digi 001 and other similar systems have dipped below the $1,000 mark with powerful capabilities that were ten times more expensive just a few short years ago. All this digital power means there are a few new things to learn and some things to be aware of before you start working with digital hard disk recording systems.

The first item of business is always to make sure the interface is properly configured. If the sample rate and bit rate are selectable, make sure they are set correctly. Pro Tools LE presents a dialog box when a new file, or session, is created that will set the session's bit depth. Bit depths cannot be mixed. Once a session is begun at a specific bit depth, all sound files must be at the same bit depth to play back properly. Remember that the bit depth for standard audio CDs is 16-bit. Using 24-bit depth for tracking is possible, but the final mix must eventually be converted to 16-bit before an audio CD can be burned; more about this in chapter 18.

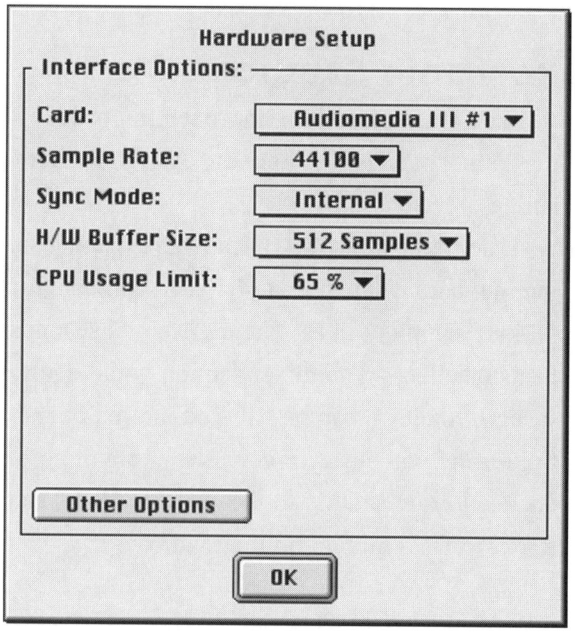

Once the bit depth is set, the resolution or sample rate must be set. This is usually a part of the hardware setup, or settings for the computer card or interface. The sample rate for audio CDs is 44,100 hZ, or 44.1 kHz. The same rules apply for sample rate as with bit depth. The entire

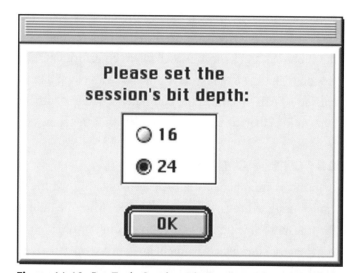

Figure 14.10. Pro Tools Session Bit-Depth Setting Dialog Box

Figure 14.11. Pro Tools LE Hardware Setup Dialog Box

session must be at the same resolution or the audio files will not play back properly. Audio CD data must be at 44.1 kHz and 16-bit depth to play properly on any commercial CD player. Figure 14.11 shows the Hardware Setup dialog box for Pro Tools LE. The bit depth is set when creating a new session and the sampling rate is set separately.

The next setting to deal with is the Sync Mode or Clock Source. In the previous chapter, I mentioned the importance of setting the proper clock source for connecting computer hard disk recorders to other digital audio sources such as DAT decks. This is also true for connecting to digital microphones, MDMs, and any other digital medium that involves real-time transfer of audio data.

Any digital device playing a sound can be set as the source for clock or sync data. If recording an analog source, such as a cassette deck, or recording live players in a tracking session, the sync or clock should be set on internal. Failure to properly set the clock source will affect the audio data in several different ways. Audio will play back pitched up or pitched down, or it will have sporadic little white noise bursts in it. Pitch problems are usually the result of external sync during playback instead of internal sync. In this case, the files are all right and correcting the sync setting will fix the problem. If there are white noise bursts in the

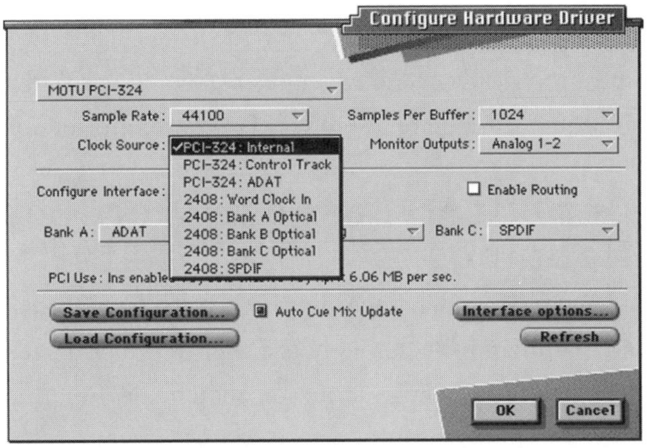

Figure 14.12. MOTU 2408 Hardware Driver Configuration Dialog Box

recorded files it indicates that the sync was improperly set during recording. In this case the damage occurred during recording and the files cannot be fixed.

Managing Hard Disk Space

Another factor to consider is the actual hard disk being used for recording. Digital audio files can be quite large and the software will stop recording in mid-take if it runs out of storage space on the drive. If there is less than a gigabyte of space left on the computer's internal drive, consider purchasing another drive solely for digital recording use. Any drive will fill up over time and eventually space will be tight. Fortunately, there is a way to calculate just how much room, in file size, a newly recorded file will need. This will require a little math but you can handle it. The equation looks like this:

Sample Rate * Duration (in seconds) * (Resolution/8) * Number of Tracks = Size of the Audio Files

The first two calculations of the equation give the total number of samples for the file. For example, to calculate the space required to record a new 60-second track at 16/44.1 kHz, multiply the sampling rate (16) by the duration (60 seconds) and that comes to a total of 960 samples. Next, take the resolution (44,100) and divide by 8. Computer data is not measured in samples but in 8-bit words called bytes, so dividing by 8 converts from digital audio numbers to computer numbers. The computer number for the resolution is 5512.5. Multiply the number of samples (960) by 5512.5 and you have the file size in bytes, 5,292,000, for one track of digital audio data. From there on, it's computer numbers; 1,024 bytes is a kilobyte (K), 1,024 kilobytes is a megabyte (MB), and 1,024 megabytes is a gigabyte (GB). If you are recording more than a single track, the number will need to be multiplied by the number of tracks.

Backing-Up Audio Files from the Hard Disk

Backing up files at the end of a session is a good habit to acquire. Blank CDs are now cheaper than analog cassettes, making them an economical storage medium. For active projects at 3 IPS we use CD-RWs to back up after each session. Removable media such as Jaz or Zip disks are also good for this purpose. Mark the date each archive was made so there is no confusion over which set of files is the most recent. Once the backup is made and verified, the files can be dumped from the hard disk if room is required for another project. For more information on backup systems see chapter 9.

Computer-Based System Capabilities—Old Terms, New Meanings

Many familiar recording terms are used to describe the elements and functions of digital audio so that the new technology is easier to grasp. That's why digital audio programs use terms like tracks and channels. These terms do match the functions, but for judging the actual capabilities of the system, they are a bit inaccurate.

In the analog world, a track is the area on which a signal is recorded on a strip of magnetic tape. A stereo machine records and plays back two tracks at a time. Since physical space on the recording head and magnetic tape was involved, more tracks meant wider heads and tape. It also meant more electronics to manage all those tracks for both recording and playback. This is not only apparent in the size difference between 2-track and 24-track machines, but also the cost of the machine. The number of tracks a studio had involved prestige and the mark of being a professional recording facility. The largest analog tape machine available is twenty-four tracks so any professional level studio would have to have at least one 24-track machine.

When sequencers were introduced they used the term "track" to refer to the individual streams of MIDI data that were recorded. These tracks weren't physical in any way, just a familiar term attached to a way of separating data. The term track is also used by computer-based digital recorders for the way they separated data. This is fine for describing the interface but the total track count becomes a bit misleading. Computer-based hard disk recorders in the mid- to high-end all use either a computer card, or combination of computer card and interface setup, for analog-to-digital conversion when recording, and digital-to-analog conversion for playback. The interface capabilities are what control the number of tracks available, not the software itself. This is indicated as the number of voices that the interface supports. The software may support an unlimited number of audio tracks and allow recording until the hard disk is full, but playback will be limited to the number of voices specified by the interface and/or card. This is similar to polyphony in the electronic keyboard world, where

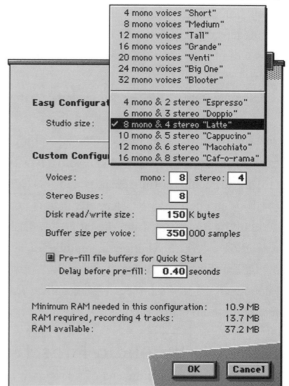

Figure 14.13. Audio Desk/Digital Performer Voice Configuration Dialog Box

the instrument has a maximum number of sounds and when that number is exceeded, the oldest sounds are cut off.

MOTU's Audio Suite or Digital Performer, running on the 2408 system, has a maximum of thirty-two voices, which can be split up between stereo and mono tracks. The 2408 is a computer-based system, also referred to as host-based. Its power is relative to the computer's power. This means that the software uses the computer's processors and RAM for all digital audio handling. This differs from systems such as Pro Tools that use a card in the computer for all of the digital audio processing. At the bottom of the dialog box in figure 14.13, the RAM requirements are listed for each voice configuration selected. The top two numbers display in red if the amount of RAM required exceeds the bottom number, which is the total RAM available to the application.

Channels are to mixers what tracks are to tape decks. Large format mixing consoles are the hallmark of top pro studios. Turn off the control room lights and they become the best Christmas light display on the block. With Pro Tools LE, I can easily create a 24-channel, 8-bus mixer with five sends and five inserts per channel. However, the Digi 001 interface does not have twenty-four inputs to feed those twenty-four tracks, so recording to them all simultaneously is impossible. The Digi 001 can play back twenty-four tracks of audio, but the interface only supports a maximum of eighteen tracks. Depending upon your needs, the interface specifications may be more important than the specifications of the software.

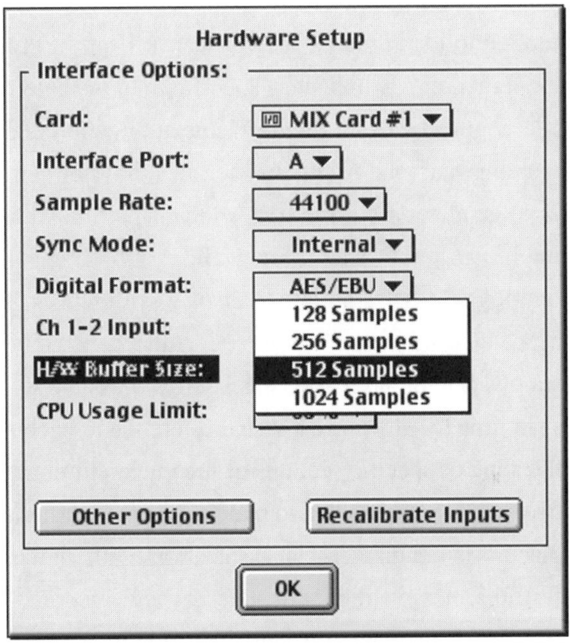

One issue when using a computer or host-based system with both MIDI and digital audio is latency. The first four letters of the word indicate what the problem is—events occurring

Figure 14.14. Pro Tools LE buffer dialog box

later than expected. In MIDI connections, this is when there is a noticeable delay between pressing a key and hearing sound. In digital audio, it is when different audio tracks are not properly in sync with each other. This is usually compensated for in the computer's RAM with a buffer that stores the audio before it is sent out.

Please do not take these remarks as negative comments about these systems. They are both very powerful systems in this price range, and have established a standard other products must match to compete. But as a purchaser and user, you need to be fully aware of the capabilities of anything you purchase and not get confused by terminology. The power of the host computer will affect the ultimate capability of these systems, so be mindful that to really get the most out of the software, a CPU upgrade may be in your future. Even the latest models of computer may require more RAM. This is especially true if you are running several different software plug-ins.

Markers

Markers, or memory locations, are the software equivalent of locate points. The advantage in the computer world is that markers are an unlimited resource. It is possible to label every part of song for easy identification and instant access. Most software packages offer a list view of markers so that clicking on one instantly moves to that point in the song. Click the play button and the file plays from that point.

Depending on the software, marker information ranges from a simple name tag to view settings for a specified region. In Digital Performer, markers are limited to identifying a specific bar or beat. In Pro Tools LE a marker can indicate a specific time or region in the file. Figure 14.15 shows the Memory Location dialog for creating markers. Additional settings determine the percentage of zoom for the area, which is helpful when editing. Using the Track Show/Hide and Track Height options also helps automate display preferences. This is especially helpful when screen real estate is in short supply. Setting up markers as soon as possible will help save time by providing a visual reference to each part of the song or specific sections of the track, eliminating the need to constantly listen to make sure you are in the right place. Using markers in association with the pre-roll features in most digital sequencers and recorders is an excellent technique for punching sections of a track. Create a marker at the location you wish to record and enter the desired amount of pre-roll. Selecting the marker will always bring you to the correct starting point so that all you have to do is press the record button.

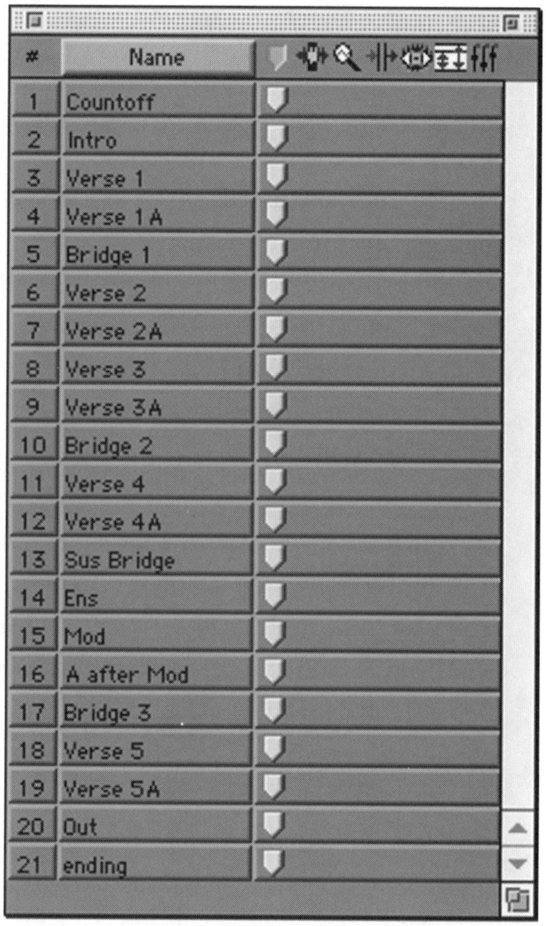

Computer-Based System Capabilities—Reality Check

A reality check is when you look in your checkbook and reality hits you square in the face. Computer-based systems offer some of the best capabilities of any of the systems mentioned in this book; however, there is a price to be paid to get each

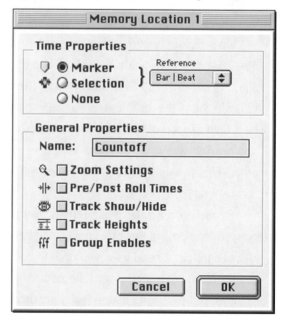

Figure 14.15. Pro Tools LE Memory Locations List

Figure 14.16. Pro Tools LE Memory Location Dialog Box

system up to its full potential. Host-based systems, such as the MOTU 2408 and Digi 001, get their horsepower from the host computer—particularly the processor speed and amount of available RAM. Hard disk size is also a factor, but only in the amount of recording time available.

Pro Tools uses PCI cards to handle the digital audio processing, relieving your computer of those chores and allowing it to concentrate on refreshing the screen. Pro Tools runs alongside another application called DAE (Digidesign Audio Engine). DAE functions as the operating system for Pro Tools and other supported applications such as Sound Designer and Digital Performer.

Tracking with High-End Gear

The high-end digital studio contains several modular recorders or a computer-based hard disk recording system. The current trend in product development is toward more powerful hard disk recorders in both modular systems and computer-based systems. The systems we discuss in this book are considered high-end for this audience but in the pro studio and post production world there are more expensive and powerful systems. This will be the area to watch as super high-end features work their way down to lower price points.

Modular Systems

All of the lessons learned in development and field use of the original ADAT and DA-88 make the top of the line tape machines a pleasure to work with. Hopefully at this level they are being fed from digital mixers or quality pre-amps for the best possible signal quality. Just having a great recorder isn't enough; the signal must be kept clean all the way through the chain. Just as with all tape, high-end tracking is straightforward.

Modular hard disks have advanced to the level of twenty-four tracks in a single unit. The computer editing options available with both the Mackie and TASCAM machines give these modules many of the advantages of computer-based systems. The advantage these systems have is the portability of the unit and the removable hard drive itself. A removable hard disk can easily be moved from studio to studio and can be changed faster than a reel of 2-inch analog tape.

Computer-Based Hard Disk Recording

Computer-based systems at this level are among the most powerful recording systems offered. For demonstration purposes I've chosen Digidesign's Pro Tools software, but similar features can be found in other packages, including many of those in the mid-level category (see chapters 7 and 8).

The Name Game, Part I

Proper labeling of the patch bay is essential for easy routing of signals through the studio. Hard disk recorders such as Pro Tools and Paris have the equivalent of a digital patch bay built-in to route audio signals from the interface to tracks, to plug-ins, and back out again. It is possible to label some of these connections for easy reference and save this information as a part of a session setup or template. There are eight ins and eight outs on the interface and each one should be labeled with what is connected to it.

Labeling information can include the instrument, microphone, or name of the person being recorded. A properly labeled routing system results in easier recognition of the bus network so signals are set from the correct input to the correct channel or bus assignment. Inputs and outputs deal with the interface, in this case the Digidesign 888/24 I/O .

Inserts should also be labeled. An insert is a specific point in the signal path where it is sent outside the mixer or I/O to an external device for processing, then returned through the mixer or I/O to the same point to continue its journey through the signal chain. In short, an insert is a point at which another signal is inserted into the signal chain. Inserts are located on individual channels so the processing does not affect any other channel. The most common use of an insert is for adding EQ or compression.

Labeling bus and insert routes and saving them as a part of a session template can save setup time for future sessions. The names you enter will show up in

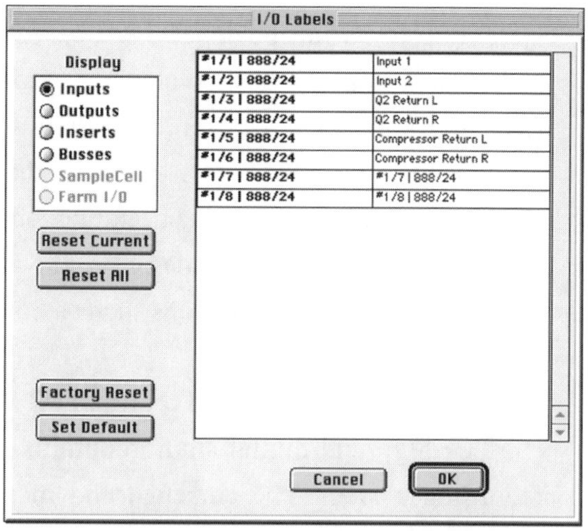

Figure 14.17. Pro Tools Input Labeling Dialog Box

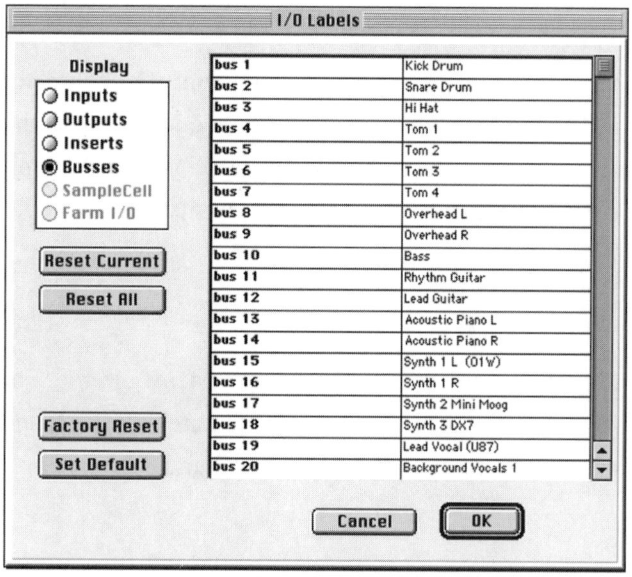

Figure 14.18. Pro Tools Bus Labeling Dialog Box

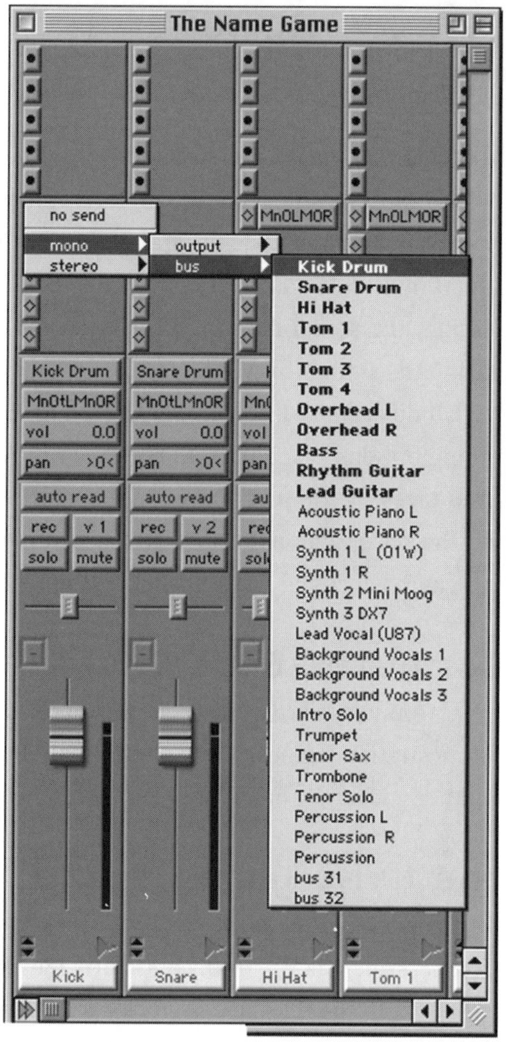

Figure 14.19. Pro Tools Mix Window with Bus Menu Selected

the pop-up menus on the channel strips in Pro Tools' Mix window. Once a bus is assigned to a channel, it is bolded in the menu.

Tracks, or channel strips in the Mix window, can also be named. All this technology is wonderful, but in the end the important thing is the product being recorded. Once the session begins, fumbling with the technology will only hurt the session, and in the end, the product.

A *bus* is a route inside a mixer that signals from any channel can be routed to, usually for routing to effects devices. A bus is different from an insert because it is designed to handle signals from multiple channels instead of just one. The number of busses is limited by the equipment for computer-based programs and for hardware mixers. An 8-bus board, as in the Mackie Digital 8 Bus mixer, has eight separate routes available. Busses can also be used to create sub-mixes from a group of channels. This feature can create monitor mixes going to the players' headphones or to a mix group that allows a number of faders to be controlled by one or two faders for mixing purposes. In computer hard disk recording systems, these routings occur in the software itself and are limited only by the capabilities of the system.

Destructive and Nondestructive Recording

Tracking on a computer-based system offers the nondestructive option to keep every take or destructively record over the previous take. Destructive recording is similar to using tape. Each time a track is recorded, it overwrites the previously recorded audio data with the new performance. The old performance is erased and/or destroyed as it would have been on an analog recorder.

Selecting nondestructive recording allows the same audio track to be used for each take but with each subsequent take that is recorded, the previous take is moved to and preserved in the main file, or session file. This allows additional takes without making more tracks in the software. The previously recorded audio files can be reinserted in a track later and edited to produce the final track.

Loop Recording

Loop recording is a kind of nondestructive recording that allows multiple takes to be recorded back to back, without touching the software controls. Set the begin point and end point in the software, most software will also allow for a preroll, and select record. The software will repeat or loop the section over and over until you select stop. This is helpful when

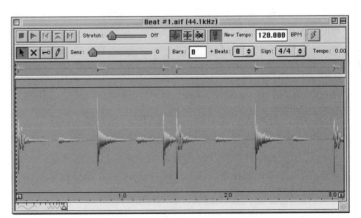

Figure 14.20. Steinberg ReCycle Groove Editor

working alone or on a specific section of a track such as a solo or voice over that needs several passes of the same copy. Later, each take can be selected and played back. The final performance can be any one take or edited from several different takes.

Sample-Based Recording

Sample-based recording involves editing loops and sounds before any tracks are laid down. This can be done using a digital sampler, a groove box, a stand-alone hard disk recorder, a digital sequencer, or some other digital recording software. For drum loops there are programs like Recycle from Steinberg that process drum loops. Files edited in recycle can be exported in a variety of file formats.

When working with drum loops, take extra care to trim the beginning of the sample right to the downbeat of the loop. Even a small amount of excess can be enough to ruin the feel of the track. Since many drum loops come from analog sources such as vinyl records and cassettes, the exact tempo of the piece may be decimal places off a metronome marking. Digital Performer offers a feature that will take any sample and match its length to a specified number of measures. A sample can be defined as being a 2-measure sample and Digital Performer will calculate the exact tempo for the sequence so that it will match the loop.

Digital Performer can also alter the length of a loop to match the sequence tempo. Select the loop and define it as two measures of the sequence and it will compress or expand the length of the loop so that it fills two measures at the sequence's tempo. Using DSP to speed up or slow down the speed, or tempo of the loop is a popular effect.

Managing Sound Files While Tracking—The Name Game, Part II

Managing all the files created while recording to a hard disk is a task unto itself and a definite justification for detailed session notes. In any digital audio recording application, the audio files are automatically given a name when they are recorded. In Pro Tools this name is taken from the track name—adding to the importance of naming the track. This way all of the kick drum audio files will be labeled Kick, followed by a number to indicate the order in which they were recorded. Files are displayed in a box on the right hand side of the Pro Tools edit window. Figure 14.21 shows a list from a recent chorus

Figure 14.21. Pro Tools LE Edit Window

recording session. The piece was recorded in sections so the list is quite long. Managing this list requires naming and properly logging all of the takes so the best ones are easily identified.

One last tip for managing audio files: eliminate unwanted files. Most sequencers have an Undo Record command and Pro Tools has a handy keystroke command to instantly erase the current take.

Improvising When Things Go Wrong

Every now and then you will be faced with a situation where something in your studio ceases to function as advertised. This behavior is most often observed in the hours after tech support and your local supplier have closed for the evening and your deadline is already too close for comfort. This has lead me to theorize that these little devices can smell fear and know the precise time to break down and cause the most angst. Do not give in to the Dark Side. Release your anger and remain calm. Only then can you concentrate on getting out of this predicament and meeting your deadline.

Seriously, situations like this is are all too common. You will learn a lot about how and why things work during these times, so learn all you can while you are dealing with the emergency because this will allow you to instantly deal with any reoccurrence of the problem. You may also bear witness to a dealer or manufacturer earning your business by coming through for you in the clutch with support, answers, tips, or replacement gear.

Steps for Troubleshooting

As soon as a crisis occurs, power down your hardware and then power up again. If possible, let your equipment cool down if it has been on for a while. For software, quit the application and reboot, and if the problem persists, quit, restart the computer, and then reboot. Another software option is to locate the preferences file for the application and trash it. The program will create a new one when it boots.

If you have Web access, most companies have Web sites with FAQ and Tech Support sections that may help and save a phone call. Software updates may be available that can correct the problem.

If problems persist place a call to tech support. Give a clear and concise report of the problem and any steps you've taken to fix it. Tech support can only help you if you can accurately explain the problem and the circumstances surrounding it. Yelling at them won't solve the problem or enhance your reputation. Have a notepad handy to write down any steps they suggest you try.

If tech support's diagnosis is a trip to the repair shop, find out if it's a repair that can be done locally or if it needs to go back to the factory. This is a good reason to save those original boxes if you have the space. Also inquire if it's possible to get a loaner or rental unit. If you take it back to where you bought it, you may be able to get a loaner unit there.

When in trouble it's great to have friends. Here's where some local networking can save your life. You may be able to save the day with a few phone calls. Someone else may have experienced the problem you are having and be able to help you fix it, or at least get around it. They also may be able to lend you a piece of gear, or even give you a break on using their space if you are really in a bind.

Hybrid Recording Setups

A hybrid studio is one that contains several different types of recording gear. This is another way of acknowledging that nothing ever gets thrown away, sold, or traded-in on the next new wonder box. Older equipment can still serve you in a pinch, so if the resale value is not going to help you in buying something new, hold on to it. I know of a few studios, my own included, that have and use Pro Tools but still find plenty of reasons to keep the MDMs around and busy. Using an MDM as a backup unit can also mean having a plan B at the ready in case the computer does not want to play nice with the other children on a day when you need it.

Anyone with enough computer experience knows that there are times when the machine boots up and what worked fine yesterday seems to have mysteriously vanished over night. This can cost money in the end, so be ready for those little gremlins. An original ADAT may not have all the sexy features of the latest and greatest software but it still works every time you start it up. It serves nicely as a portable unit for location recording and is still used as the primary recording device for a lot of the sessions here. Finding new uses for older equipment can be an economical way of growing your studio until the budget for the big upgrade comes along.

Powering Up Your Gear

Before you turn on your equipment, check the manuals for startup instructions. Some pieces of equipment emit a loud pop on start up. This is unpleasant to listen to and potentially damaging to other pieces of equipment. As a rule, turn on your recorders, outboard gear and synths first. Leave the mixer and power amp as the last two things to power up. It is important to turn things on in this order. Tube gear needs time to warm up, so power it up at least fifteen minutes before it is needed in the recording session. If you have a computer with external hard drives attached, power them up first and make sure they are spooled up (the disk access light is not blinking) before powering up the computer's CPU. When powering down, work backwards. Begin with the power amp, then the mixer, then the outboard gear and synths.

Writing Up a Session (No Job Is Finished Until the Paperwork Is Done)

Documenting the setup used in a session is vital both for continued work on the project and for new projects as well. This is where the arsenal of favored equipment settings is stored for the days when someone asks, "How'd you get that great guitar sound?" Chances are that during the tracking session EQ and compression have been applied to various instruments, reverb has been added, and effects settings have been changed to some extent. Finally, a rough mix has been worked up. Take note of every detail.

You may think it's no big deal to remember how the reverb is configured but just try to get that sound back next month when it's time to mix or cut something else or fix that one little part that's bothering someone.

All of this information is essential to creating the final mix, so it must be documented. This can be accomplished in a number of ways. Before automated gear, studios used Polaroid cameras to take snapshots of the gear to record the settings of the knobs, dials, and faders that were set at the end of the session. This is how the snapshot feature in digital mixers got its name.

Most outboard gear allows the creation of user presets. These can be valuable for saving settings, but it also may be necessary to use a log sheet and write down anything that cannot be saved, as well as the location and name of anything that is saved in a unit's memory.

Recording software and plug-ins can save most data as a part of each file. Plug-in data is usually saved separately in the individual plug-in. Check the manual for the correct procedures before all edits are gone for good.

Lastly, at the end of the session, make sure the musicians leave with everything they brought, and only what they brought. I have heard stories of everything from patch cords to microphones missing at the end of a session. It's sad to think some of our fellow musicians would do something like this, but it happens, intentionally or not. The best plan is to be observant and take a thorough inventory at the end of the session. The longer something is gone the less likely it will be recovered. Mark your equipment, so it can easily be distinguished, especially if you do any location recording. This includes labeling patch cords with markers or colored tape, engraving your name or phone number on mics and other metal components, and placing distinguishing marks on any road cases.

Summary

Recording is a relatively simple process that exponentially increases in complexity. Therefore it is important to plan appropriately in advance. Setting up for a session is as important as the session itself in making the business of recording music a productive one. Being prepared for everything means no surprises, or at least no surprises you can't successfully resolve. Once the session starts it is important to know your equipment and how to get the best out of it. After the session, the engineer's work is still not done. Logging the session is as important as the setup. Detailed notes on the settings of every piece of equipment used will make continuing work on the project easier.

Chapter 15.
External Controllers

If you use a computer as the central component of a digital recording studio, you have two basic options for controlling data. First, it is possible to use digital audio software to move virtual sliders or faders on the computer screen (see chapter 14). The word *fader* is used to describe a sliding controller that is often used to fade the volume of a particular track in or out. Faders, or sliders, can also be used to control other parameters such as effects.

The second option is to use a separate piece of hardware that has a control surface that is more responsive to subtle moves and adjustments than a computer mouse or track ball. The screen controls built into digital audio software (see chapters 7 and 8) do not respond with the same feel or response time as a fader or slider on a mixer. Virtual knobs are especially difficult to manipulate with a computer mouse. The need for a separate control surface or controller has resulted in a variety of products for almost any budget.

Controller Types

External controllers can be grouped into two categories. Some are designed for a specific piece of software and will only work with that software such as the HUI, which was designed for use with Pro Tools. Others are generic and can be connected to a computer and will successfully interface with most of the popular digital audio programs on the market. Like other gear reviewed throughout this book, these devices can be grouped into the entry-level, mid-level, and high-end categories; I will tell you which pieces are software specific as we go along.

Entry Level

At the entry level, Motor Mix, by CM Automation (list $999), is designed to work with many different applications including MIDI sequencers, software-based synths, samplers, and digital audio recording software. It has eight motorized faders. A motorized fader can respond to data sent by the software instructing it to move up or down. This means that you can set the levels for various tracks throughout the piece and then instruct the software to perform the mix on its own, referred to as automation. This can save literally hundreds of hours in the mixdown stage of the recording process.

Motor Mix has eight knobs and sixty-eight switches. For console automation Motor Mix can perform fader moves, mute, solo, and record ready functions. Motor Mix can control plug-in values

Figure 15.1. CM Motor Mix

and enter them for automation. At a size of 10.5 inches wide and 12.5 inches deep it fits almost anywhere. Up to four units can be joined together to function as a single mixer.

Mid-Level

The MCS-3800 by JL Cooper (list $2,999) works with a number of different applications. The basic configuration includes eight motorized faders, five rotary controllers, sixty user-definable function

buttons, and a jog and shuttle wheel. It can be expanded both internally and externally. The maximum configuration is sixty-four faders with two rotary controllers per channel. There are two internal expansion slots for adding controller cards. Interface cards include RE-422, GPI, USB, and others so it can be connected to most computer brands and models. Other add-on units include a 3-axis joystick controller for onscreen editing functions and a T-bar transition controller for transitions in editing and animation software.

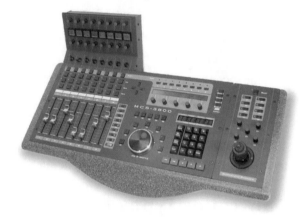

Figure 15.2. JL Cooper MSC-3800

The HUI by Mackie (list $3,499) looks like the little brother of the digital 8-bus mixer (see chapter 10) but is a control surface for Pro Tools (see chapter 8). The HUI, or Human User Interface, has two mic preamps so it can handle sessions that require no more than two microphones. The motorized faders can control Pro Tools' on-screen tracks in groups of eight. There are also controls for changing Pro Tools

plug-in values. The transport section includes a jog and shuttle wheel as well as cursor controls. There is also a control room monitor section that can accommodate three sets of speakers or headphones and a talk-back mic (so the engineer can talk back to the people—hopefully musicians—in the recording studio). In addition to Pro Tools, the HUI is now supported by Digital Performer (see chapter 8), beginning with version 2.7.

Figure 15.3. Mackie HUI

High End

Pro Control by Digidesign (list $11,995) is the ultimate Pro Tools controller. There are two basic units, the Pro Control Interface for Pro Tools and the 8-channel expander units that can be chained together for up to thirty-two channels of control surface. Pro Control uses Ethernet communication so response is faster than the previously described units (they use MIDI to carry the control commands to the computer).

Pro Control is designed to access every Pro Tools parameter than can be automated. There is a touch pad built in for times where a point-and-click is necessary. The controller works with both Mac and PC versions of Pro Tools.

Figure 15.4. Digidesign Pro Control

Summary

An external control unit can be a useful device for those who want to have a piece of gear for precise control of faders and other controllers. These units are designed to be used with a variety of hardware and computer MIDI/digital audio software. Like other gear there are units designed for the entry, mid-, and high-end budgets.

Chapter 16.
Digital Editing

In the old analog world, editing meant a razor blade, a splicing block, and a reel-to-reel tape deck whose reels could be rocked back and forth to find the precise point to cut the tape. This spot was usually marked with a white china marker. The tape was removed from the head, placed on the splicing block, and cut. The excess tape was wound off the reel and onto the floor. The back end of the edit was cut at the appropriate place and the tape was joined with the help of a piece of adhesive tape applied to the back of the recording tape to hold it together. Once a cut had been made and the tape was on the floor, it was next to impossible to recover the track. Analog editing was, by definition, destructive.

Today we've replaced those crude tools with digital software and hardware. Disk based systems (see chapters 5 and 6) have raised editing to a new level. Even the most basic recorders and software have editing capabilities way beyond what is possible with analog tape splicing. Because of this, the old saw, "we'll fix it in the mix," has been changed to, "we'll edit it in post-production." In fact, editing has expanded into all phases of production from being strictly a postrecording activity.

Ever since the early days of recording, with records like the Beatles' *Sgt. Pepper's Lonely Hearts Club Band,* The Beach Boys' *Pet Sounds*, and Pink Floyd's *Dark Side of the Moon*, pop music has been affected by editing. These recordings manipulated analog editing with stunning results. Digital editing offers a greater number of options at a fraction of the cost to anyone who cares to try their hand. With today's digital equipment, the possibilities are immense.

Digital Editing Options

All of the digital recording options mentioned throughout this book offer some level of digital editing. This includes MDM, portable hard disk recorders, and computer-based systems. Recording options that do not include a computer have a limited number of editing features, but typically the editing capacity is greater with the more expensive units.

The most flexibility comes when a computer (Windows or Macintosh) is used for editing. For example, it is possible to record tracks on an MDM and then use a computer software editing tool to prepare the final mix for DAT or CD.

If you are using a computer-based system, then editing options include using the recording software's built-in editing features or purchasing a separate digital editing program. The latter option is the one that most professional studios employ. In most cases it is best to use digital editing software that was designed just for this purpose.

Destructive and Nondestructive Editing

The concepts of destructive and nondestructive recording were introduced in chapter 14. Like recording, there is destructive and nondestructive editing. Nondestructive editing does not alter the original file. In other words, no matter many edits there are, it is always possible to go back to the original and start from square one.

Digital audio programs include a variety of ways to maintain the original version. With some, you simply make a backup copy of the original and then apply the edits to a copy. Other programs have ways of displaying the edits on the computer screen. For example, when examining a list of audio files that represent edits in Pro Tools, it is easy to recognize the original audio file because it is in bold type. The edited files are in plain type.

The nondestructive editing feature makes it a snap to apply a wide range of edits to a digital recording. The advantage is that an unlimited number of edits can be performed all without affecting the original recording. They can be saved and recalled with the click of a mouse.

Block Editing

There are two types of digital editing: block editing and wave editing. The term block is derived from the manner in which audio track data is displayed on the screen. Most multitrack digital audio software (see chapters 6 and 7) uses block editing. In figure 16.2 the Pro Tools Edit window shows the audio waves in blocks. These blocks can be edited in several ways. The start and end points can be shortened to trim excess data, usually silence, from the beginning or end of a particular block. Blocks can also be resized so that only a certain part plays back. When performing various edits, the original block with all audio data is preserved intact and any trimming can be undone at any time. Just go to the Edit menu and select undo.

Blocks can be divided into smaller blocks for compositing (see chapter 14). In addition, blocks can be shifted or nudged forward or

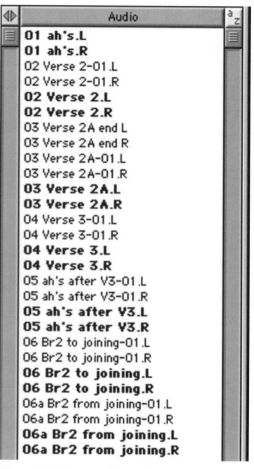

Figure 16.1. Pro Tools Audio Files List

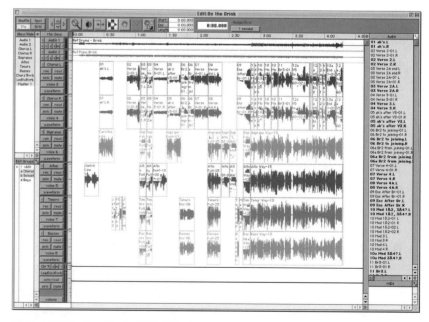

Figure 16.2. Pro Tools Edit Window

backward to correct for timing problems. They can also be positioned on more than one track at more than one time and copied and pasted to other locations. All of this can be undone at the click of a mouse button.

Some software-based multitrack digital audio packages, such as those mentioned in chapters 7 and 8, use SMPTE time code to manage blocks. For example, each block in Pro Tools is assigned a time stamp when it is recorded. Using this information it is easy to reposition any moved block back to its original spot. If the block is moved to correct timing problems a user time stamp can be entered, but the original time stamp will always remain.

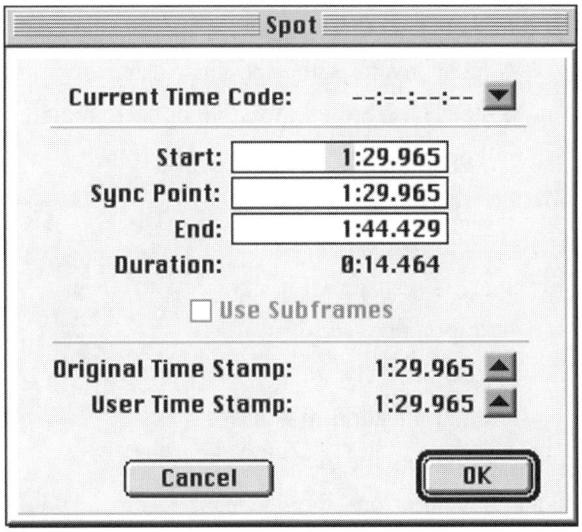

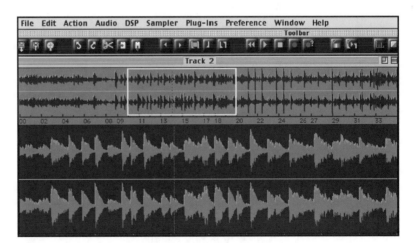

Figure 16.3. Pro Tools Spot Dialog Box

Wave Editing

The second type of editing is wave editing. Wave editors handle two or more tracks at a time and display the audio data as a continuous waveform. Wave editing serves a different purpose than block editing. Block editing focuses on the overall performance and sound of the recording. Wave editing is usually used to fix small problems in the recording, to apply effects, or to make transfers between different file formats.

Situations that might require wave editing are clicks resulting from rough block transitions, digital noise or pops, unwanted vocal noise, harsh sounding breaths, and any number of other unwanted noises that can creep into a recording. These noises can be a performer accidentally hitting a music or mic stand, dropping a pencil, or coughing. Wave editors are used to remove or change the sound wave. They offer more flexibility, control, and options than block editors.

Some digital audio programs can do both block and wave editing, while others can only do one. If you do not have wave editing capabilities, you will need to export your files to a separate waveform editor. Most block oriented programs,

Figure 16.4. Wave Editing Using Peak by Bias

such as MIDI/digital audio sequencers, have the ability to export audio to a wave editor. So the options are either to purchase a program that includes both block and wave editing or purchase two programs.

Editing Basics

Almost anyone with experience using a computer is familiar with the basic editing concepts of cut, copy, and paste. These are all available in basic digital editing. These simple tasks alone can save time and trouble by copying chorus vocals or any other phrase that repeats without change. Removing even the most minute section of a file and replacing it with a better performance is a snap. All it takes is a little practice, and learning how to use the software.

Each application may have different names for these functions but they are the power center of digital editing. The audio tracks shown in Figure 16.5 are the left and right chorus tracks from a recent project. Several different takes were recorded. After the

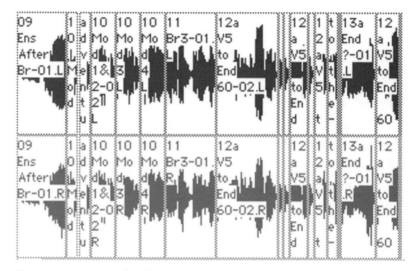

Figure 16.5. Pro Tools Chorus Tracks

session, I determined the best take of each phrase. The recording engineer then cut and pasted all the selected takes together, sixteen sections for each track. We were even able to make adjustments for phrases that were not quite in time with the track. This was block editing at its finest. It allowed us to record a number of takes of a phrase and then choose parts from each one to make the final version. Cool stuff!

Imagine for a second that this file (Figure 16.5) contains the hook of a pop tune. It would be simple to copy and paste the tracks, edits and all, to every section in the tune where it repeats. This technique can save lots of studio time.

The trick to digital editing is finding the correct spot to edit and cover any problems that result from a rough edit. Figure 16.6 shows two tracks that have just been edited together. The left (top) track is fine but the right track produces a click at the edit point in playback. This requires wave editing. Again, some packages offer both block and wave editing, others do not. Either way, this particular file required both block and wave editing. One does not replace the other.

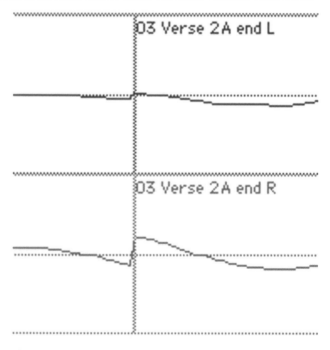

Figure 16.6. Bad Edit

This example was in Pro Tools, so I simply selected the wave editor and zoomed in on the edit location and checked for problems. I found a major gap in the waveform. I corrected it using the pencil tool (there is also a wave drawing feature) to redraw the wave so that it became a smooth line, or curve, from one section to the next, thus eliminating the unwanted sound.

Crossfade is another tool for smoothing over an edit point. With a crossfade, the first file is faded out while the second file is faded in. Any unwanted audio that results from the edit is lost in the fade. The software usually includes several choices for the curve, or rate, of the fade and how long the complete cross-fade will take.

The goal of all editing is to make the edits as clean as possible when listening to the track alone, also referred to as *solo*. Even after making several edits and crossfades, some

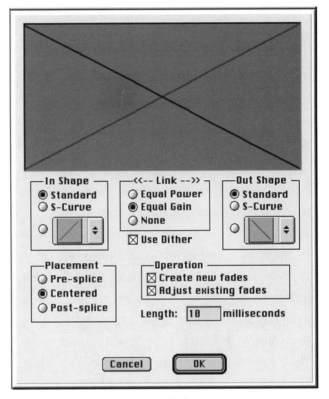

Figure 16.7. Pro Tools Fade Dialog Box

roughness may still be present. If this is the case, sometimes the solution is adding an effect like reverb. Effects will be discussed in chapter 17.

Editing a vocal track can be difficult if the singer is experiencing pitch problems. Even the best of takes may have a few notes that land short of the mark. Since most high-end (and some mid-level) software includes pitch correction, be sure to use it before beginning major surgery to assemble a composite take. This simple adjustment may save a few hours of smoothing over edit points.

If you find that the software you are using to record has sufficient editing features, you are in luck. Of course, the more a program costs, the more editing features will be included. However, if you find that you would like more control, then consider purchasing a second, dedicated editing program such as those described in the following section.

Digital Editing Software

Digital editing software was introduced in chapter 7. These programs are designed to provide you with tools to edit files in a variety of ways and go far beyond the basic cut, copy, and paste functions that are often included with all digital audio software. Digital editors are able to convert from and export to a wide variety of file formats. For example, if you want to convert files to QuickTime, avi, wav, aiff, or other formats (see chapter 20), digital editing software is the way to go.

There are two categories of digital editing software available: stereo, or 2-track, and multitrack. Stereo programs are designed to be the last step in the mixing process. You record the digital tracks using any one of the recording options discussed in chapters 4 through 8. Then, the stereo editing software is used to make edits, apply effects, and create the final mix in DAT or CD format.

Multitrack editors have similar capabilities as stereo or 2-track software with the obvious difference being that they can handle more than two tracks. Examples of multitrack and stereo editing software are described in the following section.

Stereo (2-Track) Editing Software

No matter how you record your original tracks, whether it is through use of MDM, hard disk, or computer-based, you will eventually need to mix it all down to a 2-track stereo mix. One of the best tools to use at this stage is stereo or 2-track editing.

First of all, all stereo or 2-track editors are waveform editors. There are several stereo programs on the market for Macintosh and Windows. On the Windows side, Sound Forge and Sound Forge XP (by Sonic Foundry) and Wavelab 3.0 (by Steinberg) have been more or less the industry standard for years. Sound Forge XP is an entry-level option. Cool Edit 2000 (by Syntrillium) is an excellent entry-level option that is shareware and sells for under $100. For Macintosh users, Peak (by Bias) and sonicWORX Studio (by Prosoniq) are excellent stereo (2-track) editing programs. Peak LE is a "lite" version designed for entry-level Mac users.

With these programs it is possible to cut, paste, move, delete, mute, fade, and crossfade. These programs usually come with a few effects plug-ins (see chapter 17) including common and not so common effects such as reverb, delay/echo, and others. After the editing of the files is complete, stereo editors can save files in a variety of formats for burning a CD or for use in multimedia environments (see chapter 20).

Now, on to how to take advantage of all this stereo technology. Typically, you would first create your music using any of the various ways mentioned throughout this book—MDM, hard disk, and so forth—to create the digital audio recording. After creating the file, you would then mix the music down to two tracks. This is where the 2-track editing software comes in. If you are using a stand-alone stereo editor, the file is imported into the editor to process the

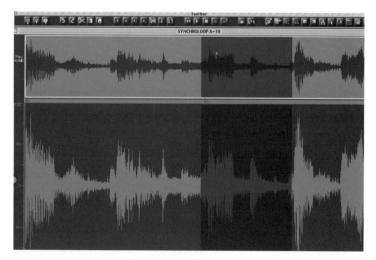

Figure 16.8. Selecting a Portion of a File in Peak

information using digital signal processing tools. Stereo editors can work with stereo and mono signals. Because they are wave editors, they have the advantage of being able to edit and alter minute parts of a file. It is possible to select a specific part of the file and then apply any one of many DSP (digital signal processing) functions and/or effects.

Multitrack Editing Software

Another option in the editing category is multitrack editing software. These programs are designed to do many of the same editing functions as stereo editors. The major difference is that they can import multiple tracks of data whereas the stereo editors can import only stereo and mono files.

Some multitrack editors can also function as multitrack recording software similar to the programs mentioned in chapter 8. However, their main objective is to provide editing capabilities. An excellent multitrack editor for Windows is Wavelab 3.0 (by Steinberg). This program was mentioned in the stereo digital editors section; however, the 3.0 version can also import multitrack files or files with more than two tracks. Other Windows multitrack editors include Cool Edit Pro (by Syntrillium), SAW (by Innovative Quality Software), Vegas

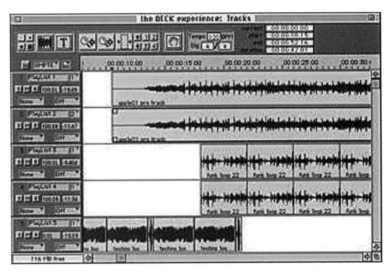

Figure 16.9. Multitrack Editing Software (Deck by Bias)

Pro (by Sonic Foundry), and Samplitude (by Sek'd). There are many more options from which to choose for Windows users. Deck (by Bias) is an excellent, powerful multitrack program for Mac users.

Selecting the Best Digital Editing Program

Selecting the best digital-editing program can be a confusing task. You might start by looking at the recording software you are using. Does the company offer an editing program? If so, try it out, because it may have a similar look and feel and be easier for you to learn. It may also interface smoothly with your existing software. Also be sure to purchase the program that has the editing features you require. It is not uncommon to pay more than $500 for a high-end digital-editing program, but if you don't need the top of the line options, consider one of the "lite" or entry-level offerings.

You may not need a multitrack editing program if you are using a MIDI/digital audio sequencer such as Cakewalk or Digital Performer. These programs have powerful editing capabilities built-in. If this is the case, you can then go with a stereo editor for the final mix down.

It is also a good idea to check out the software before purchasing it. Try to get your hands on the software by visiting someone you know who is using the software or download a copy from the company's Web site.

Summary

Perhaps the most significant enhancement of digital audio recording is the ability to edit. This includes both destructive and nondestructive editing. There are two types of editing—block and waveform. Some of the high-end digital audio programs include both types while others just support block editing. To get the most editing power, a separate digital editing program should be considered. These programs come in stereo and multitrack formats. There is a wide variety of software from which to choose for the entry to high-end user. Spend time reviewing the various options and be sure to select a program that has the necessary features that you require.

Chapter 17.
Effects Processing

Effects or effects processing refers to any form of audio signal processing such as reverb, delay, chorusing, and so forth. This chapter introduces the basic types of effects that can be used in a digital studio. In addition, specific applications of effects will also be addressed.

Outboard and Plug-Ins

There are two ways that effects are packaged. In the analog studios (and in some digital studios), effects come in separate rack-mount units referred to as outboard effects. These units are patched to the other equipment in the studio via the patch bay (see chapter 10).

When using a computer and digital audio software, effects plug-ins are used (see chapter 8). Plug-ins are outboard effects cousins designed to be integrated within the software environment. For example, when using a digital audio recording software program, software plug-ins add effects processing functions to the program.

Types of Effects Processors

Effects processors can be broken into four basic types. This applies to all effects, whether they are in the form of outboard effects or software plug-ins.

1. Effects that handle balances in the frequency spectrum.
2. Effects that process the signal over time.
3. Effects that control the dynamics, or loudness, of the signal.
4. Effects that enhance the audio image of the signal.

Mixer EQ

Equalization is built into just about every mixer available, including digital models. Most EQs are parametric, with the number of bands changing from mixer to mixer. These EQs may be enough for most basic recording and mixing needs. More bands of EQ allow for more precise shaping of the tone. Some mixer EQs also have a switch to select a broad band or narrow band of frequencies to be affected around the main selected frequency.

A mixer's EQ is solid state construction for analog consoles, digital in digital consoles. For tube EQ, it will be necessary to add an outboard EQ unit. Microphone preamps can do double duty for this purpose, so consider that when choosing outboard gear. Outboard EQ may not be necessary for every situation, so a dedicated EQ unit may not be very high on the priority list.

EQ Applications

Chances are that anyone who owns an audio playback system has experience with EQ. The treble and bass controls on stereos, boom boxes, and car radios are very basic forms of EQ. Want more thump in the bass? Then turn up the bass control. Want to hear more of the vocal? Turn up the treble, or turn down the bass. Think of this as the jumping off point for exactly how EQ works in the studio, only with much more focus and precision.

Frequency Spectrum Effects

Frequency spectrum effects include all types of equalization (referred to as EQ) and filters. There are two types of equalizers: fixed frequency and variable frequency. The most common fixed frequency equalizer is the graphic equalizer. Its front panel has a row of sliders, each controlling a specific frequency. A graphic equalizer gets its name because the sliders form a visible frequency curve when positioned. Graphic EQs are available in single- or dual-channel configurations. The number of bands varies; for example, a single rack space dual-channel unit such as the dbx 2215 has sixteen bands. The dbx 2031 (see Figure 17.1) has thirty-one bands and is a single rack space, single-channel outboard unit. The dbx 2231 is a 31-band, 2-channel unit and is two rack spaces high.

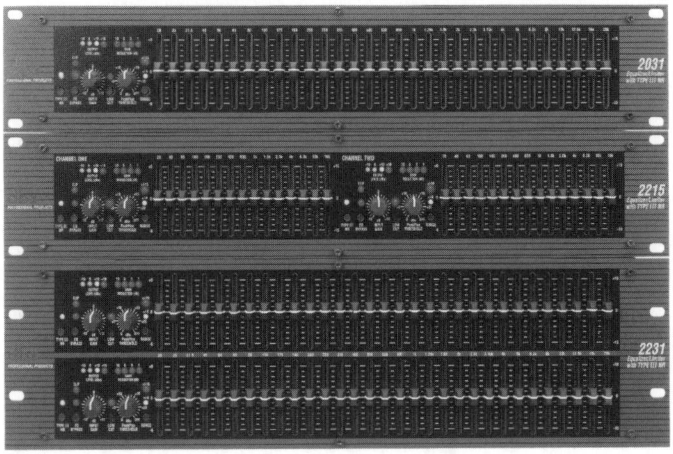

Figure 17.1. Dbx 20 Series Graphic Equalizers

In addition to being used to process recorded signals, graphic EQs have another important use in the studio. They are inserted in the signal path going to the control room monitors and are used to compensate for unwanted frequency boosts in the room. This is commonly referred to as "tuning the room." Since many digital studio control rooms are converted spaces, adding a graphic EQ is essential. A properly positioned room EQ setting should look like a smooth curve, not the skyline of New York City. Once the EQ is set up, it doesn't need to be changed unless there is a major change in the physical or acoustical layout of the space.

The EQ unit should be mounted somewhere out of the way to avoid accidental bumps that will move the sliders. Rack space covers are also available to mount over the front panel to prevent the controls from being touched.

Prices for outboard graphic EQs cost from $250 to $2,000. The features included on most EQ units are the same in all price ranges with the exception of the number of EQ bands. What makes one unit worth more than another is the quality of the internal electronics. Only a few units currently available are digital units. The Yamaha YDG2030 is a 2-channel digital unit with thirty bands of EQ. Each band covers a third of an octave. It displays the bands on a view screen on the front panel.

Parametric equalizers perform the same basic function as graphic equalizers but they also can be used to fine-tune the frequencies they effect. Instead of sliders at fixed frequencies, the parametric EQ has knobs that adjust to the exact frequency that will be the high or low point of the frequency curve. This allows a precise cut or boost to only the desired or problem frequency.

Figure 17.2. Yamaha YDG2030 Digital Graphic EQ

Figure 17.3. Focusrite Red 2 Parametric Equalizer

Figure 17.4. Yamaha YDP2006 Digital Parametric EQ

Pricing for outboard parametric EQs begins at $300 for entry-level units and runs up to $4,000 for high-end tube gear. Once again, the feature set is very similar for all units with the quality of the circuitry being what separates the entry level from the high end. Since tube EQs, such as the Focusrite Red 2, are the most sought after, true digital outboard units are not plentiful at the moment. The Yamaha YPD2006 is one of the few digital units. It uses 20-bit A/D converters and offers two channels of 6-band EQ. There are twenty preset locations for saving settings for easy recall in future sessions.

Filters

Filters process signals by eliminating unwanted frequencies. There are four types of filters: high-pass, low-pass, notch, and band-pass. The high-pass, or low-cut, filter reduces frequencies below a selected frequency. The low-pass, or high-cut, filter reduces frequencies above a selected frequency. High-pass filters allow signals higher than the selected frequency to pass and remove frequencies lower than the selected frequency. Low-pass filters allow signals lower than the selected frequency to pass but remove the frequencies higher than the selected frequency.

The high-pass filter can be used to remove low rumbles that may result from recording in a nonsoundproofed environment. A low-pass filter can eliminate sounds like tape hiss at the top end of a recording.

A notch filter is designed to eliminate a narrow frequency band and is most useful for corrective surgery on recordings with problems like 60 Hz ground hum. It eliminates the selected frequency without noticeably effecting surrounding frequencies.

Band pass filters set both a high and low point for filtering, allowing everything in between to pass by unaffected. This is used mostly for corrective surgery on existing recordings rather than on new recordings.

High- and low-pass filters are included with most equalizers and on some mixers. Notch and band-pass filters are not as common since their use is limited to specific situations not encountered in normal recording. They are common in many digital audio packages since they are used to clean up older or problem recordings.

Recording

In the recording process, EQ is used to shape the tone of a signal by altering its frequency content. It may be necessary to compensate for a poor quality instrument, an inadequate microphone, or a less than ideal recording space. EQ can also be used to shape a sound into something completely new and different. In most circumstances, sound is always recorded flat with the EQ applied to the signal for mixdown. The term *flat* refers to a signal with no EQ. This allows for additional tweaks in the EQ settings that may be required to blend all the tracks together for the final mix.

Selecting the appropriate EQ is like making a good stew: Bring many diverse ingredients together, season to taste, and hope the results are an effective overall blend. EQ is a tool for blending frequencies together to produce a pleasing result. Unlike a stew, ingredients can be removed as well as added. Sometimes instruments can clash in a specific frequency range and one or the other sound is obscured or made less effective. EQ is used to reshape one or both sounds until there is no longer a conflict. One of the chief sins of EQ usage is constant boosting when sounds conflict. The EQ knob turns both ways, and many times cutting or reducing certain frequencies is the best way to solve a problem and get a cleaner mix. People who think they have to apply it to everything often misuse EQ. If it sounds good flat, or unprocessed, then it doesn't need EQ. As always, your ears are the final judge, so choose effects wisely.

Time-Based Effects

Time-based effects involve repeating the signal in different ways to produce different results. Time-based effects include reverb, delay, flanging, phasing, as well as others. Reverb blends the repetitions and fades them to produce the sound of the waves decaying in a specific room environment. Delay repeats the signal with a variable time delay that can range from barely perceptible to very obvious, depending on the effect desired. Flanging and phasing are two specific effects produced by using short delays to produce a unique special effect. The signal can also be stretched or reduced in its duration to produce various effects or to adjust for time or pitch problems.

Types of Reverb

Reverb, short for reverberation, is one of the most used and overused effects in recording. To return to the stew analogy, reverb is like salt. It is one of those seasonings that some folks like a lot, and others prefer only a little. I can remember drowning my first few mixes in reverb. It was a cool sound and I finally had it in my rack. Then the novelty wore off and I learned to be a little more tasteful in its application. The initial problem is that *everything* sounds better with reverb, even performances that are not too good to begin with, so the effect can cloud good judgement. Overuse of reverb can lead to a sonic washout, where nothing has punch or definition. As you build your equipment rack, listen to the music in your own collection for how reverb is applied, both in the overall mix and as a special effect. Learning and experimenting are never-ending processes in studio.

When paging through the presets on a reverb unit, there are several terms that will appear over and over in preset names. Here's a little guide to help interpret them. There are three common types of room sizes: room, chamber, and hall.

Room is the smallest of the three types. Room settings provide ambiance and size but with short decay times so they do not ring for long periods of time. This allows for greater definition when mixing sounds together. Room settings are the most common type of reverb for basic use in pop styles of music.

Chamber settings replicate a small to medium sized room with hard, tiled surfaces. The decay time is still short so chamber settings are a bit more flexible than hall settings but they create a bigger sound and take up more room in the mix. The resulting sound may not be realistic, so be careful when using chamber settings. Listen to be sure they provide the sound and impact you desire.

Hall settings are an emulation of a large concert hall or stadium. They add both a sense of size and distance to the sound. The decay time of a hall reverb is long, and low frequencies can continue well after the initial sound, which can create problems in the low end of the mix. Use the hall option judiciously.

Other types of reverb are also available. These are electronic simulations or completely synthetic creations. Plate reverb is a simulation of early reverb when the sound waves were sent through a metal plate to produce the effect. Plate reverb is good to use on vocals or other sounds that need to be up front in the mix.

Reverse reverb flips around the decay envelope of a sound. The amount of reverb builds from the end of the decay to its maximum amount and is clipped off at the end.

Early reflections are simply the first echoes that can be heard in a real space. This is not a true reverb but rather a way of adding some space to a sound without adding the full decay of a reverb. It can be used in conjunction with a reverb setting to help further define the space, like creating a virtual room.

Gated reverb uses a noise gate to cut off the sound below a certain decibel level. The result is a short, choppy sound that packs a lot of punch. The effect is used frequently on professionally recorded CDs and introduced on Phil Collins' "In The Air Tonight" from the *Face Value CD*. This effect should be sparingly applied and is most effective on drum and bass sounds.

Reverb Presets

A reverb preset name may also include the adjective bright or dark. In bright rooms, the high frequencies have a greater decay time. Since they last longer, there is more of a shimmer to the sound, making it brighter to the ear. In dark rooms, high frequencies decay faster, leaving more mid-range and low frequencies. In performance, furnishings and people more quickly absorb high frequencies so the dark effect is more realistic.

Delay and Echo

Delay and echo involve exact repetitions of the signal. With delay and echo, the idea is to control the amount of time between repetitions and the number of repetitions. A slap back delay, or echo, is a delay that is perceptible as a distinct repeat of the original sound. The delay times for this effect are anything greater than 35 milliseconds. Some outboard units allow for the delay to be set for a specific tempo by taping it manually on the front panel of the unit. Other options include a choice of feel, such as a triple feel for shuffle grooves.

Flanging and Phasing

A flange is the metal part of a tape reel that is attached to either side of the hub to keep the tape from coming off the hub in handling. As the legend goes, flanging was discovered in a studio where two identical tapes were playing on two separate open reel decks. The engineer leaned on the flange of one of the reels, slowing the tape slightly. The result was a jet-like sound that became one of the more popular effects in rock and pop recording. Flanging is part delay, less than 30 milliseconds, with some pitch shifting thrown in to complete the effect.

Phasing is similar to flanging but without the pitch shift. The sound is mellower than flanging, with a vibrato-like waver. If flanging sounds like a jet plane, think of phasing as hearing the sound under water. The delay times used for phasing are shorter than for flanging, making the effect less pronounced.

Chorus

No, this is not a large vocal ensemble, but the name is taken from that context for a reason. The chorusing effect takes a signal and makes multiple copies pitched slightly higher and lower than the original sound. This produces a fat overall sound. For example, start with a single vocalist. The sound is basically thin. Now add another vocalist and the blending of the voices makes a fatter sound. Add more, and the sound becomes huge, even when singing in unison. The reason for this is the slight variations in tuning from voice to voice actually works to make a better overall sound. The delay time for chorusing is usually between 15 and 35 milliseconds.

Pitch Shifting/Harmonizing

Pitch shifting can be used for a number of different effects. The original intent for pitch shifting was to correct notes that were slightly out of tune. There are, however many more effects that can be produced with this process. Vocal harmonies can be created, but care must be used to make sure there are no clashes with the harmony of the song since harmonizers are set to a specific interval and not to follow the harmony of the song. Radical shifts in pitch can be used to create exotic sound effects or alter the quality of a human voice. On a subtler level, listen to the voice of actress Natalie Portman in *Star Wars: Episode I—The Phantom Menace*. As Queen Amidala, her voice is pitched down, giving her a different, more authoritative sound than her natural voice when portraying the handmaiden Padme.

Dynamics Processors

Dynamics processors deal with the loudness of a signal. This was introduced in chapter 11. This section will address some of the specific applications of these devices.

Compressors

Think of compression as a tamer of wild signals—signals with large dynamic leaps that tend to pin meters in the forbidden red zone. Compression can also add a certain punch to a sound that will help it cut through the mix. In order to become familiar with the functions of a compressor, be it an outboard unit or plug-in, become familiar with the knobs and switches on the front panel.

Compressor Front Panel Explained

There are several key concepts when dealing with compressors: threshold, attack time, release time, hold time, gain reduction, and output level. Threshold sets the level at which the compressor begins compressing the signal. Attack time indicates how quickly, or slowly, the compressor will respond to signals above the threshold. Release time governs how long it takes for the compressor to return to a 1:1

Figure 17.5. Dbx DPP Dynamics Processor

ratio of sound, after the signal has dropped below the threshold. Hold time is the absolute minimum time that the compressor will alter the signal after it crosses the threshold. Gain reduction indicates the volume, or decibels, being stripped from the sound as it passes through the compressor. Output level, or *gain*, is used to boost the compressed signal as it leaves the unit and heads back to the insert point.

Outboard compressors come in groups of two or four in a single rack space unit. They usually function independently since each sound is coming from a different source. For compressing mixes or stereo sources, engaging the stereo link allows two units to function together for better results. With stereo link, two units function as one, reacting to sounds on both sides of the stereo field so any compression is applied equally to both sides of the signal, not just to the side where the threshold is crossed.

Other Compressor Functions

Other processors that can be combined in the same unit with a compressor or in a separate outboard unit include limiters, de-essers, expanders, and noise gates.

Limiting is a radical form of compression. Instead of reducing the signal by a selected ratio of decibels, limiting holds the signal at a specified decibel level and does not allow it to get any louder. This is most useful in situations where levels can be uncontrollable, such as live recording. The attack time should be short in order to respond to loud sounds quickly, before the level peaks. Limiting has a much greater effect on frequency response, especially with very high frequencies, so be prepared for the signal to noise ratio to drop if limiting high sounds.

Figure 17.6. Dbx 166XL Compressor

De-essers compress the strong, high frequencies associated with "s," "z," "ch," and "sh" vocal sounds. These sounds are compressed without effecting the overall level of the track. This is discussed in the preamp section of chapter 11.

Expanders perform a role opposite to that of a compressor. They increase the decibel level of a signal by a set ratio. This is used to boost the level of quiet sounds or to function as a noise gate. Gating can be used as an effect to punch up drums or bass or to eliminate unwanted background noise when using mics in a live or non-soundproofed situation. With this process the gate shuts when sound falls below a set decibel level, essentially turning off the mic. This way the mic does not pickup unwanted ambient noise when it is not being used.

Side-Chain Input

Many compressors have a side-chain input that allows a separate signal to be routed into the unit to trigger the effect. This signal can be different from the one actually being effected. EQ is usually used to brighten the signal being routed to the side-chain. De-essers use this method and brighten the 5-kHz range where the "s" sound of sibilants is found. This setup is also popular for radio voiceovers so that the music is lowered in volume to allow the announcer to be heard over the music. This technique is called *ducking*. The microphone is connected to the side-chain input. Whenever the announcer or DJ speaks, the compressor is triggered and the music is compressed. The lower volume makes it easier to talk over the music. When the voice stops, the music is gradually returned to the 1:1 level. Any sound can be used to trigger the compressor for various results.

Outboard Multi-Effects

In the early days of project studio development, effects units were still an area that clearly separated the haves from the have-nots. Effects units were expensive and for the most part, dedicated to a single task. This meant purchasing several units. With the birth of the multi-effects unit it became possible to have the processing power of spectral, time, and dynamics processing all in one unit. The units became affordable for the smallest studios.

Entry-level units have come a long way in sonic quality. Size ranges from tabletop, to 1/3 rack space, to full rack space. In mid-level units there is more programmability for tweaking, creating, and storing presets. The sonic quality has improved and some units have digital connections, usually TOSlink, or Lightpipe on Alesis products. The high-end units are state of the art in sound quality, offering digital connections, large selections of presets, and flexible programmability.

Chances are the multi-effects unit will be the choice of many for entry- and mid-level studios. A typical multi-effects unit typically will contain several EQ options including multi-band, graphic EQ, and filtering. Chorus, flanging, phasing, and pitch effects should also be onboard. The reverb and delay sections will probably be the most used sections of any multi-effects processor. Audition these sections first when selecting a unit.

The more units in the rack the more individual signal processing power, so there may be a tradeoff between purchasing one expensive piece or purchasing several less expensive units. When comparing units from different manufacturers, you may find certain presets that make the unit really shine. Effects units can be mixed and matched in your rack and each unit may take on a specific role, such a favorite unit for vocals, or guitars, or overall room ambience. Effects units can also be added as your budget allows.

Internal Keyboard Effects

Many keyboards and tone modules have some internal effects built-in, or as optional add-ons. This can be helpful for some recording situations. In smaller setups, keyboard effects can be helpful because they allow any other processor to be dedicated to handling other signals. On the down side, most built-in effects do not have the best sonic quality.

When I am recording using keyboards and synths, I decide if the keyboard sound requires reverb. If not, the reverb section of the keyboard's effects is bypassed during recording and then added back, using outboard or plug-in effects, in the final mix. An example of this would be to use a piano patch that sounds like it is in an empty stadium while the rest of the mix is in a small room. Bypassing the stadium reverb allows the whole mix to sound like it is in the same room. There are times when the effects are a part of a specific patch, or sound, and cannot be turned off without the sound itself being compromised. In these cases the effect must be considered part of the sound and cannot be removed or replaced externally. Some keyboards can bypass the effects section with a single command, others require it to be edited on a sound-by-sound basis. Consult the manual for the keyboard to determine how best to work with its internal effects.

Placing Effects in the Signal Chain

Routing a signal to the effects processors can follow one of two paths. If the signal is to be recorded flat, or without the effect, the signal is routed directly from the channel to the recorder via the direct output. Then it is sent to an auxiliary output, or bus, which is connected to the outboard effects unit. The signal from the effect is brought back into the mixer for monitoring in the control room and for the headphone mix.

If the effected sound is to be recorded, for example compression on a vocal, an insert connects the effect. An insert routes the signal from the channel to the effect, back to the channel at the point it left, and then to the recorder. The signal may also be bussed to a second effect to add reverb for monitoring and headphones. A bus is a route that can be used by all channels of a mixer so many different signals can be combined and sent to a single destination or effects device.

Effects that are specific to a single sound, such as compressors, are best routed in as inserts. A compressor is not the sort of device to share among other sounds since it responds to peaks in the audio signal and does not differentiate one sound from another. On the other hand, adding reverb to tracks as a whole can be done with a bus. Even the signals processed with inserts can be routed through a bus as well, since they occur in different points along the signal path.

Effects Plug-Ins (Software)

Computer-based hard disk recording software have their own unique type of effects processors called plug-ins. Plug-ins are special programs that can be added to digital recording software to add additional functions. Several basic plug-ins are usually included with the software, such as EQ, compression, limiting, filtering, delay, and sometimes reverb. Additional plug-ins can be purchased and added to the software. The difference between plug-ins comes down to audio quality and price. In the plug-in world, there are expensive and inexpensive plug-ins. As with any purchase, listen and compare first. The following section will explore some of the different types of plug-ins and the tasks they perform.

Plug-In Formats

There are two basic plug-in types: real-time and non-real-time. Real-time plug-ins can be heard during playback or while recording. Non-real-time plug-ins only allow a short audition of the effect to be heard but the actual effect is written directly to the audio file and is not heard during playback or while recording. The resulting file can, however, be played back with the plug-in added. If there is a problem, the process can be undone, or, with nondestructive editing, the effected file can be erased and the process begun again with the original audio file. Depending upon the software and hardware being used, it is possible to have both types of plug-ins available in the same application.

There are several plug-in formats available, each of them developed by a software company for their particular package. Many of the actual plug-ins have been created by third-party companies and are available in several different formats. Before purchasing a system, be sure to check out the plug-in availability for the system. Analyzing your needs will help guide your purchase.

Using Plug-Ins

For real-time plug-ins, applications use an interface similar to the effects routing scheme of a mixer, inserts, and busses. For example, in Pro Tools, the real time effects use Digidesign's TDM format and are accessed through the inserts and bus routings in the Mix window. The non-real time plug-ins are called Audiosuite plug-ins and are accessed from the Edit menu. Plug-ins are also available in MIDI/digital audio sequencers, such as Cubase, Logic, and Digital Performer, and digital editors mentioned in chapter 16.

There is good news and bad news about using plug-ins. First the good news. When using an outboard unit, for example the Focusrite Red 2 EQ, only two channels are available. Routing two signals fills the capacity of the unit so any other signal requires another Red 2 outboard unit. Listing at $3,995, these units are not cheap. However, using the TDM plug-in version of the Red 2, it is possible to have as many channels of Red 2s as your computer hardware will allow.

The catch is, "as the computer hardware will allow." Plug-ins require computer power to run. In the case of a Pro Tools TDM plug-in, that power is a DSP chip on the card that is installed inside the computer. Systems like the MOTU 1208 or Digi 001 use processor power in the computer. The bad news is that computer processing power can be consumed in a hurry. One good reverb plug-in can bring a computer-based system to its knees unless fortified with the speediest processor and sufficient RAM

(Random Access Memory). TDM users can add additional cards inside the computer to add more DSP chips but that means additional cost. Once the card slots inside the computer are full it means adding an expansion chassis at further cost. The bottom line is, plug-ins are one of the most powerful aspects of using a computer-based hard disk systems, but there are limits. Find out as much as you can about plug-in power requirements before purchasing to be sure that you have sufficient power to run them.

Automation

Some programs allow for plug-in settings to be automated. In Pro Tools it is possible to choose only specific settings for automation or automate everything at once. Figure 17.7 shows the automation window for the D-Verb TDM plug-in. Items in the list on the left are parameters that can be selected for automation. Items on the right are parameters that already have been selected for automation. Automation can be created and edited in the Pro Tools Mix or Edit windows. Automating effects saves time since the software will execute them automatically.

Plug-In Management

Getting the most out of plug-ins involves a little knowledge of what their requirements are and how to use them effectively. Like their hardware cousins, a little creativity in management can get around their limitations.

Consider using a bus for effects instead of placing them on every channel. This way there is only one software processor created instead of many. Also, it is possible to combine outboard effects and plug-ins together. This can lighten the load on the computer components and makes it possible to keep on using

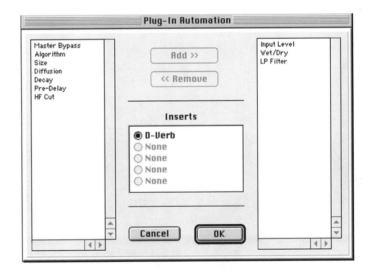

Figure 17.7. D-VERB Automation Window

the outboard effects equipment in the rack along with the new plug-in toys simultaneously.

I have a saying that there is no problem in my studio that a few thousand dollars won't cure. For more effects signal processing power there are two options: add more cards to the computer (referred to as *farm cards*), so there are more digital signal processing (DSP) chips available, and/or add more RAM to the computer. If that is not in the budget there are still plenty of tricks in the arsenal.

For example, Pro Tools uses TDM plug-ins that come in two versions: real-time and non-real-time. For basic effects like EQ or compression, usually a single setting is used for the entire track. Once the track is recorded and the amount of effect determined, the audio file can be processed with the Audiosuite (non-real-time) plug-in. This frees up DSP power for other effects. Since all editing in Pro Tools can be nondestructive, the original, unprocessed file is still available should you need to go back and rework any processing.

If no Audiosuite version is available, the bounce to disk function in Pro Tools can be used to create a new audio file with the processing included. The bounce to disk function is normally used for mixdown to create the stereo master file but can also be used to create submixes of tracks in addition to single tracks with processing added. This process can also be used to assemble complex special effects in a separate file or Pro Tools Session and the resulting stereo or mono file can then be imported into the main file.

Plug-In Roundup

Plug-ins are constantly growing in number and function. A list of plug-in developers for digital audio software that you are using can be found on the company's Web site. Most companies that produce plug-ins have demo versions that can be downloaded. There are two types of demos available: demos with a time limit on processing that work for couple minutes and then stop processing, or demos that function fully for a specific number of days. Some companies, like Digidesign, Waves, and Arboretum, sell packages of plug-ins that work with most digital audio software. These tend to provide all of the basic types needed such as compressors, limiters, filters, EQs, and reverb. Because they offer several plug-ins at an attractive price, these packages are a good place to start.

Just as with outboard effects gear, different plug-ins have their own unique characteristics. The windows and commands are unique for each plug-in. Which one works best for you may take a

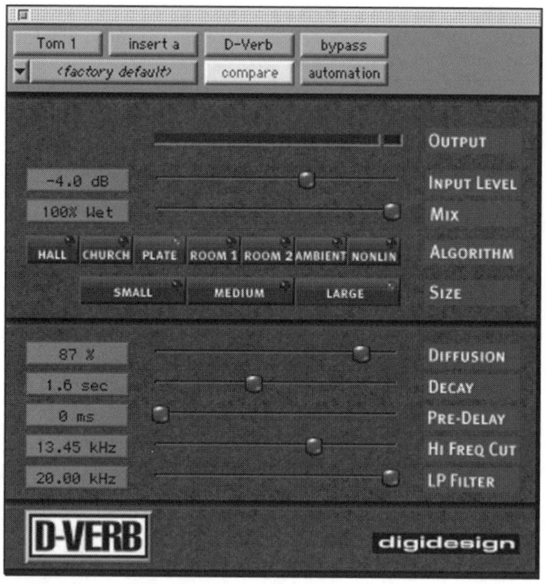

Figure 17.8. Digidesign D-Verb Plug-In

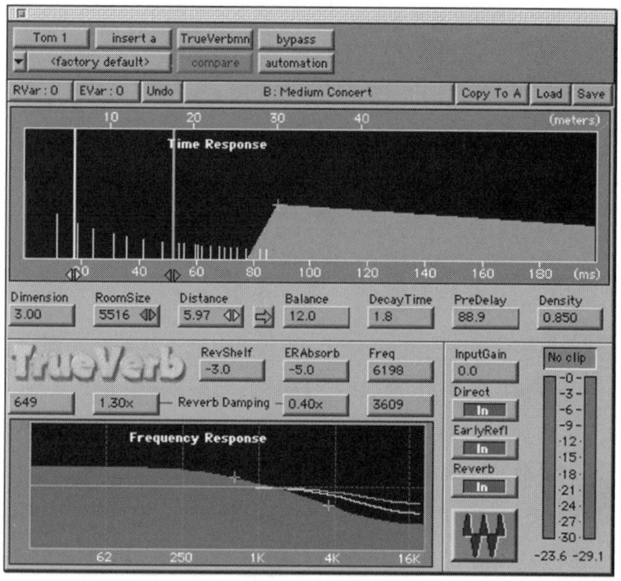

Figure 17.9. Waves TrueVerb Plug-In

little bit of research. There are several reverb plug-ins currently available; two are shown in Figures 17.8 and 17.9. The interfaces are very different but the function is the same.

Mixer Plug-Ins

One of the drawbacks to using a computer program such a Pro Tools is that the mixer channels are still not truly configured with the same exact features as a hardware mixer's channel strip. A solution for this is Metric Halo's Channel Strip plug-in. This plug-in provides controls for input and output, gain and trim, polarity inversion, and 6-band parametric EQ, just like a hardware mixer. In addition there is a compressor, expander, and gate, with a side chain that can be switched between pre- and post-EQ thrown in. This saves an additional insert routing and an additional DSP chip. High resolution meters are provided for each output section of the plug-in including a master for stereo or mono signals. The graphic display is a plus with software plug-ins that many developers take advantage of and it allows visual feedback and the ability to tweak settings by clicking and dragging the line to adjust the values.

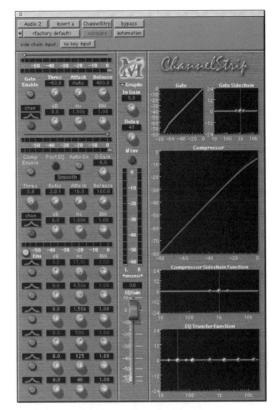

Figure 17.10. Channel Strip Plug-In

Hardware Emulators and Vintage Gear

Since plug-ins perform the function of outboard processing gear it would seem logical that some of the top names in outboard gear would have plug-in versions of their own. Recognizable names, like Focusrite, Lexicon, TC Electronic, and Drawmer, all have software versions simulating some of their famous hardware.

Focusrite is well known for their quality outboard devices and they also produce plug-in versions. The Focusrite software interface bears the unmistakable look of the Red series. The Focusrite d2 is a graphic EQ based on the hardware d2 and the Focusrite d3 compressor is represented as well.

Figure 17.11. Focusrite d2 Plug-In   **Figure 17.12. Focusrite d3 Plug-In**

Lexicon's Lexiverb plug-in is one of the most graphically interesting in its display of reverb decay times. The sound quality is excellent and the automation feature makes this plug-in a very powerful tool for the digital studio.

Vintage gear is also represented in offerings from plug-in manufacturer Bomb Factory. The LA2 plug-in is an emulation of the Teletronics LA-2A tube compressor/limiter. The 1176 is based on the Urei 1176 solid state compressor. Both of these units offer the classic sound but with all the advantages of modern technology. You may fully automate all parameters. Their functions are expanded to include stereo or mono compatibility.

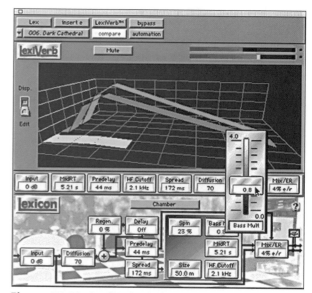

Figure 17.13. LexiVerb Plug-In

Figure 17.14. Bomb Factory LA-2A Plug-In

Figure 17.15. Bomb Factory 1176 Plug-In

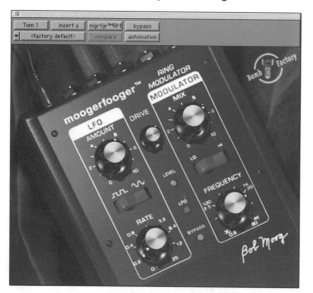

Figure 17.16. Bomb Factory Ring Modulator Plug-In

Figure 17.17. Bomb Factory SansAmp Plug-In

Bomb Factory produces some other classic effects including the Moogerfooger lowpass filter, Ring Modulator, and SansAmp—a tube amp simulator. These plug-ins are great for adding some extra sizzle to instrumental tracks.

Another piece of hardware that is also being emulated is the microphone. Antares has released a microphone modeler. This plug-in takes the source mic you are using and attempts to make it sound like other microphone models. The microphone can be chosen from a long list that includes many classic manufacturers and models including Neumann, AKG, B & K, RCA, and Telefunken.

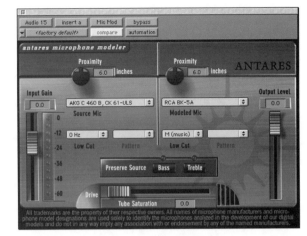

Figure 17.18. Antares Microphone Modeler Plug-In

Figure 17.19. DUYdadtape Plug-In

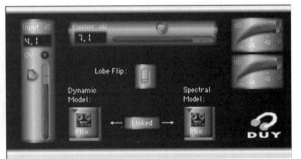

Figure 17.20. DUYdadvalve Plug-In

Analog sound still has a place in digital recording. Emulating the best parts of analog recording is a big part of digital recording. DUY has created some plug-ins that emulate the sound of analog tape decks and valve gear.

Amp and Virtual Synth Plug-Ins

Amp and virtual synth plug-ins can be used to when recording tracks. Amps Farm is a guitarist's dream come true. Forget lugging heavy amps around or bringing different heads and cabinets to a session in case the producer wants a certain sound. Amp Farm can do it all internally. This plug-in simulates the sound of an impressive list of amps.

The cabinets list is equally impressive and includes choices for several mic positions.

Amp Farm's plug-in interface changes to match the style controls on the original amp. Mix and match the

| 1959 Fender Bassman |
| 1964 Fender "Blackface" Deluxe |
| 1967 Fender "Blackface" Twin |
| 1960 Vox AC30 |
| 1966 Vox AC30 with Top Boost |
| 1965 Marshall JTM 45 |
| 1968 Marshall Plexi |
| 1986 Marshall JCM 800 |
| 1995 Mesa Boogie "Recto" Head |
| 1994 Mesa Boogie Trem-O-Verb |
| 1989 Soldano SLO Head |
| 1987 Soldano X-88R Preamp |
| 1996 Matchless Chieftain |

Figure 17.21. Amp Farm Plug-In's Amp menu

amps and cabinets, then tweak the knobs and switches to further refine the sound. It's just like the real thing only there's no unplugging to switch from one to the other. In my studio the resident guitarist and engineer tried this plug-in and decided to nix getting their old amp fixed since, "We won't be needing it now."

For keyboard players there are also plug-in options. The Virus Synthesizer plug-in from Access, O.S. is a TDM version of a hardware synthesizer complete with control that can be fully automated. The synthesizer uses the DSP chips on the Digidesign computer interface card, and can achieve 80-voice polyphony on a Pro Tools/24 Mix Plus system. The synthesizer's output can be processed through other TDM plug-ins and the synth's filters can process audio routes as well.

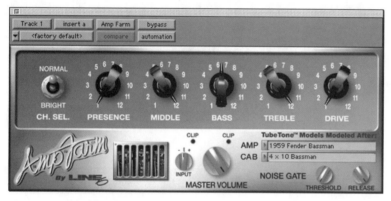

Figure 17.23. Amp Farm Plug-In

| 4 × 10 Bassman |
| 4 × 10 Bassman (near) |
| 4 × 10 Bassman (off-axis) |
| 4 × 10 Bassman (near/off-axis) |
| 4 × 12 Marshall |
| 4 × 12 Marshall (near) |
| 4 × 12 Marshall (off-axis) |
| 4 × 12 Marshall (near/off-axis) |
| 2 × 12 Twin |
| 2 × 12 Twin (near) |
| 2 × 12 Twin (off-axis) |
| 2 × 12 Twin (near/off-axis) |
| 2 × 12 AC30 |
| 2 × 12 AC30 (near) |
| 2 × 12 AC30 (off-axis) |
| 2 × 12 AC30 (near/off-axis) |
| 1 × 12 '52 Deluxe |
| 1 × 12 '52 Deluxe (off-axis) |
| 1 × 12 '64 Deluxe |
| 1 × 12 '64 Deluxe (off-axis) |
| Big Cab |
| Big Cab (off-axis) |
| None |

Figure 17.22. Amp Farm Plug-In's Cab menu

Figure 17.24. Virus Synthesizer Plug-In

The Direct Connect plug-in from Digidesign allows direct connection between many software synthesizers and samplers such as the Bitheadz Unity Sampler and Retro

Figure 17.25. Direct Connect Plug-In

Synthesizer (see chapter 2), the Koblo 9000 synthesizer. Audio generated by the synths and samplers is recorded directly into Pro Tools with no external connection.

Plug-Ins for Editing

One of the biggest problems in recording is a vocal performance that has a few pitch problems. Pitch correction software plug-ins makes this a relatively simple problem to fix. This plug-in can even be used to create special vocal effects.

In many pop styles, the bass needs to have just the right EQ. Plug-ins such as MaxxBass can create a virtual subwoofer and be more effective than EQ for that thumpin' bass sound.

Noise Removal Plug-Ins

One of the handiest plug-ins I have is DINR from Digidesign. This plug-in removes unwanted noise from tracks. This is especially useful when recording in locations that are not soundproofed, like basements, bedrooms, and live or location recording. This may single-handedly save the day if tracks suffer from air conditioner or heating system noise, tape hiss, ground hum, or other constant noise.

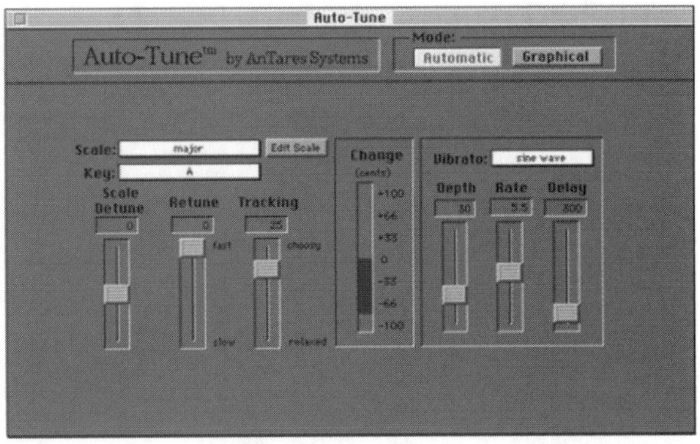

Figure 17.26. Antares Auto-Tune Plug-In

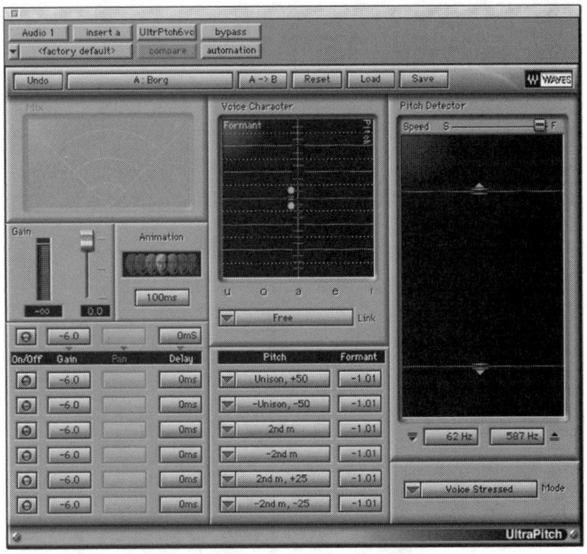

Figure 17.27. Waves UltraPitch Plug-In

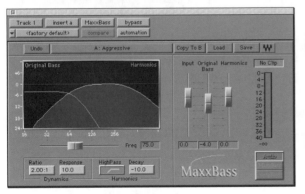

Figure 17.28. MaxxBass Plug-In

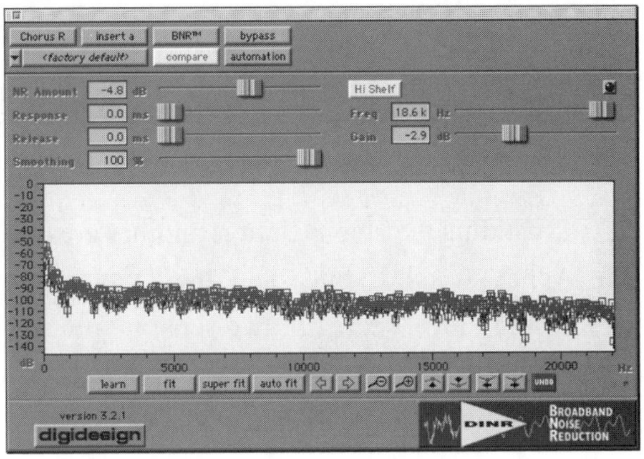

Figure 17.29. Digidesign DINR Plug-In

Stereo Field Processors

Plug-ins can be used to convert mono source sounds to stereo. This can be useful when working with mono sounds and sample loops, remastering or restoring old recordings, sound design, or multimedia creation.

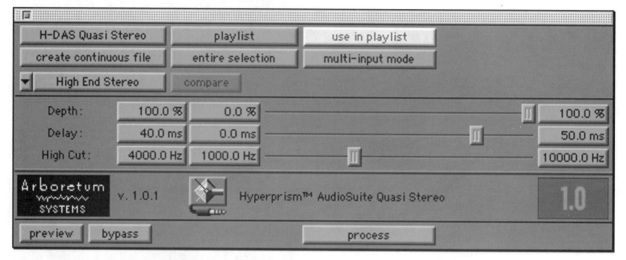

Figure 17.30. Arboritum Systems Stereo Plug-In

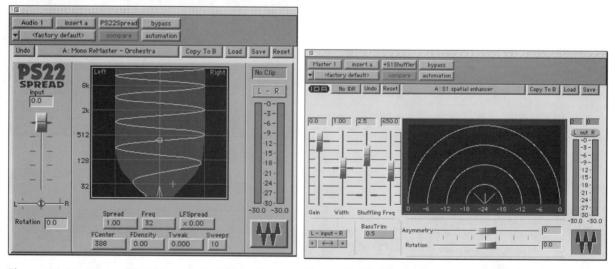

Figure 17.31. Waves PS22 Stereomaker Plug-In   **Figure 17.32. Waves S-1 Stereo Imager**

Expanding the stereo field is another area being explored in DSP processing. Plug-in versions of the Aphex Aural Exciter and the QSound process recreate the effects developed in outboard processing units. There are two separate plug-ins available for QSound. The QSYS TDM plug-in is intended for the processing of individual tracks, or mono files. This process is used to place individual tracks in a 3-D space. The QX/TDM plug-in applies the same encoding to stereo mix files without loss of image integrity or mono compatibility.

The Waves S1 Stereo Imager is a group of four plug-ins that control the width and spaciousness of the stereo image.

The stereo field is also a good place for special effects. The Waves MondoMod can add motion to a sound for subtle or exaggerated effects. The amount of rotation can be a simple tight to left, a Doppler type effect, or a full 360-degree rotation.

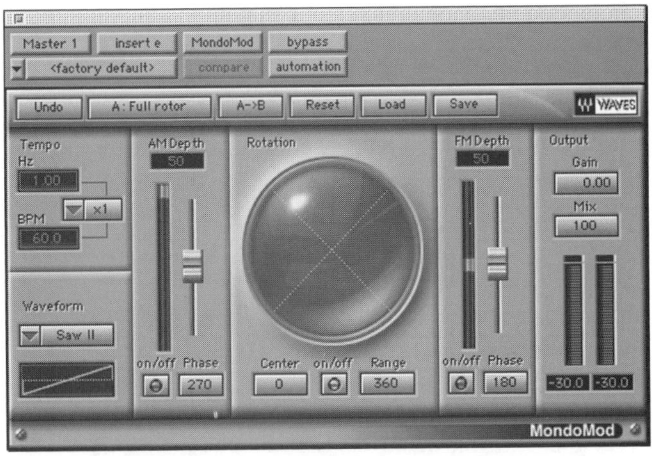

Vinyl Records

Ray Gun is available as a plug-in or a stand alone application. Its purpose is to remove all the clicks, pops, and other grunge from audio file transfers of vinyl recordings. After listening to the files and tweaking the amount of noise reduction, pop sensitivity, and rumble, the file is processed and a new, cleaner version is ready for transfer to CD, or other digital medium.

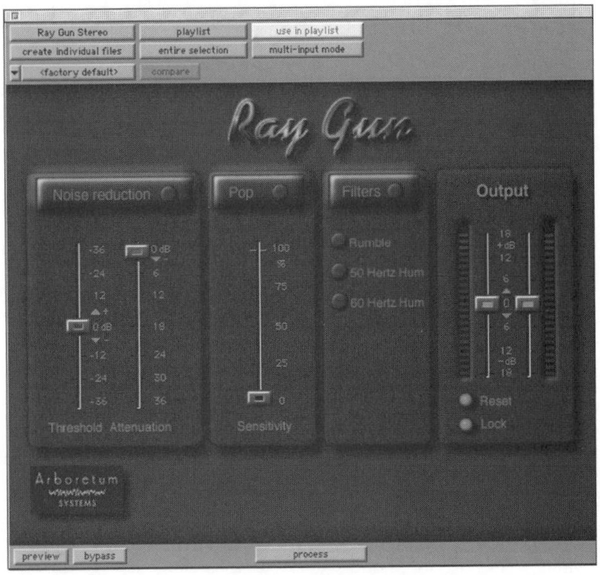

A Plug-In for Making Plug-Ins

The company DUY has created DSPider and ReDSPider plug-ins that emulate a multi-effects device. These plug-ins use modules of reverbs, delays, EQs, and compressors as building blocks to allow you to construct custom plug-ins.

Surround Sound

Surround is the current buzzword in the industry. Already common in film and television sound, the growing popularity of DVD audio and home theater systems makes it a reality for audio production on any level. Plug-ins from Dolby Labs and Kind of Loud Technologies allow 5.1 surround sound format mixing and encoding.

For the working with a surround mix, Kind Of Loud has created a special version of their RealVerb plug-in.

Figure 17.33. Waves MondoMod Plug-In

Figure 17.34. Arboretum Systems Ray Gun Plug-In

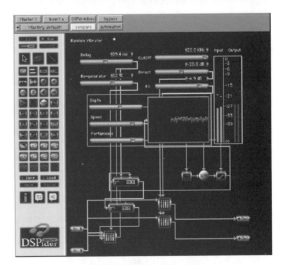

Figure 17.35. DUY DSPider Plug-In

Mastering Plug-Ins

TC Electronics' MasterX plug-in is a software version of their Finalizer processing unit. The plug-in is a high quality compressor, limiter, and expander. There are presets to use either as is, or as a starting point for developing personalized settings. These can be saved and recalled for future use. Chapter 19 is dedicated to exploring the mastering process in detail.

Additional MasterTools are produced by Apogee and marketed by Steinberg. Apogee is renowned for its converters. The MasterTools plug-in is a necessity for sessions recorded at 24-bit since they must be converted to 16-bit for

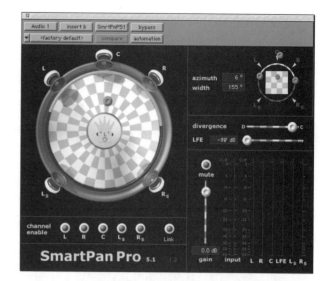

Figure 17.37. Kind Of Loud Technologies RealVerb 5.1

CD production. The UV 22 encoding plug-in preserves the resolution and detail of recordings made above 20-bit when creating a 16-bit file. There is a Nova feature that removes any digital clipping that may result during the mastering process. It works like a limiter, trimming all spikes off at digital zero. It also keeps a log of all instances of clippings, or "overs," in the terminology used by Apogee.

Hardware vs. Software Effects

This chapter has outlined both software (plug-ins) and hardware (outboard) effects options. There is actually a third option—using a mixer with built-in internal effects. The choice, as usual, comes down to personal preference and budget. It is possible to use all three types of effects (hardware, plug-in, and built-in to the mixer) for various needs in the studio.

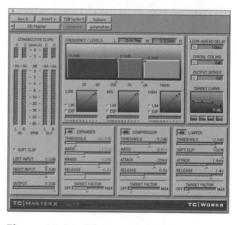

Figure 17.38. TCMasterX Plug-In

Hardware Effects Pros and Cons

Dedicated hardware effects, referred to as outboard effects, are designed to do a specific job and do it well. There is never an issue of running out of DSP chips or overtaxing a computer's CPU. Outboard effects are self-sufficient and do not

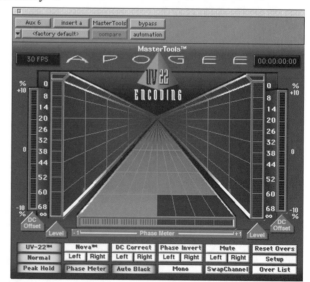

Figure 17.39. Apogee MasterTools Plug-In

require any additional software to run. It is possible to use your studio's audio system when rehearsing or during writing sessions. Many units support MIDI for program or parameter changes for changes on the fly from a controller keyboard or MIDI sequencer. They are easier to use than plug-ins in hybrid systems where recording can take place on a number of different media, for example on MDMs or hard disk.

On the down side, the additional connections introduce noise into the signal chain. High-end outboard effects usually cost more than plug-ins. Entry-level hardware effects can be noisy. The interface is limited to a small screen and individual pages of parameters. Also, editing can be difficult and there is a limit on user-programmable presets.

Plug-In Effects Pros and Cons

Plug-ins are digital and do not add noise to the signal chain. They interface easily with recording software and can be routed as inserts or busses. Some plug-ins can be used in real time or non-real-time environments. The parameters are usually visible on a single screen, often with graphs for visual feedback. Plug-ins can be easily automated. It is possible to have multiple versions of the same plug-in running at the same time, each with different settings. Plug-ins make it possible to create emulations of classic equipment no longer available, with additional functions added. Plug-ins can also be designed by the user for processes that are not practical using hardware (outboard) units. It is easy to create and save a large number of user-defined settings.

On the down side, plug-ins require a computer. It is easy to run out of DSP power using entry- or mid-level systems in a complicated mix. Working around this limitation takes valuable time in creating submixes or extra tracks that also eat up hard disk space. In some applications it is not possible to have more than one plug-in on the screen at a time. Some plug-in interfaces are large and hide the mixing controls while displayed. The many different formats of plug-ins make it difficult, or expensive, to have access to the same rack of effects for all software in the studio.

Summary

Effects are essential in the digital studio. They come in a variety of packages, including hardware, or outboard, effects, and effects built in to the mixer. They can also be software effects, called plug-ins. This chapter listed most of the popular effects with a short description. Popular outboard effects units were also introduced. Effects plug-ins were described and several examples were listed.

Chapter 18.
Mixing

The last step in the recording process is to produce the final mix. There are several ways to go about this, depending upon your setup. Obviously, the goal is to produce the best possible sounding performance on some form of digital media. To that end, this chapter is broken into two parts. The first is an overview of the hardware options for mixdown in the digital world. The second part is a variety of tips and tricks on preparing and creating the best mix.

Choosing the Mixdown Deck

To get the best possible results, you will need to save your final project on some form of digital media, with your basic choices being MiniDisc, CD, or DAT. As with other aspects of digital recording there are entry-level, mid-level, and high-end gear.

Selecting the right mixdown deck is a complicated choice. It is affected by your studio setup, budget, and history. Ultimately the goal is to produce the best possible sounding audio file in the format for CD burning or for use on the Web. Here's a quick overview, and then all the options will be explored in greater depth.

The first widely used digital format was Sony's beta format, which Sony no longer supports. Next was the DAT format, which failed as a consumer replacement for analog cassettes, but which grew to be the number one mixdown choice. Another consumer oriented format, the MiniDisc, also found a niche in the studio as both a multitrack and mixdown recording machine.

There are other mixdown solutions. A CD burner can be the mixdown device for a computer digital audio workstation. A relatively new format is the Alesis Masterlink, a combination of hard disk recorder and CD burner with some DSP (effects) thrown in. A rack of modular machines can mix to two tracks of an ADAT, DA-88 family, or modular hard disk machine. (Surround sound mixes are also usually mixed down to a DA-88 or ADAT so the entire mix is on one tape.) Computer hard disk-based systems can mixdown to an external deck or, more ideally directly to disk.

DAT

DAT is the mixdown recorder of choice for many studios and is priced in the mid- and high-end range. DAT is a popular medium for both mastering and CD production. A few DAT recorders can be purchased for under $1,000. Among these are the TASCAM DA-20 mkII and the Sony PCM-R300. These units provide the same quality digital sound as the

Figure 18.1. TASCAM DA-20mkII DAT Recorder

more expensive decks without some of the high-end bells and whistles. DAT decks under $1,000 usually have the Serial Copy Anti-Theft Management System, or SCAMS, installed, which prevents digital dubbing. This is not recommended if you want to make digital copies of your work.

Figure 18.2. Sony PCM-R300 DAT Recorder

DAT decks costing more than $1,000 typically have AES/EBU connections in addition to S/PDIF digital connections. The TASCAM DA-45HR has 24-bit recording capability. Panasonic's SV4100 DAT recorder also supports five modes of external sync.

Figure 18.3. TASCAM DA-45

MiniDisc

The MiniDisc is following in the footsteps of the DAT deck. It failed to catch the general public's fancy as a replacement for the cassette, but it has found a place in low-end audio production and sound design. The Sony MDS-E11 and TASCAM MD-301mkII are MiniDiscs in the

Figure 18.4. Panasonic SV-4100

$500 price range. MiniDiscs are conveniently portable and can be a great way to audition mixes on the road or anywhere outside the studio. In this price range digital connections are usually S/PDIF only. Track naming is a cool feature and is one of the reasons MiniDisc has become popular in live and broadcast mediums. The nonlinear format offers editing features, random access, and shuffle modes so the order of tracks can be customized. If you are on a tight budget, a MiniDisc can be an excellent solution. As with the DAT, digital connections are limited to S/PDIF at the entry level.

The TASCAM MD-80mkII is more expensive, listing for $2,699, and offers more features including AES/EBU connections, word sync, a frame accurate jog and shuttle wheel, and advanced 20-bit

Figure 18.5. Sony MDS-E11 MiniDisc Recorder

Figure 18.6. TASCAM MD-301mkII MiniDisc Recorder

Figure 18.7. TASCAM MD-80mkII MiniDisc Recorder

converters. This unit also contains a built-in sample rate converter. Live sound extras include serial and parallel ports for computer control and separate monitor and online outputs.

CD Burners

CD burners come in two forms: built-in to a computer and stand-alone units. Both can be used for mixdown. Computer-based CD burners can be purchased for under $500, and blank bulk CDs are cheaper than blank analog cassettes. This adds up to a bargain for producing digital recordings that can be played on any commercial CD player. Even reference mixes can be played back in any environment from a home system, car, or portable player. The trade-off is that it takes longer to burn a CD than it does to save a file to MiniDisc or to DAT.

Stand-alone CD burners, also referred to as real time burners, are dropping in price as more units become available. Units cost in the $1,000 to $2,000 range and excel at burning CDs quickly without taking the extra time required to burn a CD on a computer. However they cannot be used to create computer data or multimedia CDs.

Figure 18.8. TASCAM CD-RW5000 CD Burner

Figure 18.9. HHB CDR-850 CD Burner

Hard Disk/CD

The Alesis Masterlink is part hard disk recorder and part CD burner. It is a self-contained unit with a hard disk, CD burner, and software, and it has built-in signal processing capabilities. The Alesis has all the advantages of a computer-based system without the computer and costs less than $2,000. The mix is recorded to the hard disk, mastered using internal DSP, then burned to the CD burner, which supports 24-bit format CDs.

Mixing Tips and Tricks

Once you have all the required gear, you are ready to create the final mix. It is a mental and physical challenge. Rule number one is start fresh. Don't try mixing at the end of a recording session or at the end of a long day. Mixing involves shaping and blending all the parts created in recording and editing. You must have a clear image in your mind of how the final product should sound. Rule number two is to have a record of everything done in the recording and editing process so you can realize the clear image in your mind.

Figure 18.10. Alesis Masterlink

No matter how great the basic tracks are, the mix will determine whether the whole is equal to, greater, or less than the sum of its parts. A great mix can do a lot for a song but a bad mix will ruin the best of tracks. How each track is blended into the whole is crucial. Creating a great blend is a skill that comes from experience and patience. Just as a chef combines basic ingredients with spices to make a great meal, an engineer combines basic tracks with effects to produce a great mix. How well the two are blended determines whether the end result is sonic mastery or sonic mush.

Preparing for Mixing

As with recording, all equipment should be cleaned and checked before beginning the mixdown process. Check the cable connections and run a simple test tone to make sure everything is functioning properly. If the connection to the mixdown deck is analog, use a 1-kHz test tone to calibrate the deck's inputs and make sure the tone goes up to 0 dB. If mixing to DAT, record 30 seconds of the tone to the DAT tape. This will aid level calibration for mastering.

Make sure each channel is correctly labeled on the mixing console. This is especially important on larger consoles with many channels. Keep a note pad and pen handy to write down any notes and have a copy of the music or lyric sheet there as well. Set the volume for monitoring at a comfortable level. Once set, try to maintain it for all of your mixing so you will have is a common reference point. This will provide continuity from track to track, making mastering a bit easier.

Digital 0 (and Ways to Avoid It)

Since digital 0 is an absolute barrier, even a slight peak may send an attempted mixdown back to the beginning. Old habits die hard and those of us with analog experience learned to drive the meters to the limit for a strong signal. DAT decks and other digital media do not have the high noise floor that analog did, so mixing to the limit does not accomplish the same objectives. In fact, crossing digital 0 can cause you to damage your file.

When setting a level with the test tone, do not set it at zero. Try setting a level between –14 dB to –8 dB. This way any peaks in the sound will still be under the dreaded zero level and allow more attention to be paid to metering on the console rather than the DAT deck's meters.

Approaches to Mixing

From an artistic standpoint, each mix needs a vision. It could be as simple as placing the instruments on a stage, as if the listener were watching a performance. Or, on the more complex side, if the material calls for something more theatrical, all sorts of effects can be used to create illusions and soundscapes. It all begins with some basic tools. Panning controls (short for *panoramic*) place the sound to the left, right, or center of the stereo field. These can be used to position instruments on a virtual stage or move a sound around the stereo field for an effect.

Creating the front-to-back depth of the image involves volume control and possibly some reverb. Sounds "further away" will always be softer, so cutting back on things in the background will assist in creating a more natural environment. Chapter 17 dealt with the various reverb settings: room, chamber, and hall. In the mix these qualities can be applied to create a feeling of space and define the size of the virtual room in which the performance takes place.

In actual practice there are a few different ways of mixing. The beginning usually involves starting from scratch—moving all faders down to silence and bringing each instrument in one by one. In most pop and jazz recordings the mix begins with the drum set, starting with the bass drum, and moving along the tracks as they are laid out on the mixer: snare, hi hat, and so forth. Set the bass drum at 10 dB lower than 0 to start. Another approach is to begin with the most prominent part in the mix, say the vocal, and work down from there. Set the prominent part at 5 dB less than 0 and then continue by bringing in one instrument or part at a time. Setting that first decibel level is important, because there should be plenty of room left for the mix to increase slightly in volume. Never take the mix level up to 0. Again, leave 2 or 3 dB at the top to leave room for a little more volume to be added in mastering.

Next, listen to each instrument, one at a time. Establish a balance of grouped instruments like drum sets, strings, and horn sections. Set the panning positions for each instrument and make any volume adjustments necessary. Then begin to add effects. Other engineers wait until there is a rough mix before applying effects. The choice is partly personal preference and partly the material nature of the project.

All too often, mixing becomes a gradual climb up the decibel level ladder. Whenever you have a part that is not prominent enough, the obvious solution is to move the fader up thus increasing the overall volume. Later on in the mix that part becomes too loud. What is the typical solution? Move another fader up to increase the volume. The result is an unnatural sound. The cure is remembering that faders also move down! If a part is not coming through clearly, maybe everything else needs to be brought down a little. With EQ, other instruments may need to be trimmed back in certain frequencies to make room for one that is being obscured in the mix.

Applying EQ

EQ is the tone shaping tool. It alters the sound's harmonic structure, allowing selected frequencies to be amplified or reduced (see chapter 17). Twisting the EQ knob is playing with a delicate balance, too far one way or the other will send perfection careening into excess noise or unsatisfying thinness. EQ is best applied on a track by track basis, but its effects are cumulative. If too many track EQs are boosted in the same frequency range the overall effect on the mix may be a large frequency boost in that particular range. This will unbalance the overall mix, making it heavy and muddy in that frequency. Boosting the sound can also increase noise on the track or expose unpleasant aspects of the sound itself. Every tone contains overtones that are effected by EQ in a range other than the sounding pitch. For example, it is possible to add presence to a bass by boosting the mid-range rather than the low end, which may make it muddy or boomy rather than louder or more present.

If you are trying to be subtle, remember that an EQ change of 1 dB is inaudible and most people cannot detect even a 2 dB or 3 dB change. Not every sound can be the most interesting or the most important. Sometimes the changes needed to make a sound blend properly may make them a disappointment to listen to by themselves. Focus on the overall effect and make sure that each part is fulfilling its function to your satisfaction.

Being able to understand producer-speak is a boon to all engineers. Even when working in a home environment you may be called upon to translate a cryptic word or phrase into sonic results. Consider this list of phrases as part translation and part problem solving guide.

Low-Frequency Terms

Power, weight—Try boosting under 200 Hz if more is needed.

Woody, tubby—Try cutting between 200 and 300 Hz if it's too much.

Fat, warm—Try boosting below 500 Hz to add.

Muddy, boomy—Try cutting below 500 Hz to reduce.

Full, rich—Leave low end flat, no EQ.

Rumbly—Try cutting low frequency.

Thin, anemic—Try adding low frequency.

Mid-Frequency Terms

Presence, clarity, definition, punch—Try anywhere from 500 Hz up to 1.5 kHz depending on the instrument.

Muddy, tinny, nasal—Try cutting in the 500 Hz to 3 kHz range.

Hard—Try cutting in the 2 kHz to 3 kHz range.

Strident, piercing—Try cutting in the 2 kHz to 5 kHz range.

Twangy—Try cutting around 3 kHz.

Metallic—Try cutting in the 2 kHz to 5 kHz range.

Sibilant—Try cutting in the 2 kHz to 5 kHz range.

Natural, smooth—Leave mid-range flat, no EQ.

Lacks punch or color—Try boosting mid range.

Hollow—Try adding between 500 Hz to 1000Hz.

Muffled, muddy—Try adding at 5 kHz.

High-Frequency Terms

Bright, crisp—Try boosting above 7 kHz.

Glassy, edgy, sibilant—Try cutting above 7 kHz.

Airy, transparent—Try leaving flat, no EQ.

Too close or detailed—Try cutting high frequency.

Mellow, round, smooth—Try cutting high frequency.

Dull, muffled, distant—Try adding high frequency.

To better understand EQ and its capabilities, spend some time listening to different tracks in solo and experiment with the EQ in each frequency and notice its effect on the overall sound.

Using Compression

Compression is part effect and part necessity. Compression controls the dynamics of a part by smoothing out peaks in the performance. If there is a track that alternately peaks the meters then disappears in the mix, it is a candidate for compression. This allows the track to be at a volume where the softer parts do not get lost and the louder parts do not distort. Not every track needs compression. Use of compression should be limited to the tracks that actually need it and tracks on which it is used specifically for effect. Compression can add punch to a part but it can also flatten it if too much compression is applied.

Vocals are almost always compressed. The amount depends on the singer's style and recording technique. Large shifts in signal level will cause the compressor to react differently, noticeably altering the sound quality. Extremely high compression ratios may bring out sibilance and background noise.

Reverb

Reverb is the most obvious and identifiable effect. Most of us bathe our early mixes in it because it makes almost anything sound better. When contemplating how much reverb you want and when to add it, consider that what the listener hears first when an instrument is played in a room is the natural sound of the instrument; then, the early reflections of that sound off of the walls and other reflective surfaces; and lastly, the later reflections as the sound continues to bounce around the room as it is absorbed and deflected by materials in the room. In a small room there is more direct sound of the instrument, and the early and late reflections come very quickly. As the room size increases, the direct sound from the instrument begins to decrease and more of the early reflections are heard. With the increase in room size there is also a longer decay time for the late reflections. With large halls there is more early reflection than there is direct sound from the instrument and the decay times are even longer.

Since most project studio tracks are cut directly or by tight miking in a natural sound source, the "room" in which the performance takes place must be added synthetically after the fact. Reverb helps create a sonic signature and can be a simulation of a natural environment, through its ability to create a virtual club, concert hall, or church. It can also be effectively unrealistic if some or all of a mix is very dry (as in New Age music) or very wet (as in '70s disco recordings). In reverb jargon, the word *wet* is used when reverb is applied. *Dry*, conversely, means little or no reverb. One tip: always apply EQ before reverb because EQ differences are easier to hear when dry.

Volume and reverb help define the space in which the performance occurs. With a single reverb there will be only one setting available, so choose one that best suits the style of music and sound you are trying to achieve. Pop music typically uses small size rooms; translation—short reverb time. Jazz and chamber music use a little larger space, a large room where the instruments can blend naturally; translation—longer reverb time. Classical orchestras use large halls for blending large numbers of instruments; translation—longest reverb times. Putting part of a mix in a small room setting and the rest in a large hall will result in an unnatural and unpleasing sound.

Positioning the Sound

When positioning instruments in space, there are two dimensions in which to work. Stereo involves positioning sounds from the left to right in the "room," whereas reverb involves positioning sounds from the front to the back in the "room." The most obvious is the left to right space in the stereo field. In that field there are five identifiable positions: hard left, mid-left, center, mid-right, and hard right. The front to back dimension of the mix will depend on the size of the reverb's room.

Center is the most prominent position and should be held by the lead vocal or other soloist front and center. Pulling back the volume moves an instrument to the back of the room. In pop recording the bass drum and bass are usually positioned center but in back of the vocal.

If there is more than one reverb unit available, dedicate one unit to the vocal. Using a specific setting, such as a plate reverb, will help keep the solo out in front and isolated in the mix. For acoustic ensembles panning is important to maintain realism. For example, an orchestra has a standard seating arrangement on stage and orchestra tracks should be positioned accordingly in the mix. For example, the strings are in front of the winds and positioned with the first and second violins to the left of center and the violas and cellos to the right of center; the woodwinds are left of center and the brass right of center, etc.

If there is more than one reverb unit in the rack, make sure the settings complement each other. A level of reverb, or any effect for than matter, that makes an interesting sound in solo may not make an interesting or pleasing sound when combined in a mix. It is hard cutting back on something after you have spent hours coming up with the perfect sound, but it happens all the time. The bottom line is how the tracks finally play together.

It is ultimately your vision, judgement, and taste that must be used when applying effects to a track. The best way to learn what each effect does, and what each setting within the effect does, is to experiment with different settings and see what is being changed. As with any instrument, it takes some time to master each effect. Don't be afraid to explore.

Mixer Automation

Automation is a definite upside of digital recording. Chances are that during the recording and editing stages, some rough mixes were made for work tapes or just to document the session. By saving snapshots of these mixes, including EQ and internal effects settings, you will already have a skeleton of a final mix.

Final mixes can be auditioned, then tweaked a day or two later. With enough memory it is possible to store several versions of a mix to choose among. Automation may not save time in the long run, but your time will be spent more productively. The mix will always be consistent allowing more attention to detail. Automation is especially helpful on fades, making them smooth from start to finish. The only decision you will need to make is the length. Always err on the long side for fades because they are easily shortened in mastering. The only way to lengthen a fade is re-mixing. Save and document mixes just as you would the master tapes or disks. They can be worth their weight in gold if a song has to be re-mixed.

Stereo to Mono Compatibility

There are situations where mixes will be played in mono, for example with multimedia and Internet files. Keep this in mind while mixing, because there are some things that sound good in stereo but not in mono. Many mixers have a mono switch that converts the mix to mono. Mono conversion eliminates the stereo's left to right placement by putting everything in the middle. The result is that when a stereo image is converted to mono, center panned sounds may be too loud and anything panned hard left or hard right suffers a 3 dB loss in level. Technically speaking, the problem is that phase signals increase in volume and out of phase signals cancel each other out. This is why some sounds will increase in volume while others seem to disappear no matter how much level is added. Keep this in mind during signal processing and mixing if you will be need a mono compatible mix.

Mixing Surround Sound

The demand for mixing for surround sound has increased to the point that most digital mixer manufacturers include surround sound capability into many units. The surround sound concept has been around since the Quad experiment in the '70s. The difference with surround sound is that the current format comes from the motion picture industry, not audio component manufacturers. The currently adopted standard is the Dolby Digital 5.1 format developed by Dolby Labs. It has been adopted for use in DVD video releases and digital television (DTV). This consists of six channels of audio, five full sound channels, and one channel that exclusively handles low frequencies. Speakers for the five full frequency channels are placed around the listener: three are positioned in front in a left-center-right pattern (forming a 60° angle with the listener), two are placed slightly behind the listener (from 100° to 120° from the front-center line). The low frequency signal is fed to a special speaker called a *subwoofer*, which is usually placed on the floor between the center speaker and the left or right speaker.

Begin the list of equipment needed for surround with extra speakers and a subwoofer. All those speakers will need amplifiers to drive them, so add two stereo amps to the one already being used to drive the current pair of stereo monitors in the studio to bring the channel count to six. There are also mono amplifiers available for this purpose called monoblocks, or you could use powered monitors.

The audio signal on a DVD is compressed to conserve bandwidth. The compression algorithm used is called AC-3. When playing a DVD in a home theater setup, the AV receiver decodes of this signal and routes it to the correct speaker channel. To create the correctly encoded signal, an encoder is required. Currently, hardware encoders are extremely expensive and certain types may only be available by lease. On the software side, there is Sonic Foundry's SoftEncode application for Windows and APack from Astarte in both Mac and PC versions.

The surround sound mix itself will need extra panning capabilities for a 6-channel setup. This technology is already built into mixers such as the Mackie db8, Yamaha's 02R and 03D, the Panasonic DA7, and the new Roland VM series mixers (see Chapter 10). For computer-based systems there are plenty of options. For Windows users, the Mx5.1 by Minnetonka Software can accommodate 5.1 mixing with either the Digital Audio Labs V8 card or the Yamaha DSP Factory. Smart Pan Pro from Kind of Loud Technologies can perform 5.1 or 7.1 mixing on a Pro Tools TDM system. Look for this market to grow rapidly as home theater systems become more popular and DVD audio becomes a commercial reality.

In the end, what makes a great mix is attention to every sonic detail. Whether it is a solo artist or massive production, everything should sound clear and natural across the entire frequency spectrum. Each element should have its own place and not conflict or obscure any other element. You should also have cool toys to play with!

Summary

The basic mixdown options are MiniDisc, CD, or DAT. MiniDisc and CD burners are the least expensive. For the high-end, consider DAT. There are several models of each format to suit almost any budget. After selecting the mixdown deck, sitting down to create the final mix is the next step. This chapter presented an overview of tips and tricks for mixing.

Chapter 19.
Mastering

The very last step in the digital audio recording process is to create the final version called the *master*. The process of creating the master is referred to as *mastering*. Before digital studio, mastering was always done in a professional studio. However, with the current level of digital technology it is possible to create your own masters. This chapter presents the basic concepts and the hardware and software required to make a good master.

Assembling the Order

The process of mastering molds the project into a cohesive final product. The first part should be completed before the mastering session even begins, namely determining the order of songs on the CD. This is important, because part of making the final whole is the flow from track to track. This impacts both the sonic quality of the songs and the amount of space between them. First, create a possible order and listen to it out for a while. Make changes if necessary, listen again, and then establish the final order. Repeat this process until the desired order is reached. Once the order is established, create a log sheet with the order and the duration of each song.

The Mastering Process

Up until the digital explosion a few years ago, most mastering was typically done in professional studios with large consoles and a rack of outboard processors. The equipment in the professional studios is top of the line and the environment is ideal for critical listening. The mastering engineer knows both the equipment and the space well and this helps in judging what needs to be done to a recording to bring out its best while minimizing any flaws in the recording. One of the advantages of using a mastering engineer is having another set of skilled ears listen to the tracks and assess them. It also allows you to hear your work in an ideal listening environment and it may point out shortcomings you need to address in the future.

Today, many people are mastering in their own digital studio thanks to the availability of the necessary hardware and software. Though most entry- and mid-level studios lack the sophistication of equipment found in a mastering studio, there are a few things that can be done to compensate for this. First, know your studio space. Listen not only to your work but also to other recordings in your collection. Compare your sound to the same recordings played in other systems in other spaces. Listen for the sound in different frequency ranges. Is the bass present, muddy, or booming? Is the high end bright, dull, or piercing? Is the mid-range full or nasal? Listening to a recording that has been well mastered on the best equipment can help you adjust whatever equipment you are working on. Listen to music in the style of the music you want to master and then compare it to your current project. Compare them frequently and try to imitate the mastered CD. This will give you a model to help you in the mastering process. I also recommend getting a copy of Donald Fagen's *Nightfly* CD. It is an excellent digital recording that many engineers use to test monitors.

If you are mastering through outboard processing, purchase the cleanest sounding processors, primarily graphic EQ and compressors, that your budget will allow. Since outboard gear, especially low cost gear, can add noise to the recording, a second pass through that equipment will add another layer of noise. Mastering on computer-based systems has an advantage in this area. Plug-ins are an affordable and quieter solution to the problem.

The Mastering Approach

Just as with mixing, the best way to approach mastering is to start fresh. Mastering is a mental process. It involves critical listening and a more subtle hand in shaping the sound. It is important that your ears are fresh and you are ready to be your own toughest critic. If there is a problem that cannot be fixed in the mastering process, the track must be re-mixed (see chapter 18).

Shaping sound starts with using EQ to cut or boost certain frequencies. If there is a problem with a sound in a specific frequency range, fixing it may undesirably effect another sound in the same range. If the problem cannot be resolved with EQ, re-mixing the song with improved processing on the sounds in question is the only way to fix the problem. This is where automated mixing can save the day. Recreating a mix is a tedious process since everything must be set and patched exactly as it was for the sound to be similar. Automation, snapshots, and session notes will all make the reconstruction process an easier task.

Maintenance and Testing

Some basic maintenance and testing should begin any mastering session. If mastering to DAT, make sure the deck is in optimum condition, with clean heads and a fresh, high quality tape. Use the 1-kHz test tone recorded on the mix tape to calibrate levels for the recorder used for the master. Also, make sure all audio connections are secure and functioning properly. If the mixer does not include a test tone generator, external tone generators are available.

Listening Clues

When beginning a mastering session, start by listening to the whole project from start to finish. Assuming that there are no problems with the order of tracks, focus on the sound. Will volume adjustments be required to keep each song at a comfortable listening level? If they are, that problem must be rectified. Are the ballads softer or louder than the up-tempo tunes? If yes, add this to the list. Listen to each track as it begins. Does it seem to come out of nowhere? Is there noise at the beginning? Is there any noise when moving from the end of one track to the beginning of another?

Now critically listen to each track. Listen for anything that is not the way you want it to be, for example, a part that is being buried or is a little too loud. Are certain instruments jumping out in the mix? Are there parts of a song that peak the meters but the overall sound of the track is not very loud?

There are a lot of potential loose ends to tie up. Not every project will suffer from all or any of these problems. There may be some tracks that require very little processing. The goal is, as always, to make the best music possible.

If you can find the money in your budget, master one project at a professional mastering studio just to observe the process. This experience will be worth more than all the words I could write on the subject.

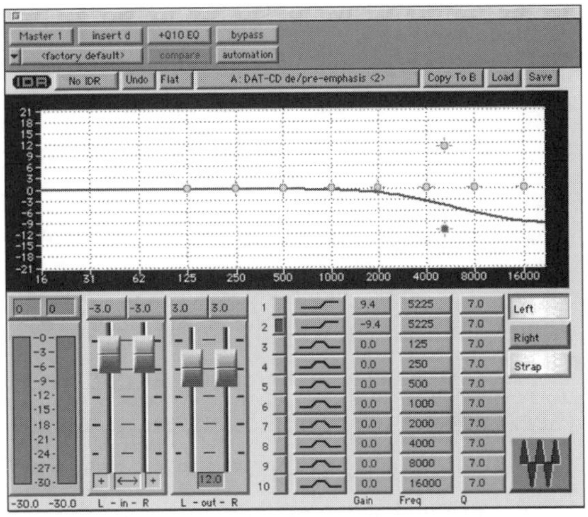

EQ

In the mixing process (see chapter 18), EQ is used on an instrument by instrument or track by track basis to shape and blend different tone colors into a proper balance. When mastering, EQ is applied to specific frequency ranges to bring out ranges that need more presence or pull back ranges that are too predominant in the overall mix. As

Figure 19.1. Waves +Q10 EQ Plug-In

mentioned in chapter 18, the trick is to avoid fixing one problem and creating another. An example would be cutting anything in a frequency shared by the lead vocal. Therefore, EQ must be applied carefully. A top quality multiband EQ is best because it allows for finer tuning of the frequency to be tweaked. As with applying EQ in mixing, it is usually the first effect added to the mix.

Compress to Impress

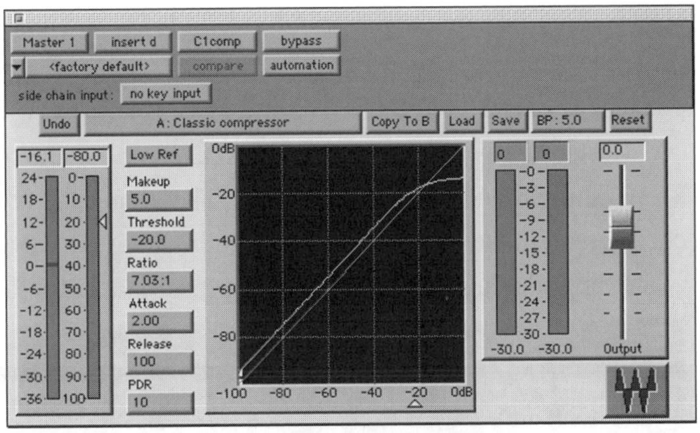

Compression has the reputation of being the tool to make a recording louder. To some extent this is true, but the flip side is that it can suck the life out of a recording just as easily if too much is applied. Try beginning with a very slight level of compression and increase the settings until the effect is just audible, then back off a little until it sounds natural again.

Figure 19.2. Waves C1 Compressor Plug-In

Multiband compression is similar in concept to multiband EQ, except it effects a frequency band dynamically. With a multiband compressor there are three bands of compression, each effecting its own frequency range. The advantage is being able to address problems in the bass, mid-range, and high end separately and independently.

In addition to compression, some limiting or expansion may be necessary to smooth or bring up specific sections. It is during the compression phase that levels of each song should be checked against each other to make sure there are no major dif-

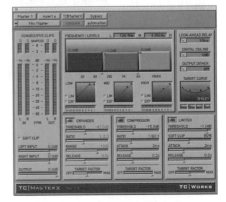

Figure 19.3. TC/MasterX Plug-In

ferences. There may still be some tracks that must be reduced in volume because they peak and distort when brought up to match the others.

A limiter is another effect that is designed to squash those nasty peaks and bring up the volume level of the track. Unfortunately, when the overall volume is brought up, some noise may be brought up in volume along with the music.

An expander can be added to clip off any excess noise at the beginning and end of the track. Care must be used in the setting so reverb trails

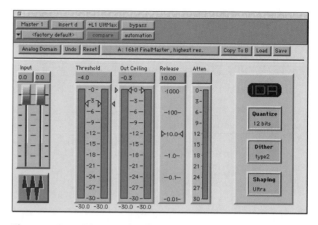

Figure 19.4. Waves UltraMax Expander Plug-In

are not clipped accidentally. Always set the expander's threshold lower than the compressor's threshold.

One tool in digital processing to be wary of is *normalizing*. The process of normalizing is supposed to take advantage of all available headroom by locating the highest peak in a sound file and moving the entire sound file up in decibels until the peak is at the loudest point possible without distorting. It sounds like a good idea, but it is often not the best thing for a track. Our ears follow the average decibel level of the track, not the peaks. Our analog ears do not track information the same way digital equipment does. What sounds like a good idea for making a track optimally loud may not bring the desired results. However, normalizing a track can be a good idea when preparing files for multimedia (see chapter 20).

Mastering Tools for the Digital Studio

Mastering has only recently come to the home studio thanks to outboard gear like the Finalizer from TC Electronic and the dbx Quantum. These specialized units combine a multiband EQ, multiband compressor, limiter, and expander with other tools for enhancing digital recordings. Both units can work at the top sampling and bit resolution rates available for the cleanest sound possible.

Figure 19.5. TC Electronic Finalizer

Figure 19.6. Dbx Quantum Digital Mastering Processor

Alesis Masterlink

Currently in a class by itself as both a mixdown deck and mastering tool, the Masterlink functions as a stand-alone hard disk mastering tool. After the files are recorded onto the internal hard disk, a 3-band parametric EQ, single band compressor, limiter, and normalizer are available to process the files. They all work in real time and edits are nondestructive. Tracks can be cropped destructively to eliminate unwanted

Figure 19.7. Alesis Masterlink

space before and after the track. For determining song order, it is possible to construct play lists of files on the hard drive. This makes experimentation easy and is great for turning out shorter length CDs from a full project for press kits or demos. The CD burner records standard Red Book CDs at 4X speed and can burn 24/96 CDs using its own CD24 format at 2X speed. Current generation CD players will not play 24-bit CDs. However, Macintosh, Windows, and UNIX computers recognize 24-bit files as aiff format audio files.

Mastering on a Computer

Computer-based systems have become popular in professional and home or project studios. It is difficult to judge the full effect of processing on the entire track with just a short preview. Therefore, programs with real-time processing capabilities are best for mastering.

Surgical editing is also possible in the computer. Problem peaks can be squashed directly without applying compression to the entire track allowing for a more natural sound. Short, subtle fades can be applied to the beginning and end of a track to eliminate the sudden appearance or disappearance of noise. With the added feature of nondestructive editing, anything can be tried and instantly undone without a significant loss in time.

The digital revolution first made it possible to record basic tracks in digital, then edit them in digital, mix them in digital, add effects in digital and now master them in digital. Equipment that once filled an entire room can now fit on a desktop.

Creating the Final Product

Creating or burning the final CD is usually the end of the digital audio yellow brick road. Or should I say red or orange or blue brick road? In this case, the road should be red since standard audio CDs are called Red Book CDs. When you buy a commercial CD from a store it is a Red Book CD. Orange Book CDs are like Red Book CDs in the making. They become Red Book when they are finalized. Orange Book CDs can have audio files added incrementally as opposed to being burned start to finish in one session. Once they are finalized, which involves adding a table of contents to the disc, they will become Red Book CDs. Blue Book CDs are called enhanced CDs on the market. They combine audio data with data that can only be read by a computer. This data can include video clips, text files, or graphics.

If the master will be recorded to an external CD burner or DAT tape, all that is left to do is hit the record button and record the track. Most stand alone CD recorders accept Orange Book CDs. This allows the CD to be constructed track by track over time by pausing the burner between tracks or removing the CD and reinserting it at a later time. As long as the CD is not finalized, and there is enough room available, more tracks can be added.

Go Directly to 16/44.1 (Do Not Pass Go, Do Not Collect $200)

Anyone working at a bit rate and resolution higher than 16/44.1, it is now time to come down from the mountaintop and join the rest of the digital world. The purpose of recording at higher resolutions and bit rates is to record a more detailed digital image of the performance. Unfortunately,

all of those 20-bit or 24-bit, 48-kHz or 96-kHz files must be converted to 16-bit 44.1 kHz files before burning the final Red Book CD. Conversion can be performed by a hardware converter or, for computer-based systems, a software converter.

Apogee developed the UV22 encoding process for this and uses it in both their hardware units and a TDM software plug-in for Pro Tools. The UV22 system does not use dithering as do most other conversion systems. It uses a periodic signal higher in the audio spectrum than dithering noise, around 22 kHz that effects the signal less than the dithering process. Dithering introduces a

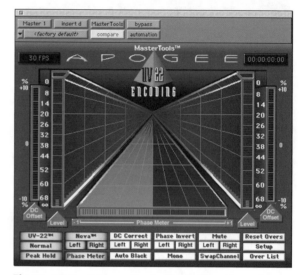

Figure 19.8. Apogee MasterTools Plug-In

low level of white noise to the recording. The purpose of dithering is to help keep as much audio detail as possible while the excess data is being truncated down to the lower bit rate and resolution. Truncating digital audio without dithering can produce low level distortion. Dithering introduces a low level of noise to the recording that helps boost signals that would otherwise be lost in the conversion process.

CD Burning Software

Special software is required to access a CD burner attached to a computer and make the connection and send the studio files to the burner. This software can provide functions and flexibility not available in

stand-alone, real-time CD writers. All burners ship with at least a basic CD authoring program. Most computer users will want to consider a more powerful program and some of these options are outlined below.

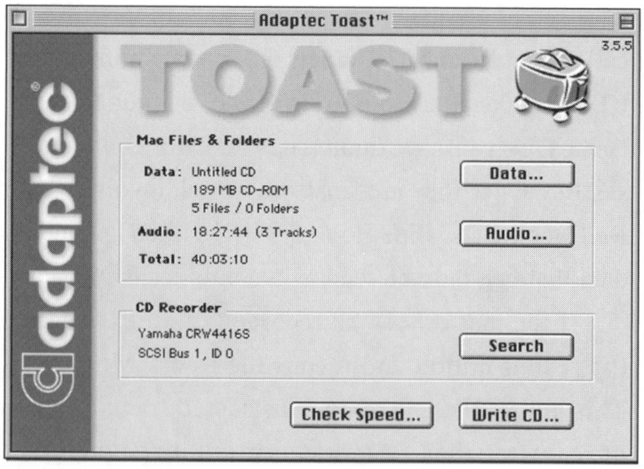

For Macintosh, this is usually Adaptec's Toast software. Toast is a versatile program that is capable of creating a number of different types of CD, including Red, Orange, and Blue book, as well as several computer data configurations. This allows it to easily create a basic audio CD for everything from

Figure 19.9. Adaptec Toast Main Screen

rehearsal tracks and reference mixes to a final mix and also create a data backup of files along the way. For final archiving, I like to create a Blue Book CD that contains all the sequencer, digital audio, music notation, and text files needed for a track along with an audio track of the finished mix. This makes it easy to refer back to past projects because everything I need on one disc.

When creating audio CDs, the software offers options over the space between tracks and can also indicate the total length of the CD. The

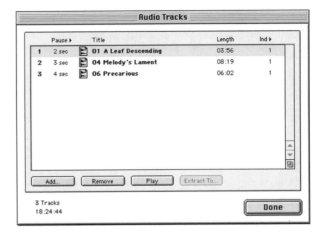

Figure 19.10. Adaptec Toast Audio Tracks Window

information from this window can be copied and pasted into a word processing or page layout program to create a track log or print a tray card.

Additional CD-Burning Software Options

You should consider purchasing a dedicated program for burning CDs as it provides more control and options than the basic software that comes with the burner. There are many to choose from on the market.

For Macintosh users, the options include Toast 4 Deluxe and Jam by Adaptec, Waveburner by Emagic, and Masterlist CD by Digidesign.

Windows users also have a variety of CD burning software to choose from including Easy CD Creator by Adaptec, CD Architect by Sonic Foundry, Red Roaster by Sek'd, and Wavelab by Steinberg.

Which CD-burner software is best for you? If you are using a program that supports CD burning/ mastering software, consider that using a program designed to be used with the program. For example, if you are using Sound Forge, then you might want to go with CD Architect because the same company designed it. If you are a Mac Pro Tools user then checkout Masterlist CD. It is also a good idea to get recommendations from friends and colleagues and to download a demo and review it. There are entry-level offerings that cost under $100. For the mid-level and high end expect to pay in the $150 to $500 range for more powerful CD burning/mastering software.

The mid-level to high-end CD burning/mastering software brings a greater level of control to the desktop. Some of the options in the mid-level to high-end offerings include allowing for changes to be made to the gain of each track to bring tracks into line with one another. Cross fade control allows for greater control over segues between tracks.

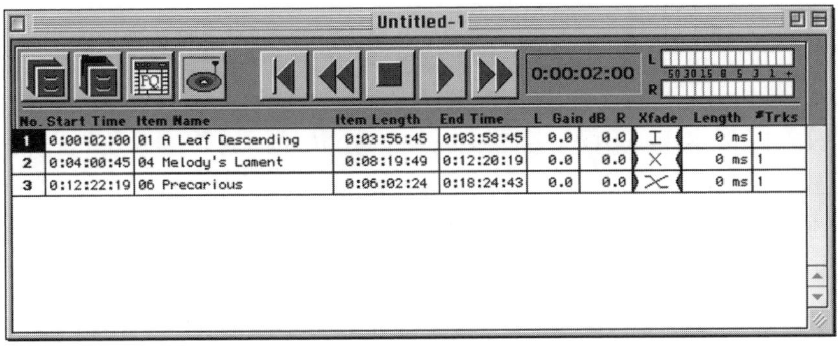

Figure 19.11. Masterlist CD Main Window

Many options are programmable including setting the time and fade in/out between tracks. This allows creation of special effects such as one track fading into another, direct segues, or simply controlling the space between tracks for dramatic effect.

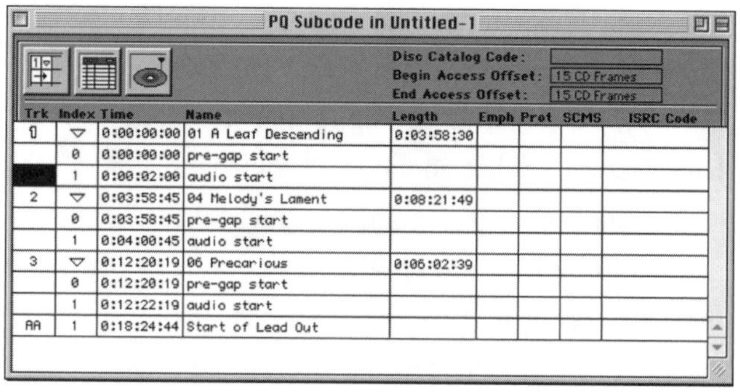

Masterlist by DigiDesign also allows access to the PQ subcode of the CD. This allows a single, long audio region to be broken up into a series of separate tracks. This is

Figure 19.12. Masterlist CD PQ Subcode Window

helpful for creating audio CDs from live performance tapes or other situations where no break is desired in the performance. Start IDs can be inserted anywhere in the PQ sub code to allow the CD player to be advanced to a particular point on the CD.

Converting MIDI Tracks to Audio

Digital Sequencers (see chapters 6, 7, and 8) allow for mixing of digital audio tracks and MIDI tracks in the same file. The computer can play back both types of data simultaneously, resulting in a complete performance of the piece. However, the file cannot be transferred directly to an audio CD

or mixed down to a waveform file. The MIDI tracks have to first be converted to audio data. This can be done individually, track by track, or by combining several tracks into a submix. The best result will be achieved if each track is kept separate, if sufficient hard disk space is available.

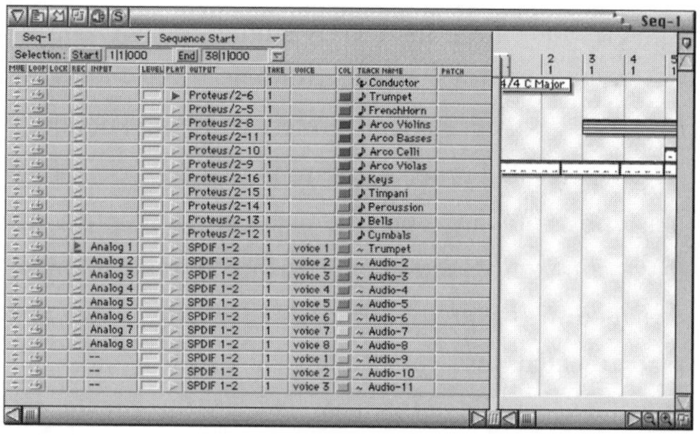

The steps are relatively simple. Create a new audio track for every MIDI track. Play enable the MIDI track, or tracks if creating a submix, to be recorded. Record enable the audio track, or tracks, if transferring more

Figure 19.13. Digital Performer Tracks Window

than one track at a time or creating a stereo sub mix.

Play a little of the MIDI sequence at its loudest part to ensure that the level does not exceed digital zero. Then select record and let the sequence play through until the end. The MIDI data flows out through the MIDI interface to the MIDI keyboard. The audio from the keyboard is recorded back to the digital sequencer through the digital audio interface or computer card and is recorded as audio data in the digital sequencer. Depending on your studio and the digital audio interface setup, it may be possible to record more than one track at a time.

In the end, there will be an audio track duplicate of every MIDI track. For digital sequencers with DSP plug-ins, the digital audio tracks can be processed with any DSP effects included in the system such as compression, EQ, or reverb. Digital sequencers with mixing console features can control the volume level and panning of the converted audio tracks.

The last step on the road to making an audio CD is to create a stereo file in a file format supported by your CD burning software. The command for this process, and its menu location, varies from sequencer to sequencer. In Digital Performer and Pro Tools LE it is called Bounce To Disk. In Cubase VST it is called Export Audio. This provides several options for file format, resolution, and sample rate. Check the CD burning software first to determine what type of file is required. Once the stereo file is created, launch the CD burning software and create the audio CD.

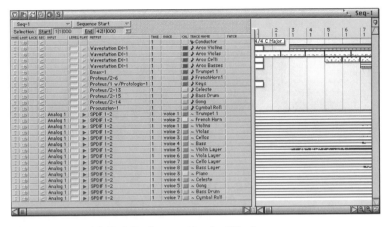

Figure 19.14. Digital Performer Tracks Window

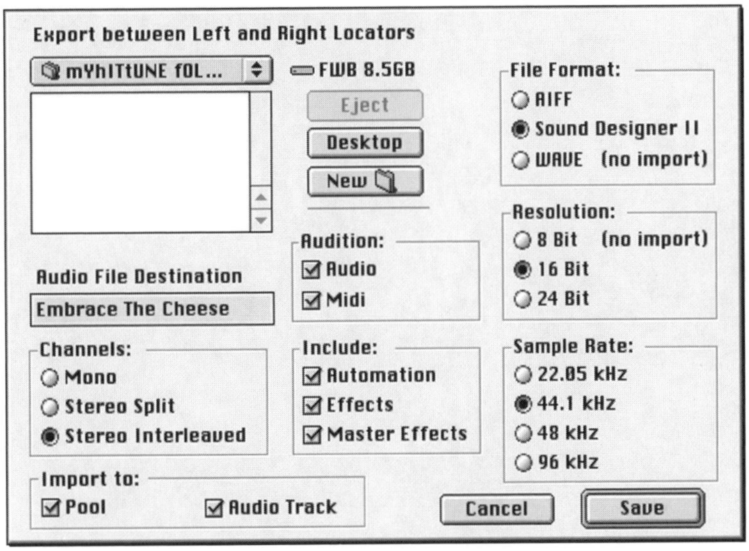

Figure 19.15. Cubase VST Export Audio Dialog Box

Summary

This chapter introduced mastering, the last process in the creation of a digital recording. You not only need to have the right tools, but you must pay significant attention to the mastering process itself. You also must decide if you are going to create the mastered CD yourself or take it to mastering studio. If you produce your own masters, then you will need either outboard equipment or specialized mastering software. It takes time to become familiar with the process, but with practice, you will be creating your own mastered projects in your studio.

Chapter 20.

Digital Recording, Multimedia, and the Internet

The previous chapters have dealt with digital recording with the main output or product being an audio recording, such as a CD. This chapter will introduce and provide an overview of the various multimedia options in the digital world.

It is possible to record music in the digital world for other applications, such as video, computer games, the Internet, and CD and DVD-ROM programs. Digital audio and MIDI files can be incorporated into Web pages and shared over the Internet.

Overview of Multimedia Applications

There are many ways that audio can be used in multimedia. Some applications include:
- incorporating audio into multimedia presentations using software such as Aldus Persuasion and Microsoft PowerPoint.
- providing sound files for use over the Internet and in World Wide Web pages.
- composing music for video.
- composing music for CD-ROM and DVD-ROM projects.

This chapter is designed to provide a brief overview of each of these areas. You will need to spend time learning to use the software to become proficient with any of the described applications.

Required Hardware and Software

All of the applications described in this chapter require a computer (Macintosh or Windows) and software that can convert files into various file formats. In the digital world, computer files are stored in several different formats because computers and various programs do not all store digital information in the same manner. For example, there are different formats for audio, MIDI, and video. In addition, software often uses its own proprietary format. So a file created by one digital audio program may be unreadable by another. For these reasons it is important to be able to convert files to a variety of formats for multimedia use.

Digital File Formats

Some audio file formats have been explored in previous chapters. The most common Macintosh audio format is aiff (for audio interchange file format, which is pronounced by saying each letter separately A-I-F-F). Another popular Macintosh audio file format is sdii, which stands for Sound Designer II. This program was one of the early offerings in the digital world so the file format is very popular with Macintosh software. The common Windows digital audio file format is wav (pronounced wave).

MIDI files can also be used in multimedia and, in some cases, they are the preferred file format because they are relatively small in size compared to audio files. Therefore, MIDI files can be easily incorporated into multimedia software. Digital audio files are typically much larger in size. For example, a 30-second audio clip can be in the 300 K size range depending upon the sampling rate used. A MIDI file of the same information is approximately 65 K. However, if you want to add acoustic sounds, then an audio file is the way to go.

There are also formats that are used for movies and multimedia. Movie file formats include QuickTime and avi. QuickTime is a cross-platform format used in many applications. The format currently predominant on Windows computers is avi. To work with multimedia, you should ideally have access to both QuickTime and avi-formatted files. In some instances it may be advantageous to convert sound files (MIDI and audio) to video formats. This is necessary when composing music for a video project or if you plan to add music to multimedia software for use on the Internet. This will be explored in more detail later in this chapter.

Converting Audio Files to Various Formats

Since there are a variety of file formats that are used, software is needed to convert audio and MIDI files to various formats. The best tool to convert audio is a digital editing program. There are many from which to choose. Some of the most popular are Sound Forge, CoolEdit Pro, Peak, and Vegas. The two programs that I am most familiar with are Sound Forge for Windows, published by Sonic Foundry, and Peak for Macintosh, published by Bais. Both of these programs can import and export audio files in a variety of formats. The other nice feature is that both companies offer a "lite" version of their programs for use by entry- to mid-level users. Sound Forge XP (Windows) lists for $59.95. Peak LE lists for $99.

Converting MIDI Files to Various Formats

As with audio files, MIDI files can be converted to other formats if necessary. Each MIDI sequencer uses its own proprietary file format. However, there is a General MIDI file format that most programs can read called Standard MIDI file format (SMF). SMFs can be created by a MIDI sequencer, usually by choosing Save As from the File menu and then choosing MIDI Sequencer, or SMF format. It is also possible to convert MIDI files to various video formats for use in multimedia software and on the Internet. This will be explained in more detail later in this chapter.

Converting Audio Files to MIDI

Sometimes people will ask, "How can I convert audio files to MIDI?" The short answer is that you can't. Currently, it is not possible to convert audio to MIDI.

Converting Sound Files to Video/Movie Format

If your goal is to add sound files to multimedia files from presentation software and word processors, converting sound files to a movie format is usually the best option. This is because file formats for movies are the most common and can be read by most multimedia capable software.

Both MIDI and audio files can be converted to a movie format. To convert a MIDI file to a movie format, I usually convert the audio or MIDI file to QuickTime, a free program for Macintosh and Windows from Apple Computer. A copy of QuickTime can be downloaded for free from www.apple.com/quicktime.

Converting Files to QuickTime

Both MIDI and digital audio files can be converted to QuickTime format. To convert an audio file to QuickTime, first check to see if the audio software you are using offers QuickTime as an option. Choosing Save As from the File menu will usually reveal your options. If the digital audio software cannot export the required format, then you will need to use a digital editing software program such as Sound Forge or Peak to convert the file.

MIDI files can be converted to QuickTime by using the free software that comes with QuickTime called QuickTime Player. This program will allow you to convert MIDI files to QuickTime format.

Once the MIDI file is in QuickTime format, it can be incorporated into most word processing and multimedia software, since QuickTime is a universal format. Just look for an "insert" or "insert movie" command and the converted sound file will become part of the file, and the playback will be identical to the original version. For example, in Microsoft's PowerPoint, there is an Insert menu that lets you inserting both movie and sound files.

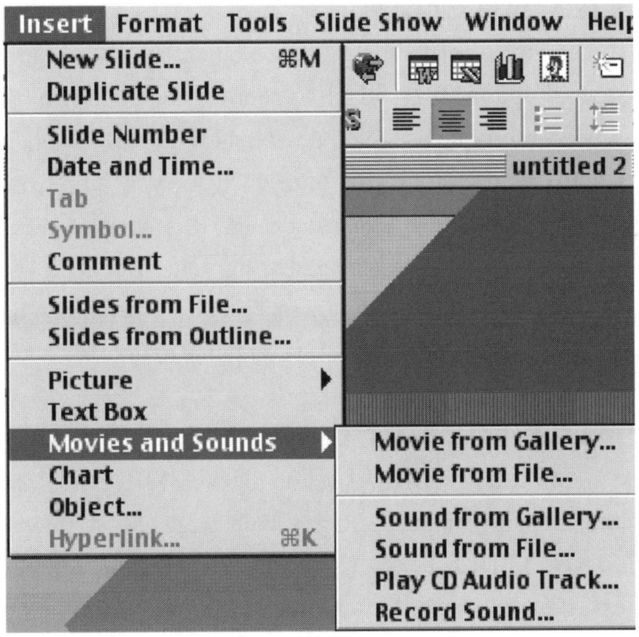

Converting Audio Files to QuickTime

There are times when you may want to use audio files instead of MIDI. Perhaps

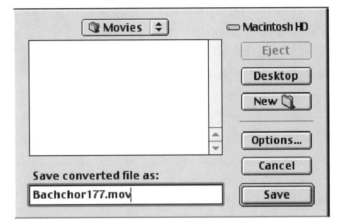

Figure 20.1. Converting a MIDI File to a QuickTime Movie

Figure 20.2. Inserting a QuickTime Movie into PowerPoint

you want to combine MIDI and digital audio tracks and/or use audio tracks in a presentation. The best way to convert digital audio files to QuickTime and other formats is by using digital editing software mentioned earlier in this chapter.

These digital programs can open audio files and include a variety of editing and processing tools. Simply open the file into the software and then make any edits or changes necessary. Silences can be removed, a fade-out can be inserted, and effects can be added. The last step is to save the file in the desired format.

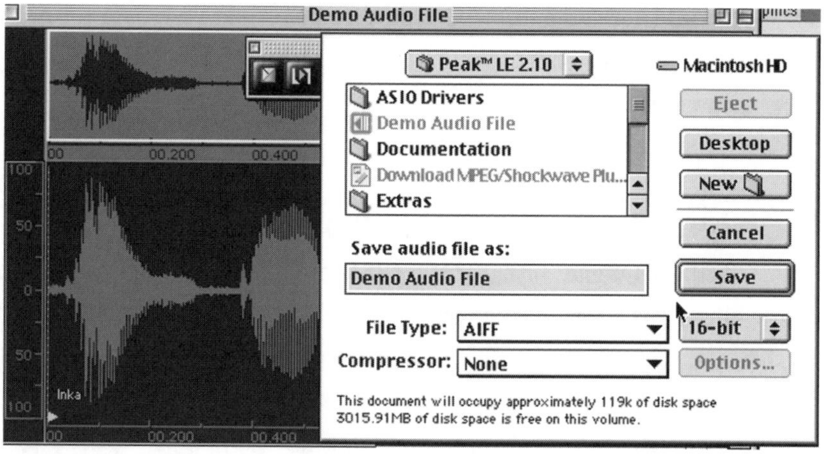

Figure 20.3. File Formats Using Peak LE

For multimedia presentations, QuickTime again is the best option, as most programs will recognize QuickTime formatted files. With Peak (Mac) and Sound Forge (Windows), saving files in a variety of formats is as simple as choosing Save As from the File menu and selecting the desired format.

Once converted, a file can be imported into many programs, including Microsoft Word, Appleworks, and other word processing programs. Movies can also be inserted into presentation software programs, such as PowerPoint.

The Internet

If you want to incorporate your music files onto the Internet for use on a Web page, there are several options from which to choose. There are two basic objectives when incorporating sound files for the Internet: playback and downloading. For example, if in creating your Web page you want to include sound files your visitors can listen to, you will want to use a streaming technology. The two most common streaming technologies are RealAudio for audio and QuickTime for movies and audio.

If you are interested in sharing your files with others over the Internet so your listeners can copy them to their own computers for listening, then downloading is the best route. Downloading occurs when a file is transferred from one computer to another.

MIDI Files and the Net

You can post MIDI files on the Net. MIDI files can be saved as Standard MIDI files (see chapter 1) and then incorporated into a Web page. Most Internet browsers can play MIDI files. You can also convert MIDI files to QuickTime movies as mentioned earlier and use these in a Web page. This is an excellent option, as QuickTime is a common format and just about every Web browser can read it.

If you're interested in using MIDI as a Web designer, consider Beatnik (www.headspace.com). The Beatnik program and the JavaScript authoring language can be used to create interactive playback capabilities in a Web page.

Audio Files for the Internet

If you want to place audio files on the Internet, you have several options. If the purpose is to provide something for the user to hear, then RealAudio or QuickTime are the best choices, as they are ubiquitous. By using Peak or Sound Forge, audio files can be saved in RealAudio or QuickTime format and then posted on a Web page. Both formats allow the files to be streamed. Streaming is a process that allows a user to hear the file while it is being sent or downloaded to them. The file is sent over the Internet in chunks. When the first chunk arrives, the file begins to play.

Compression

As mentioned previously, the problem with audio files is that they can be quite large. One minute of stereo CD quality sound can take up to 10 megabytes of storage. This means waiting a long time for files to be downloaded or copied to your computer. This is one of the main reasons why the World Wide Web is sometimes called the World Wide *Wait*! In order to deal with the large file sizes, many people use compression schemes. Compression uses a mathematical formula to reduce the size of a file while maintaining as much of the fidelity as possible.

When saving audio files with digital-editing software (Sound Forge or Peak, for example), you can select a desired sampling rate. The higher the rate, the better the quality, and of course, the bigger the file size. If high fidelity is not necessary, consider lowering the sampling rate to 22,050 for music, or even 11,025 for the speaking voice.

MP3

As of this writing, the most popular audio compression format used on the Internet is MP3 (motion picture group expert audio layer 3). MP3 uses a compression scheme that reduces the size of the audio file to approximately one-tenth of its original size and does an amazingly good job of maintaining the original fidelity. The sound quality is not as good as that of a CD, but it is pretty close. MP4 (motion picture group expert audio layer 4) is under development and promises additional enhancements.

MP3 files can be played on a computer using one of several MP3 players, such as QuickTime. They can also be played on stand-alone players similar in concept to a Walkman or Discman, only they play MP3 files.

Converting Audio Files to MP3

To convert audio files to MP3 format you will need software that can save in MP3 format. First, check to see if the MIDI/digital audio software you are using will allow you to save in MP3 format. If so, that will be the easiest way to go. If not, you will need to purchase software designed to convert files to MP3 format. There are programs available for both Macintosh and Windows. An excellent source to read reviews of various MP3 software is on the MP3.com web site (http://software.mp3.com/software). Some of the options include JukeBox 4.0 (www.musicmatch.com) for Windows and SoundJam MP (www.soundjam.com) for Macintosh. Many of these programs are free or can be purchased for under $50.

There are essentially two processes for creating MP3 files. There is a "ripper" that converts songs from a CD and turns them into wav or aiff files. There is also an encoder that converts the wav or aiff to MP3. Using MP3 software, you can convert your wav or aiff files to MP3 and then put them on the World Wide Web.

So here is what you need to do to create MP3 files: Record an audio file using your recording device. Copy that file onto your computer. Then load the MP3 ripper/encoder software and encode the file as MP3. Your files are now in a format that can be uploaded to sites on the Internet and shared with others who have MP3 players.

Promoting Your Music on the Web

The topic of promoting your music on the Web is extensive enough to fill the pages of an entire book. You may want to review some of the Web sites dedicated to this including: www.mp3.com, www.listen.com, and www.mp3lit.com. These Web sites provide you with a location to post and, in some cases, to sell, your MP3 formatted files. Check out these and related sites for more information.

Adding Sound Files to a Web Page

MIDI, movie, MP3, and other files can be inserted into a Web page. If you are familiar with HTML (hypertext markup language) then the EMBED command can be used. If you are using an HTML editor, such as Adobe Pagemill or Macromedia's DreamWeaver, you can link to the file or insert it as a QuickTime movie. Consult the help menu of the HTML editor you use to review how to link and embed files.

Creating Music for a Video

Another area to be considered in the digital world is composing music for video. You may be asked to write music for a video or to create music for animations. If this is the case, there are several options to be considered. We discuss them in the section that follows.

MIDI Sequencers

Most of the MIDI/digital audio sequencers we mention in chapters 7 and 8—such as Cakewalk, Cubase, and Digital Performer—can import video files. For example, imagine you are asked to provide sound tracks for a video. The video producer would send you the video in QuickTime format. Once the video file is imported into your sequencer, you can use the MIDI/digital audio sequencer to create sound tracks. When you import a video file, such as a QuickTime movie, it appears in one of the sequencer's tracks.

Figure 20.4. Movie Track Displayed in Performer

Now you can compose music to accompany the film. When you are done, the file can be resaved in a movie format with the soundtracks perfectly in sync with the video. The finished project is then returned to the producer of the project and you get paid. This can be a fun and profitable addition to your studio.

Video and High-End Software

There are several high-end programs designed for creating and editing movies and animations. Adobe Premier is the high-end video editing software used by many video professionals for both Macintosh and Windows. Adobe Premier lists for $599.95 and can be used to create soundtracks for videos.

For creating animations such as sales presentations, interactive applications, and e-merchandising demos, Macromedia Director is the high-end choice. It lists for $949.95 and is designed for the professional user.

Taking the high-end approach is time consuming. Just learning to operate the software will take a great deal of time. This option is designed for high-end applications.

Summary

This chapter introduced a variety of applications for integrating multimedia and digital audio. In order to work with multimedia, a computer is required to convert files to the appropriate format. After audio files are converted to a usable format, they can be incorporated into most multimedia software programs for a variety of purposes, including presentations. Audio and MIDI files can be incorporated into World Wide Web pages and shared with others over the Internet. For high-end applications special software is available for use with video and animation authoring.

Chapter 21.
Making the Purchase

If you have read this far, you are certainly serious about entering the world of digital recording. As we wrote the chapters of this book, we continued to be amazed at the plethora of choices. You should now have a fairly good idea of the options and be ready to decide what to buy.

Analyze Your Needs

A good place to start is by asking yourself what you need to produce in the studio. Review the type of recording you do. Is it mostly live performance? If so, then you should consider a recording unit that is primarily portable (see chapter 5). Are you comfortable using a computer? Do you have experience using MIDI sequencing software? Then you may want to go the computer-based route covered in chapters 6, 7, and 8.

Also ask yourself what type of recording work you want to do in the future. Are you planning to expand to include more options than you currently have? Perhaps the gear you are buying will open up some new doors. If this is the case, you will need to find the hardware and software to best support these goals.

Find a Model

I often recommend to friends and colleagues that they find someone who has a studio setup that they would like to emulate. With the explosion of the market for digital audio hardware and software described in this book, the number of studios in homes and apartments has gone up dramatically.

Perhaps someone in the community does digital recording. If so, arrange to visit his studio and pick his brain regarding the gear he uses. Is he using MDMs (see chapter 4), portable hard disk recording (see chapter 5), or computer-based systems (see chapters 6, 7, and 8)? Can you see one of these options fitting your needs?

Budget Considerations

Throughout the previous chapters, we have referred to equipment and software in the entry-level, mid-level, and high end. The higher the level, the higher the cost, and, in most cases, the steeper the learning curve. So decide—are you interested in entry-level, mid-level, or high-end applications? After making this choice, you can begin to develop a budget for all of the basic elements. The areas to consider include the following:

- recording unit (stand-alone or computer-based)
- mixdown deck
- computer and digital interface hardware
- computer software
- patch bays, interfaces, and cables
- mixer

- preamp
- monitors, amplifiers and headphones
- effects
- microphones and stands
- headphones
- cables
- supplies (tapes, etc.)
- instruments (MIDI keyboards, sound modules, etc.)
- stands (mics, keyboard, guitar, etc.)
- instrument accessories
- furniture
- acoustic room treatments

Buy Only What You Need and What You Have Time to Learn

Another good piece of advice is to purchase only what you need. When you visit music stores and other studios the wide variety and power of the options will impress and might sway you. Try to avoid buying things you won't be able to use for your recording needs. Also consider the amount of time you'll need to learn to use the equipment.

Expandability and Obsolescence

When choosing equipment, keep expandability in mind. For example, if you think you will be doubling or tripling the amount of your recording capability, you will want to purchase equipment that is expandable, like the computer-based systems and MDMs. If you primarily go on location to record, other gear may be the best such as portable units described in chapter 4.

It is wise to purchase items from a company that supports a range of product lines. Most do. This allows you to learn on an entry-level product. Then, when the time comes to upgrade to a mid-level or high-end product, you will have some familiarity with the gear and the way the equipment functions.

Setups That Work, and How to Maximize Your Gear

Identify your needs as either entry-level, mid-level or high-end. The other major decision is whether you are going to make a Macintosh or Windows computer the center of the studio or if you'll be recording without a computer. Then examine the studio setups described below for guidance.

In this chapter, there are three options for the digital studios: entry-level, mid-level, and high-end. Please note you could spend much more than $30,000 for a studio. We are limiting the scope of these options to building a personal or small digital studio. For these examples we are also avoiding room-construction costs. The estimated equipment for each of these studios listed below may vary significantly according to the specific hardware and software purchased. Use these as a starting point.

No-Computer Options

Building a studio around equipment that does not require a Macintosh or Windows computer has both advantages and disadvantages. If you are not accustomed to using a computer, or if you require equipment that is highly mobile, one of these setups will be an excellent choice.

Entry-Level Digital Studio Without a Computer ($3,000 to $5,000)

This entry-level studio will allow you to record eight or more tracks of digital audio and to mix and produce professional-quality recordings. Here is one of many variations to use as a starting point when planning your entry-level digital studio.

- Recorder/mixer: At the entry-level studio without a computer, the heart of the studio is one of the hard disk portable studio mentioned in chapter 5. Consider an entry-level model such as the Roland VS-840EX, Fostex FD-8, or Korg D-8. This recorder/mixer combination will cost around $1,000 range and will allow you to record eight tracks of audio.

- Mixdown recorder: The cheapest way to go is to purchase a CD burner so you can dump your files from the hard disk portable studio directly to a CD. CD burners were discussed in chapters 9 and 18 and can be purchased for about $500.

- Monitors: The cheapest and most efficient option at the low-end is to go with powered monitors. Powered monitors (see chapter 5) have a built-in power amp, so they are all-in-one devices. The Roland DS-90 powered digital monitors run in the $1,200 range for two. You can purchase analog monitors for approximately $500.

- Microphones: You will need to select one or more microphones (see chapter 11). There are quality brands available on the low end, so you can purchase a pair of microphones for about $200. If you end up selecting a mic with phantom power, you will need to purchase a preamp that will cost approximately $150.

- Instruments: It will be helpful to have at least one good quality synth in the studio (see chapter 1). A good quality MIDI keyboard will cost about $1,000. You could also go with a guitar synth, drum set, and other gear. However, at this level, leave that for the musicians to bring.

- Miscellaneous gear: This area includes mic stands, furniture, and other accoutrements for the studio. Don't forget to install that surge suppressor to protect your gear from a voltage spike through your home or studio. Also, a backup power supply is another important piece of gear. You will want to allow an additional $1,000 for this area.

Mid-Level Digital Studio Without a Computer ($10,000 to $15,000)

The mid-level studio takes a bit more cash to get going, but you will also have more tracks available for recording and other advantages. Again, there are many ways that you can go. Some of the possibilities and considerations follow:

- Recorder: At the mid-level you have to decide if you want to go with MDM (see chapter 4) or a hard disk portable studio like the Akai DPS 12, Korg D16, or Roland VS-880EX (see chapter 5). If you decide to go the MDM route, you will need to purchase two MDMs and chain them together for a total of sixteen tracks (see chapter 4).

- Mixer: If you go for the hard disk portable studio, the mixer is built-in. If MDM is your choice, then you will need to purchase a mixer (see chapter 10). There are several entry-level models for under $2,000 including the Yamaha O1v and the TASCAM TM-1000.

- Mixdown deck. At this level you should consider going with a DAT deck for mixdown (see chapter 3). It would also be beneficial to have a CD burner for cutting CDs. A DAT deck runs about $1,500 and a CD burner about $500.

- Monitors: Powered monitors are an excellent choice for both mid-level and entry level. These monitors (see chapter 5) have a built-in power-amp, so they are all-in-one devices. The Roland DS-90 powered digital monitors are about $1,200 for two. You can purchase analog monitors for approximately $500.

- Microphones: You will want to move up to at least the $500 range for some higher quality microphones. There are several excellent choices in the range $500 to $900 (see chapter 11). You will want to purchase a variety of mics for different applications and uses.

- Preamp: Since you will be using one or more condenser mics, a preamp is required to supply phantom power (see chapter 11). Expect to pay in the $750 range for a good quality preamp.

- Instruments: A high quality synth or two will enhance the mid-level studio (see chapter 1). For a good quality synth you will want to budget between $2,000 and $3,000. You may also want to purchase a set of drums for the studio if you will be recording a lot of acoustic drums.

- Miscellaneous gear: This area includes mic stands, furniture, and other accoutrements for the studio. Don't forget to install that surge suppressor to protect your gear from a voltage spike through the home or studio. Also, a backup power supply is another important piece of gear. You will want to budget an additional $1,000 for this.

High-End Digital Studio Without a Computer ($25,000 to $30,000)

- Recorder: There are a couple of choices that do not require a computer. One option is to go with three or four MDMs and an external controller unit such as the BRC (see chapter 4). This will provide twenty-four or thirty-two tracks of audio. An alternative is to go with a high-end modular hard disk recorder that plugs into a rack system. Some of the models listed in chapter 5 can handle twenty-four tracks of audio in a single unit. Approximate cost: $7,500.

- Mixer: The Yamaha O2R and the Mackie Digital 8 Bus (chapter 10) are appropriate gear for the high-end studio. Approximate cost: $10,000.

- Effects units (outboard): A high-end studio should include multiple compressors and several multi-effects units; for sure, have one unit per bus on the mixer console. See chapter 17 for more detailed information on this area. Approximate cost: $3,000.

- Mixdown deck. At this level you should consider going with a DAT deck for mixdown (see chapters 3 and 19). A high-end system should also have a CD burner for cutting CDs. A DAT deck will run in the $1,500 range and a CD burner is about $500.

- Monitors: Powered monitors are an excellent choice for all of the digital studio options. The monitor (see chapter 5) in this case has a built-in power-amp so they are all-in-one devices. Roland DS-90 powered digital monitors will run in the $1,200 range for two. You can purchase analog monitors from Mackie and others for approximately $500.

- Microphones: You will want to own a variety of microphones including condenser and digital mics (see chapter 11). Approximate cost: $2,000.

- Preamp: A high-end preamp will be needed in the high-end studio (see chapter 11). Approximate cost: $3,000.

- Instruments: You will want to have several good quality instruments in the studio. In the high-end studio the Korg Triton or Kurzweil 2500 would be a good keyboard. In addition, several sound modules should be considered for specialized sound capabilities according to your needs (see chapter 2). Approximate cost: $5,000.

- Miscellaneous gear: Since the high-end studio will have more gear to plug together, a separate patch bay is absolutely required (see chapter 13). You will most likely need several pairs of headphones and a headphone amp if there will be times when several performers will be recording together. In addition, you will need mic stands, furniture, and other accoutrements for the studio.

Don't forget to install that surge suppressor to protect your gear from a voltage spike through the home or studio. Also, a backup power supply is another important piece of gear. You will want to budget and addition $3,000 for this area.

Computer-Based Studios

There is another list of considerations for computer-centered studios. Three sample studios that relate directly to our personal experience are described below. The number of computer-based options is virtually limitless, so use these examples as just that—examples.

Also, for the mid-level and high-end studios, you should consider dedicating a computer to the recording task and using a second computer for browsing the Web, writing checks, and running other nondigital audio software.

As mentioned in chapter 6, both Macintosh and Windows computers can be used for all levels—entry, mid, and high. The following descriptions are in general terms. You will need to spend some time at a local computer or music store researching the various hardware options because they change quickly.

Entry-Level Digital Studio with a Computer ($5,000)

- Computer: To guarantee the necessary power to process digital audio, go with a model that is designed for the graphics industry. This is usually a mid-level to high-end computer with sufficient power to process and store digital information. If you are going to use a computer you currently own, check the recommended requirements for the software to be sure it is compatible with your system. Go with the recommended specifications rather than the minimum (see chapter 6).

- Backup storage media: If you are buying a computer today, get a model that has a built-in drive for back-up. A removable drive such as Zip or Jaz is also a good option (see chapter 9). Approximate cost: $2,000.

- Software: Any of the entry-level MIDI/digital audio sequencers mentioned in chapter 6 would be fine, and there are other viable options to be considered. It is a good idea to also purchase a digital editing program (see chapter 7). Approximate cost: $250.

- Digital audio card and interface: If you purchase a multimedia computer as described in the computer section above, you will not need to add a digital audio card. You may want to consider some of the lower-priced digital-audio cards mentioned in chapter 7. Approximate cost: $500.

- Mixer: You will need a mixer in order to plug in a microphone, instrument, and other input. One of the low-end digital mixers mentioned in chapter 10 would do the job. Approximate cost: $500.

- Mixdown deck. The best solution for mix-down media is to purchase a computer with a CD burner. This is the least expensive option. Units can be installed inside the computer's CPU and external units can also be purchased. Approximate cost: $500.

- Monitors: The cheapest and most efficient option at the low-end is to go with powered monitors. These monitors (see chapter 5) have a built-in power-amp so they are all-in-one devices. The Roland DS-90 powered digital monitors run in the $1,200 range for two. You can purchase analog monitors for approximately $500.

- Microphones: You will need to select one or more microphones (see chapter 11). There are quality brands available, so you can purchase a pair of microphones for around $200. If you end up selecting a mic with phantom power (see chapter 11), you will need to purchase a preamp that will cost approximately $150.

- Instruments: It will be helpful to have at least one good quality synth in the studio (see chapter 1). A decent quality MIDI keyboard will cost about $1,000. You could also go with a guitar synth, drum set, and other gear. However, at this level, let the musicians bring their own.

- Miscellaneous gear: This includes mic stands, furniture, and other accoutrements for the studio. Don't forget to install that surge suppressor to protect your gear from a voltage spike through the home or studio. Also, a backup power supply is important. You will want to budget and addition $1,500 for this area.

Mid-Level Digital Studio with a Computer ($10,000 to $15,000)

- Computer: For both the mid-level a high-end studio be sure to get a computer that is on the high end of the manufacturer's scale. Computer companies, like music instrument manufacturers, make a line of computers from entry-level to high-end. Digital audio by its nature requires a robust computer, so budget for the high-end model. As mentioned at the entry-level, purchasing a computer designed for graphics editing will guarantee enough power to handle the mid-level and high-end applications. Approximate cost: $2,500.

- Backup storage media: If you are buying a computer today, get a model that has a built-in drive for backup. A removable drive such as Zip or Jaz is also a good option (see chapter 9).

- Software: Chapter 7 dealt with the range of options for the mid-level studio. One option is to go with a mid-level MIDI/digital audio sequencer. If digital audio is the only requirement, one of the all-in-one packages such as those mentioned in chapter 7 could be used.

- Digital audio card and interface: At the mid-level you will want to add a digital-audio card to the system (see chapter 7). There are many cards from which to choose, so be sure you get the features you want.
- Mixer: There are several excellent mixers for the mid-level studio for under $2,000 including the Yamaha O1v and TASCAM TM-1000 (see chapter 10).

- Mixdown deck. Be sure to get a CD burner for your computer. This can be used to backup data and to mix down the final product. In addition, a DAT deck should be considered at this level (see chapter 3).

- Monitors: Powered monitors are an excellent choice for the mid- and entry-level. These monitors (see chapter 5) have a built-in power-amp, so they are all-in-one devices. The Roland DS-90 powered digital monitors will run in the $1,200 range for two. You can purchase analog monitors for approximately $500.

- Microphones: You will want to move up to the $500 range for some higher quality microphones. There are several excellent choices in the range of $500 to $900 (see chapter 11). You will want to purchase a variety of mics for different applications and uses.

- Preamp: Since you will be using one or more condenser mics, a preamp is required to supply phantom power (see chapter 11). Expect to pay in the $750 range for a good quality preamp.

- Instruments: A high quality synth or two will enhance the mid-level studio (see chapter 1). For a quality synth you will want to budget between $2,000 and $3,000. You may also want to purchase a set of drums for the studio if you will be recording a lot of acoustic drums.

- Miscellaneous gear: This area includes mic stands, furniture, and other accoutrements for the studio. Don't forget to install that surge suppressor to protect your gear from a voltage spike through the home or studio. Also, a backup power supply is important. You will want to budget an additional $1,000 for this area.

High-End Digital Studio with a Computer ($15,000 to $30,000)

- Computer: For both the mid-level and high-end studio be sure to get a computer that is on the high end of the manufacturer's scale. Computer companies, like music instrument manufacturers, make a line of computers from entry-level to high-end. Digital audio by its nature requires a robust computer, so budget for the high-end model. As mentioned, at the entry-level, purchasing a computer designed for graphics editing will guarantee enough power to handle the mid-level and high-end applications. Approximate cost: $3,000.

- Backup storage media: It is possible to use removable media and CD-ROM for backup. However, since DVD-ROM drives can also read CD-ROM (see chapter 9), a DVD-ROM drive is recommended. This is built in to the price above for the computer.

- Software: There are a variety of options to consider with regard to software and hardware for the high-end digital studio (see chapter 8). Approximate cost: $1,000.

• Digital audio card and interface: The high-end options are described in chapter 8. Be sure to review your recording needs and to purchase the package that has the features you require. Approximate cost: $1,000.

• Effects plug-ins: For a high-end studio you definitely need to budget for some additional effects plug-ins (see chapters 8 and 17). Approximate cost: $2,000

• Mixdown deck. At this level you should consider going with a DAT deck for mixdown (see chapter 3). A high-end system should also have a CD burner for cutting CDs. A DAT deck will run in the $1,500 range and a CD burner about $500.

• Monitors: Powered monitors are an excellent choice for all of the digital studio options. A powered monitor (see chapter 5) has a built-in power-amp so it is an all-in-one device. Roland DS-90 powered digital monitors will run in the $1,200 range for two. You can purchase analog monitors from Mackie and others for approximately $500.

• Microphones: You will want to own a variety of microphones for the high-end studio to include condenser and digital mics (see chapter 11). Approximate cost: $2,000.

• Preamp: You'll need a high-end preamp in the high-end studio (see chapter 11). Approximate cost: $3,000.

• Instruments: You will want to have several good quality instruments in the studio. In the high-end studio, the Korg Triton or Kurzweil 2500 is a good keyboard. In addition, several sound modules should be considered for specialized sound capabilities according to your needs (see chapter 2). Approximate cost: $5,000.

• Miscellaneous gear: Since a high-end studio has more gear to plug together, a separate patch bay is required (see chapter 13). You will also likely need several pairs of headphones and a headphone amp if several performers will ever be recording together. In addition, you will need mic stands, furniture, and other accoutrements for the studio. Don't forget to install that surge suppressor to protect your gear from a voltage spike through the home or studio. Also, a backup power supply is another important piece of gear. You will want to budget an additional $3,000 for this area.

Being an Informed Shopper

You are now well on your way to becoming an informed shopper for equipment in the digital audio world. Reading this book and others in the field is an excellent way to get your feet wet. It is also a good idea to subscribe to several magazines that support the digital recording industry. Magazines such as *Keyboard*, *Electronic Musician*, *Mix*, *EQ*, and *Recording* will be helpful to you. Each magazine has a specific audience in mind, so try to pick up a copy at a newsstand or bookstore to see if it suits your needs. You will find helpful product reviews and other articles that can help to answer your questions.

Use the Internet and World Wide Web

This book was certainly enhanced by our ability to go to a company's Web site and research specs and other information. I don't know of any worthwhile company that does not have its own Web site. Many of these sites are listed in the appendix. Going to a Web site can be the best way to get up-to-date information and to download free demo software. The Web can also be helpful when you have technical questions. I often send an email to tech support of various companies. I am amazed at how quickly I typically receive responses. Company Web sites also contain a wealth of information on how to use their software and equipment. It is not uncommon to find complete tutorials on line so check out the company Web site frequently.

The Last (Final!) Summary

In order to make the best buying decisions, many factors must be considered. These include determining your recording needs and purchasing a system that adheres to your budget. The other important distinction is whether to go with a computer-based or non-computer-based studio. Once that decision has been made, the studio needs to be assembled, be it entry-level, mid-level, or high-end. It is also important to continue to be an informed shopper by regularly researching information from publications and other resources. Following these steps will help to ensure that you will design and purchase the right equipment to fill your needs.

This book covered a wealth of information. It was our hope to guide you and to help you make choices in purchasing equipment and developing your digital studio. Good luck!

Appendix A.

Company Web Site Directory

360 Systems
www.360systems.com/

A

A Plus Four Organization
www.plusfour.org/

Aardvark
www.aardvark-pro.com/

ADK Condenser Microphones
www.a-dk.com/

Adobe Systems
www.adobe.com/

Akai USA
www.akai.com/

AKG Acoustics
www.akg-acoustics.com/

Alesis Corp.
www.alesis.com/

Allen & Heath
www.allen-heath.com/

Altech Systems
www.altechsystems.com/

Altec Lansing Corporation (also DDA, Dynacord, Electro-voice, Klark Teknik, Merlin, and Midas)
www.eviaudio.com/

Altec Lansing Corporation
www.alteclansingpro.com/

Amek Techology Group
www.amek.com/

American Loudspeaker Manufacturers Association
www.ALMA.org/

AMS Neve
www.ams-neve.com/

Antares Audio Technologies
www.antarestech.com/

APB Tools
www.kgw.tu-berlin.de/~y2371/SIGMA_1/

Aphex Systems
www.aphex.com/

Apogee
www.apogeedigital.com/

Apple Computer
www.apple.com/

Applied Research & Technology (ART)
www.artroch.com/

Argosy Console
www.argosyconsole.com/

ASC-Tube Trap
www.tubetrap.com/

Ashly Audio
www.ashly.com/

Audio Accessories
www.patchbays.com/

Audio Engineering Society (AES)
www.aes.org/

Audio-Genetics
www.demon.co.uk/gallery/frameIDX.html

Audio-Technica
www.audiotechnica.com/

Audix Corporation
www.audixusa.com/

Auralex Acoustics Inc.
www.auralex.com/

Autopatch
www.autopatch.com/

Avalon Design
www.avalondesign.com/

Avid Technology
www.avid.com/

B

B&H Photo • Video • Pro Audio
www.bhphotovideo.com

BASF/EMTEC Pro Media
www.emtec-usa.com/

BBE Sound
www.bbesound.com/intro.htm

Belden Wire and Cable
www.belden.com

Berklee Press
www.berkleepress.com/

Beyerdynamic))))
www.beyerdynamic.com

BIAS, Inc.
www.bias-inc.com/

BitHeadz Inc.
www.BitHeadz.com/

Bomb Factory Digital, Inc.
www.bombfactory.com/

Bose Corp.
www.bose.com/

Bruel & Kjaer
www.dpamicrophones.com/

Bryston
www.bryston.ca/

C

CAD Professional Microphones
www.cadmics.com/

Cakewalk Music Software
www.cakewalk.com/

Carver Professional
www.carverpro.com/

Carvin Corporation
www.carvin.com/

ClearSonic Manufacturing
www.clearsonic.com/

CM AUTOmation
www.cmautomation.com/

Coda Music Technology
www.codamusic.com/

Community Professional Loudspeakers
www.community.chester.pa.us/

Consumer Electronics Manufacturers Association (CEMA)
www.ce.org/index.asp

Cool Stuff Labs Incorporated
www.coolstufflabs.com/latest.html

Countryman Associates
63.194.67.202/mainpage.html

Crane Song
www.cranesong.com/

Crest Audio
www.crestaudio.com/

Crown International
www.crownintl.com/crownintl/

Cuan An Spidéal
www.cuan.com/

D

dB Technologies
www.dbtechno.com/

dbx Professional Products
www.dbxpro.com/

DEMAS, Inc.
www.synclavier.com/

Denon
www.del.denon.com/

DigiBid Auction Site
www.digibid.com/

Digidesign
www.digidesign.com/

Digital Audio Denmark
www.digitalaudio.dk/

Digital Audio Labs
www.digitalaudio.com/index.asp

Disc Makers
www.discmakers.com/

DOD Electronics
www.dod.com/

Dolby Labs
www/dolby.com/

DPA Microphones
www.dpamicrophones.com/

Drawmer
www.proaudio.co.uk/drawmer.htm

DUY
www.duy.com/

E

Earthworks
www.earthwks.com/

Eastern Acoustics Works
www.eaw.com/

Eastman Kodak
www.kodak.com/

Electronic Music Foundation, Limited USA
www.cdemusic.org/special/grm/

ElectroVoice
www.electrovoice.com/

Emagic Inc.
www.emagic.de/

E-MU / ENSONIQ (formerly E-mu Systems)
www.emu.com/

Ensoniq
www.ensoniq.com/

Euphonix
www.euphonix.com/

Event Electronics
www.event1.com/

Eventide Audio
www.eventide.com/

EVI Audio
www.eviaudio.com/

F

Fairlight USA
www.fairlightusa.com/

Fender
www.fender.com/

Focusrite
www.focusrite.com/

Fostex
www.fostex.com/

Fuji Photo Film USA, INc.
www.fujifilm.com/

Furman Sound
www.furmansound.com/

G

Gallery
www.gallery.co.uk

GearSearch.com
www.gearsearch.com/

Gefen
www.gefen.com/

Genelec
www.genelec.com/

Gibson
www.gibson.com/

Glyph Technologies, Inc.
www.glyphtech.com/

Gvox
www.gvox.com/index.cfm

H

Hafler
www.hafler.com/

HHB Communications
www.hhb.co.uk/usa.htm

Hitachi
www.hitachi.com/

Home Recording Rights Coalition (HRRC)
www.hrrc.org/

Hosa Technology, Inc.
www.hosatech.com/

I

ILIO Entertainments
www.ilio.com/

Imation Corporation
www.imation.com/

Inline Incorporated
www.inlineinc.com/

Instrument Jokes
www.mit.edu:8001/people/jcb/other-instrument-jokes.html

Intel
www.intel.com/

J

JBL Professional
www.jblpro.com/

JL Cooper
www.jlcooper.com/

Joemeek
www.joemeek.com/

JVC
www.jvc.com/

K

Keyboard Central
www.keyboardmag.com/

Kind of Loud Technologies
www.kindofloud.com/

Klipsch Professional
www.klipsch.com/

Klotz Digital Aktiengesellschaft
www.klotz-digital.de/

Korg USA
www.korg.com/

KRK Systems
www.krksys.com/

Kurzweil Music
www.youngchang.com/kurzweil/

L

Lentine's Music Incorporated
www.lentine.com

Lexicon
www.lexicon.com/

Logic-Users Page
www.logicuser.net

Lucasfilm THX
www.thx.com/

Lucid Technology (a division of Symetrix, Inc.)
www.lucidaudio.com/

M

McDSP
www.mcdsp.com/home.html

Mackie Designs
www.mackie.com/default.asp

MAGMA
www.magma.com/

Manley Laboratories
www.manleylabs.com/

Marantz
www.marantz.com/db/

Marmalade Software
www.marmaladesoftware.com/

Mark of the Unicorn
www.motu.com/

Marshall Electronics, Inc.
www.mars-cam.com/

Martinsound, Inc.
www.martinsound.com/

Masterwork Recording, Inc.
www.masterworkrecording.com/

Maxell
www.maxell.com

Metric Halo Laboratories
www.mhlabs.com/

Microtech Gefell GmbH
www.microtechgefell.com/

MIDI Solutions
www.midisolutions.com/

MIDIMAN
www.midiman.net/

Miller Freeman PSN
www.MFPSN.com/

Minnetonka Audio Software
www.minnetonkasoftware.com/

Mitsubishi
www.mitsubishi.com/

Monster Cable
www.monstercable.com/

Motorola
www.motorola.com/SPS/DSP/

M Pak, Inc.
www.musicpak.com/

mSoft, Inc
www.msoftinc.com/

The Museum of Sound Recording
www.mosr.org/

Music Producers Guild of the Americas
www.musicproducers.com/findex.htm

MUSITEK Corporation
www.musitek.com/

N

NAB (National Association of Broadcasters)
www.nab.org/

Nady
www.nadywireless.com/

Nagra USA
www.nagra.com/nagra/default.htm

NAMM (National Association of Music Merchants)
www.namm.com/

NEAR
www.nearspeakers.com/

Neumann/USA
www.neumannusa.com/

Neutrik USA
www.neutrikusa.com/

Nigel B Furniture
www.nigelb.com/

NVISION
www.nvision1.com/

O

OMNIRAX
www.omnirax.com/

Opcode Systems
www.opcode.com/

Oram Professional Audio
www.oram.co.uk/

Otari Corp.
www.otari.com/

P

Panasonic
www.panasonic.com/

Peavey
www.peavey.com

PG Music
www.pgmusic.com/

Philips Professional
www.philipspro.com/

Planet Medley
www.medleynet.com/

PreSonus Audio Electronics
www.presonus.com/

Q

QSound Labs
www.qsound.ca/

Quantegy
www.quantegy.com/

Quiklok
www.quiklok.com/index.music

R

Rane
www.rane.com/

Recording Industry Association of America (RIAA)
www.riaa.com/

S

SADiE
www.sadie.com/

Samson, Behringer
www.samsontech.com/

Samsung Electronics
www.samsungelectronics.com/

Sanyo-Verbatim
www.sanyo-verbatim.com/

SAS Audio Labs
www.sasaudiolabs.com/newdir/index.htm

SEK'D
www.sekd.com/

Sennheiser Electronic Corporation
www.sennheiserusa.com/

Serato Audio Research
www.serato.com

Sharp Electronics
www.sharp-usa.com/

Shockwave Audio
www.shockwaveaudio.com/

ShowPro MIDI
www.showpromidi.com/

Shure Brothers
www.shure.com/

SKB Corporation
www.skbcases.com/

SLS Loudspeakers
www.slsloudspeakers.com/

SMPTE (Society of Motion Picture & Television Engineers)
www.smpte.org/

Society of Professional Audio Recording Services (SPARS)
www.spars.com/spars/

Solid State Logic
www.solid-state-logic.com/

Sonic Foundry
www.sonicfoundry.com/

Sonic Science
www.sonicscience.com/

Sonic Solutions
www.sonic.com/

Sonorus
www.sonorus.com/

Sony Corp. of America
www.sony.com/

Sony Electronics
bpgprod.sel.sony.com

Sony Professional Audio
bpgprod.sel.sony.com/proaudio/

Soundcraft
www.soundcraft.com/

SoundTree
www.soundtree.com

Spatializer Audio Laboratories
www.spatializer.com

Spirit
www.spiritbysoundcraft.com/

Steinberg N.A.
www.us.steinberg.net/

Studer
www.studer.ch/

Summit Audio Inc.
www.summitaudio.com/

Sweetwater Sound
www.sweetwater.com/home.tpl

Symetrix
www.symetrixaudio.com/

SyQuest Technology
www.syquest.com/

T

Tannoy
www.tannoy.com/

TASCAM
www.tascam.com/

TBC Consoles
www.tbcconsoles.com/

TC Electronic
www.tcelectronic.com/

TDK Electronics
www.tdk.com/

Tektronix
www.tek.com/

Thermodyne International Ltd.
www.thermodyne-online.com/

TOA Corporation
www.toadigital.com/

Toshiba
www.toshiba.com/

Turtle Beach
www.voyetra-turtle-beach.com/site/default.asp

U

Ultimate Support Systems
www.ultimatesupport.com/

V

Voice Crystal
www.voicecrystal.com/

Voyetra
www.voyetra-turtle-beach.com/site/default.asp

W

WaveFrame
www.waveframe.com/

Wave Mechanics
www.wavemechanics.com/

Wave:Space
www.wave-space.com/

WAVES
www.waves.com/

WildSync Systems
www.wildsync.com/

X Y

Yamaha
www.yamaha.com/

Z

Z-Systems
www.z-sys.com/

Appendix B.
Books and Magazines

Books

Audio in Media, 4th Edition, Stanley R. Alten, Wadsworth Publishing Company, Belmont, California, 1999.

Anatomy of a Home Studio: How Everything Really Works, from Microphones to MIDI, Scott Wilkinson, Mix Bookshelf/Mix Books, Emeryville, CA, 1998.

Digital Home Recording: Tips, Techniques, and Tools for Home Studio, Carolyn Keating and Craig Anderton, editors, Miller Freeman Books, San Francisco, 1998.

Experiencing Music Technology, David B. Williams and Peter R. Webster, Schirmer Books, New York, 1999.

Guide to MIDI Orchestration, Paul Gilreath, Music Works, Atlanta, 1999.

Home Recording for Musicians, Craig Anderton, Music Sales Corp., New York, 1996.

How to Build a Small Budget Recording Studio from Scratch—with 12 Tested Designs, 2nd Edition, F. Alton Everest and Michael Shea, McGraw-Hill Professional Book Group, New York, 1988.

The Master Handbook of Acoustics Trade Paperback, 3rd Edition, F. Alton Everest, McGraw-Hill Professional Book Group, New York, 1994.

MIDI Basics, Lee Whitmore, Warner Bros. Publications, Miami, 1998.

Musicians and Computers, David S. Mash, Warner Bros. Publications, Miami, 1998.

Musicians and the Internet, David S. Mash, Warner Bros. Publications, Miami, 1998.

Musicians and Multimedia, David S. Mash, Warner Bros. Publications, Miami, 1998.

Sequencing Basics, Don Muro, Warner Bros. Publications, Miami, 1998.

Teaching Music with Technology, Thomas E. Rudolph, GIA Publications, Inc., Chicago, 1996.

Magazines

Electronic Musician
www.emusician.com
P.O. Box 1929
Marion, OH 43306
tel: 800.245.2737
      740.382.3322
fax: 740.389.6720

EQ
www.eqmag.com
P.O. Box 0532
Baldwin, NY 11510
tel: 212.378.0448
e-mail: circulation@psn.com

Keyboard Magazine
www.keyboardmag.com
411 Borel Avenue, Suite #100
San Mateo, CA 94402
tel: 650.358.9500
fax: 650.358.9527

Mix
www.mixonline.com
6151 Powers Ferry Road NW
Atlanta, GA 30339-2941
tel: 877.296.3125 (US only), or
      770.618.0219
fax: 770.618.0347

Pro Sound News
www.prosoundnews.com
460 Park Avenue South
New York, NY 10016
tel: 212.378.0447
e-mail: editor@psn.com

Recording Magazine
www.recordingmag.com
Music Maker Publications
5412 Idylwild Trail, Suite 100
Boulder, CO 80301
tel: 303.516.9118
fax: 303.516.9119
e-mail: info@recordingmag.com

Surround Sound Professional
www.surroundpro.com
6 Manhasset Avenue
Port Washington, NY 11050
tel: 516-944-5940
fax: 516-767-1745

Publishers

Berklee Press
www.berkleepress.com
1140 Boylston Street
Boston, MA 02215
tel: 617.747.2146
fax: 617.747.2149
e-mail: berkleepress@berklee.edu

Index

Author Bios

Thomas E. Rudolph, Ed.D., is a national leader in the field of music education and technology. He is one of the founding directors of the Technology Institute for Music Educators; adjunct assistant professor of music at the University of the Arts in Wyncote, Pennsylvania; and director of music for the Haverford School District in Haverford, Pennsylvania. He has trained thousands of music professionals at many institutions, including Berklee College of Music in Boston, Massachusetts; Central Connecticut State University in New Britain, Connecticut; The University of the Arts in Philadelphia; and Villanova University in Villanova, Pennsylvania. His publications include *Teaching Music with Technology*, *The MIDI Sequencer in the Music Classroom*, and *Technology Strategies for Music Education*.

Producer and composer Vincent A. Leonard Jr. has had works premiered nationally and internationally. He is published by Arrangers' Publishing Company and Educational Programs Publications. In 1996 he and fellow producer and engineer Jack Klotz Jr. formed Invinceable Entertainment, 3 IPS Studio and released their first CD, *Magic Up Our Sleeve*. Also widely known as a copyist and arranger, he has worked on projects with Peter Nero, the Philly Pops Orchestra, Doc Severinsen, the London Symphony Orchestra, Chuck Mangione, and musicals by Duke Ellington, Alan Menkin, Kurt Weil, and Mitch Leigh. Leonard is a member of NARAS and ASCAP, and is active as a clinician and beta tester for music software for Macintosh computers.

Berklee Press DVDs:
Just Press PLAY

AS SERIOUS ABOUT MUSIC AS YOU ARE

Kenwood Dennard: The Studio/ Touring Drummer
| ISBN: 0-87639-022-X | HL: 50448034 | DVD $19.95 |

Up Close with Patti Austin: Auditioning and Making it in the Music Business
| ISBN: 0-87639-041-6 | HL: 50448031 | DVD $19.95 |

The Ultimate Practice Guide for Vocalists
| ISBN: 0-87639-035-1 | HL: 50448017 | DVD $19.95 |

Featuring Donna McElroy

Real-Life Career Guide for the Professional Musician
| ISBN: 0-87639-031-9 | HL: 50448013 | DVD $19.95 |

Featuring David Rosenthal

Essential Rock Grooves for Bass
| ISBN: 0-87639-037-8 | HL: 50448019 | DVD $19.95 |

Featuring Danny Morris

Jazz Guitar Techniques: Modal Voicings
| ISBN: 0-87639-034-3 | HL: 50448016 | DVD $19.95 |

Featuring Rick Peckham

Jim Kelly's Guitar Workshop
| ISBN: 0-634-00865-X | HL: 00320168 | DVD $19.95 |

Basic Afro-Cuban Rhythms for Drum Set and Hand Percussion
| ISBN: 0-87639-030-0 | HL: 50448012 | DVD $19.95 |

Featuring Ricardo Monzón

Vocal Technique: Developing Your Voice for Performance
| ISBN: 0-87639-026-2 | HL: 50448038 | DVD $19.95 |

Featuring Anne Peckham

Preparing for Your Concert
| ISBN: 0-87639-036-X | HL: 50448018 | DVD $19.95 |

Featuring JoAnne Brackeen

Jazz Improvisation: Starting Out with Motivic Development
| ISBN: 0-87639-032-7 | HL: 50448014 | DVD $19.95 |

Featuring Ed Tomassi

Chop Builder for Rock Guitar
| ISBN: 0-87639-033-5 | HL: 50448015 | DVD $19.95 |

Featuring "Shred Lord" Joe Stump

Turntable Technique: The Art of the DJ
| ISBN: 0-87639-038-6 | HL: 50448025 | DVD $24.95 |

Featuring Stephen Webber

Jazz Improvisation: A Personal Approach with Joe Lovano
| ISBN: 0-87639-021-1 | HL: 50448033 | DVD $19.95 |

Harmonic Ear Training
| ISBN: 0-87639-027-0 | HL: 50448039 | DVD $19.95 |

Featuring Roberta Radley

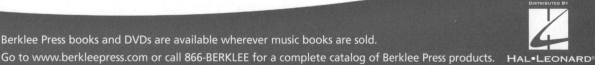